THE SOCIOLOGY OF FOOD AND EATING

For W.J.H.

The Sociology of Food and Eating

Essays on the sociological significance of food

edited by
ANNE MURCOTT
University College, Cardiff
and Welsh National School of Medicine

Gower

Published by
Gower Publishing Company Limited,
Gower House, Croft Road, Aldershot, Hants GU11 3HR,
England

Reprinted 1984, 1985, 1986

British Library Cataloguing in Publication Data

The Sociology of Food and Eating
1. Food – Social aspects
I. Murcott, Anne
306'.4'0941   TX355

ISBN 0-566-00580-8

Printed and bound in Great Britain by
Paradigm Print, Gateshead, Tyne and Wear.

Contents

Acknowledgements   vii

List of Contributors   viii

1   Introduction   *Anne Murcott*   1

SECTION I   EATING, CULTURE AND SOCIAL ORGANISATION

2   Eating Virtue   *Paul Atkinson*   9

3   Vegetarianism and the Meanings of Meat   *Julia Twigg*   18

4   Living from Hand to Mouth: the Farmworker, Food   31
     and Agribusiness   *Howard Newby*

5   The Hierarchy of Maintenance and the Maintenance of   45
     Hierarchy: Notes on Food and Industry   *Eric Batstone*

SECTION II   FOOD, HEALTH AND GENERATION

6   The Management of Food in Pregnancy   *Sally Macintyre*   57

7   A Question of Balance: Asian and British Women's   73
     Perceptions of Food During Pregnancy   *Hilary Homans*

8   Food for Equilibrium: the Dietary Principles and Practice   84
     of Chinese Families in London   *Erica Wheeler & Tan Swee Poh*

9   The Goodness is Out of It: the Meaning of Food to Two   95
     Generations   *Mildred Blaxter   &   Elizabeth Paterson*

10   The Salt of the Earth: Ideas Linking Diet, Exercise   106
     and Virtue among Elderly Aberdonians   *Rory Williams*

11   An Apple a Day...Some Reflections on Working Class   117
     Mothers' Views on Food and Health   *Roisin Pill*

12   The Sweet Things in Life: Aspects of the Management of   128
     Diabetic Diet   *Tina Posner*

SECTION III   COOKING, GENDER AND HOUSEHOLD

13   Lobster, Chicken, Cake and Tears: Deciphering Wedding   141
     Meals   *Sara Delamont*

14 You are What You Eat: Food and Family Reconstitution   152
        Jacqueline Burgoyne & David Clarke

15 The Way to a Man's Heart: Food in the Violent Home   164
        Rhian Ellis

16 Men in the Kitchen: Notes from a Cookery Class   172
        Tony Coxon

17 Cooking and the Cooked: a Note on the Domestic   178
        Preparation of Meals   *Anne Murcott*

Bibliography   186

Index   194

Acknowledgements

In the last few years a growing number of people have agreed with me that the sociological significance of food and eating is important. I am grateful to them all for their encouragement to persist, in particular to Virginia Olesen and to colleagues in Cardiff. I would especially like to thank Sara Delamont and Bill Hudson who, in addition, generously made time to help with the final practical stages of compiling this volume, and Val Dobie who prepared the typescript with such good humour.

List of Contributors

Paul Atkinson, Senior Lecturer, Department of Sociology, University College, Cardiff.

Eric Batstone, Fellow, Nuffield College, University of Oxford.

Mildred Blaxter, MRC Sociologist, MRC Medical Sociology Unit, Aberdeen.

Jacqueline Burgoyne, Senior Lecturer, Department Applied Social Studies, Sheffield City Polytechnic.

David Clark, MRC Sociologist, MRC Medical Sociology Unit, Aberdeen.

Tony Coxon, Professor of Sociological Research Methods, Department of Sociology, University College, Cardiff.

Sara Delamont, Senior Lecturer, Department of Sociology, University College, Cardiff.

Rhian Ellis, Research Officer, Economic Policy and Research Unit, Mid Glamorgan County Council.

Hilary Homans, Research Fellow, University of Warwick.

Sally Macintyre, MRC Sociologist, MRC Medical Sociology Unit, Aberdeen.

Anne Murcott, Lecturer, Department of Sociology, University College, Cardiff and Welsh National School of Medicine.

Howard Newby, Reader, Department of Sociology, University of Essex.

Elizabeth Paterson, Research Fellow, Institute of Medical Sociology, Aberdeen.

Roisin Pill, Research Fellow, Department of General Practice, Welsh National School of Medicine.

Tina Posner, Attached worker, Department of Community Medicine and General Practice, University of Oxford.

Tan Swee Poh, Research Fellow, Department of Human Nutrition, London School of Hygiene and Tropical Medicine.

Julia Twigg, Former Research Student, Department of Sociology, London School of Economics.

Erica Wheeler, Lecturer in Human Nutrition, London School of Hygiene and Tropical Medicine.

Rory Williams, MRC Sociologist, MRC Medical Sociology Unit, Aberdeen.

1 Introduction

ANNE MURCOTT

Study of the social significance of food and eating has mostly been left
to social anthropologists[1], social historians[2], social nutritionists
so-called[3] and other social commentators[4]. Sociologists, especially
in Britain, have paid the matter virtually no sustained attention (but
cf. Mennell forthcoming). There is, then, no identifiable sociological
literature dealing with British culinary practices, menus and manners,
with beliefs and concepts about food and its value, with the social
organisation of the provision of meals - leave alone how they all may
relate to the position of those able to overeat while many must go
short. Yet as Goody (1982) has observed, academic concern with these
questions is by no means frivolous. As part and parcel of the culture
and structure of the societies in which they occur they have a bearing
on attempts either to create change or to appreciate its consequences.
These original essays have been gathered together to begin remedying
this oversight.[5]

The general orientation of this collection owes obvious debt to the
anthropologists. Recognising that people eat food not feed (Douglas,
1977)[6] provides for study of 'philosophies' of eating, of what, in
other words, is believed to be food's goodness - medically and
gastronomically. Further, such beliefs are to be considered not in
isolation, but in the context of the social mores in which eating and
drinking are done. So eating habits are viewed as a matter of culture,
a product of codes of conduct and of the structure of social relationships. Indeed what and how people eat or drink may usefully be
understood in terms of a system whose coherence is afforded by the
social and cultural organisation with which it is associated.

The approach is extended here to empirical instances in modern Britain.
Only four chapters (2, 3, 8 and 17) derive from studies expressly
intended to explore what Wellin (1953) has called food ideologies, two
(13 and 14) capitalise on fairly limited evidence in order to ponder
relevant lines of thinking, and the rest are based on research in which
a concern with food and eating was either incidental, or assumed
importance only as an afterthought. All are somewhat exploratory and
speculative. They are arranged in three sections - references have been
consolidated in a single bibliography at the end of the volume and
documents, such as pamphlets or cookbooks considered as data, are mostly
identified in the footnotes to the relevant chapter.

Two major themes recur throughout the book. One concerns the way
eating is a matter of morality (cf. Turner, 1982). In order to under-

line the point, contributors have unrepentantly traded upon sayings and
cliches highlighting the commonplace equation of nutritional with social
values. 'Eat up, it's good for you' connotes not only medicinal virtues
- and perhaps tastiness - but also the moral assurance that this is the
right and proper way to behave. The right food - whether for health, in
sickness or as the appropriate menu for the occasion - also conveys a
message that the proprieties are being observed.

The other main theme goes beyond the conventional meanings with which
foodstuffs may be invested. What is eaten, how it is cooked and served,
the range of choice, who does the preparation, all are also a matter of
material and social relationships. They are integrally located in a
hierarchical social structure where power, wealth and freedom of choice
are unevenly distributed.

The four essays of Section One illustrate each of these themes.
Looking at rhetoric surrounding both so-called 'health' foods and
processed, highly refined products, Atkinson illustrates the general
issue of the way food is available to carry meanings about what is
natural, proper and virtuous. Twigg takes this up and shows that modern
vegetarianism is a philosophy of eating which, far from being isolated
from the meat-eating ideologies of the dominant culture, instead
reflects and reworks them. Newby follows, exploding the myth that those
who work on the land somehow enjoy thereby privileged access to a store
of unusually fresh and wholesome foodstuffs. Not only is the agricultural labourer's cuisine strikingly similar to that of the city
dweller, ironically it also costs more as a result of the now
corporately organised production and distribution of food. Farmworkers
and their urban counterparts are each alienated from what they produce;
the work of each constrained - and by the same token meal breaks
controlled. Based on a number of years of observational research
Batstone discusses how car workers' limited discretion over the timing
and place of meals at work contrasts starkly with the degree of freedom
allowed company directors. The extremes of the industrial hierarchy are
thus reflected and reaffirmed.

The morality of diet continues through Section Two. Good food is more
than a mere matter of nutritional value - a balanced diet more than just
a matter of health. Monitoring bodily wellbeing is reflected in notions
about suitable eating and bodily experiences impinge in ways that demand
management.[7]. Although pregnancy is widely held to be a time of
bizarre food habits Macintyre concludes that medical textbooks and
popular advice handbooks pay little attention to changes in appetite and
taste, treating them as trivial and peripheral. She draws in detail on
a study of married women expecting their first child to show that such
changes are not necessarily limited to the early stages and that they
assume a greater social, and perhaps, medical importance than is
supposed in the literature. Homans also considers the change that
pregnancy means. By juxtaposing perceptions of Asian and British women
she finds that dietary balance is a watchword for both groups. In
Wheeler and Tan's account of the views of Hongkong Chinese in London
balance, though construed differently, is once more the key. Food is
held to play a central part in maintaining a harmony between the body
and the environment that will ensure good health in infancy, during
pregnancy and motherhood and into old age.

Geographically, and more especially culturally, distant the epitome of

'goodness' for Scots grandmothers is the wholesomeness of soup, whereas
their daughters stress the value of milk. This leads Blaxter and
Paterson to conclude that 'goodness' is as much a moral as nutritional
value. Ideas about food appropriate to different states and stages in
life recur amongst the elderly Aberdonians studied by Williams. In the
process they draw a striking distinction between 'illness food' and
'health food'. Such a contrast is echoed in Pill's description of two
different folk theories of the causes of illness expressed by some
working class women in South Wales. She goes on to explore how far
notions of good food, the right diet and overeating are linked to these
two styles of reasoning. In the final essay in this section Posner
examines some of the moral ambiguities surrounding sweets and sweet
foods in advice given to diabetics.

   The third section returns to the theme of food in relation to
hierarchical social organisation but this time based on gender rather
than class. That men, women and children eat differently (in terms of
quantity and quality) is more than a matter of the physiology of average
differences in height and weight. It also reflects cultural values
about masculinity and femininity such that the privileging of men when
distributing food is, according to Delphy (1979), so well ingrained as
to be experienced as 'natural'. (See also Pilgrim Trust, 1938; Dennis
et al., 1956; Llewellyn Davies, 1978). And, of course, the conventions
governing the mutual marital obligations of men and women typically
revolve around cooking and meals. The wife's responsibility is to cook
for her husband - the corollary of the husband's responsibility to
provide for his wife. (cf. Kerr and Charles, 1982 and Murcott, 1982a).
Opening this section Delamont looks at the neglected topic of wedding
rituals and proposes that the two main types of menu she has traced
convey messages that correspond to middle and working class versions of
the 'proper' role of a wife. These versions represent an ideal. But
proprieties become peculiarly apparent when the 'normal' is disrupted.
So Burgoyne and Clark were especially struck by the way meals, cooking
and diet featured in accounts of the dissolution and reformation of
marriage. A grimmer picture of the expectations of the conventional
division of labour is provided by Ellis who reviews her own and others'
research to illustrate that failure to cook what and when he wants
frequently turns out to be the trigger to a husband's beating his wife.

   A cookery class for men is unusual, and the one Coxon describes did
not survive. His examination of the anomalous status of men with no
women to cook for them, the syllabus and the interaction in the
classroom once again points, from this different way on, to the
convention that cooking is women's work. Finally, my own chapter also
looks at men and women in the kitchen. It draws together three strands
of evidence - on the valuation of 'cooked dinners', reasserting that
women are the cooks and report that husbands do prepare food - to
suggest that it is not so much that women do the cooking as what is
called cooking describes the work women are to do.

   This collection is evidently selective, in at least two ways. First,
it touches on only a limited range substantively. It deals with food
beliefs of the elderly but not the young (cf. James, 1981), of women
more than men. The import of food for special occasions is represented
only by wedding menus, not birthday parties, visits by heads of state or
funerals (but cf. Clark, 1982, pp.129-30). School dinners, meals in

3

barracks, prisons or hospitals (cf. Paterson, 1981) scarce get a
mention. And questions about the relation of alcohol use to meals, of
so-called eating disorders, or other food related social problems are
not even raised. All these, and more, have yet thoroughly to be
considered. Second, contributors have confined themselves to rather
general statements of possible lines of enquiry and in so doing they
consciously leave more discriminating discussion of analytic approaches
to another occasion.

So this volume has been compiled with no illusions: a very great deal
more work is necessary. New data have to be collected, not as an
afterthought, but systematically, in suitably mounted research. And
further efforts are needed to develop adequate analyses that deal
convincingly not only with the symbolic significance, but also the
material and social organisation of food and eating.

NOTES

[1] As well as Richards' classic studies (1938, 1948), the work of
    Lévi-Strauss (1966, 1970, 1973, 1978) and Douglas (e.g. 1975,
    1976-77, 1977) there are various edited collections (e.g. Arnott,
    1975; Fitzgerald, 1976; Jerome et al., 1980; Fenton and Owen,
    1981; de Garine and Hladik, forthcoming), the occasional special
    study (e.g. Chang, 1977; Hugh-Jones, 1978) and textbook (Farb and
    Armelagos, 1980). Goody's Cooking, Cuisine and Class (1982) is a
    most important addition. The journal Social Science Information
    now includes a special section devoted to the 'Anthropology of
    Food', and see also articles carried by Ecology of Food and
    Nutrition.
[2] For instance Hartley (1954), Drummond and Wilbraham (1958),
    Tannahill (1975), Wilson (1976), Johnson (1977), Burnett (1979),
    also Barkas (1975); and more analytic, Forster and Ranum (1979)
    translated from the French, and Elias' (1978) tour de force
    translated from the German.
[3] E.g. Yudkin and McKenzie (1964), Barker et al. (1966) and their
    colleagues at the Queen Elizabeth College, London, and see the
    Nutrition Bulletin of the British Nutrition Foundation (BNF); also
    dietary surveys whose ostensible concerns range from health and
    welfare to market research (Boyd Orr, 1936; Barker et al., 1970;
    Crawford, 1938; Warrent, 1958; BNF, 1979; Kraft, 1979 and also
    Allen, 1968).
[4] In addition to the literature on world poverty, famine and mal-
    nutrition, are the studies of food aid (e.g. Stevens, 1979; Sinha
    1976), commentaries on the politics of national and international
    hunger (e.g. de Castro, 1967; Darling, 1941; Kotz, 1971; Balaam
    and Carey, 1981), exposés of the consequences of mult-national
    control of food production (e.g. Politics of Health Group, 1979;
    George and Paige, 1982; Tudge, 1979; Wright, 1981) and pleas for
    a more thoughtful attitude to food choice (e.g. Dufty, 1975;
    McLaughlin, 1978; Wynne-Tyson, 1975).
[5] Quite why sociologists have overlooked the study of the social
    significance of food can only be a matter of guesswork. Perhaps it
    reflects an unsociological dismissal of the topic as biological
    rather than social and thus the province of agriculturalists,
    nutritionists and so on. It may be bound up with efforts to claim

4

academic respectability. Attention has been concentrated on areas
of social life of moral and political substance and accorded
prestige such as politics, education or work. Many food related
activities in industrial society are expressly outside and beyond
the limits of work (gainful employment). Home based they belong
to the semi-visible domestic sphere. If the topic is indeed
regarded as of marginal importance socially, it may primarily have
been neglected lest the consequence of paying serious attention to
the 'trivial' risks trivialising attempts to be taken seriously.

[6] cf. 'A food has no meaning if a man does not give it a meaning by
     willingly eating it', Tremolières (1970).

[7] cf. 'On the one hand, man is a body, in the same way that this may
     be said of every other animal organism. On the other hand, man
     has a body. That is, man experiences himself as an entity that is
     not identical with his body, but that, on the contrary, has that
     body at its disposal. In other words, man's experience of himself
     always hovers in a balance between being and having a body, a
     balance that must be redressed again and again'. (Berger and
     Luckman, 1966).

SECTION I

EATING, CULTURE AND SOCIAL ORGANISATION

2 Eating Virtue

PAUL ATKINSON

FOOD AND GOOD TASTE: ETHICS AND AESTHETICS

The starting point for this essay was a BBC radio programme on food.
The presenter was talking to a representative of the food manufacturing
industry, on the topic of frozen pre-cooked foods. The general issue
that was being explored was the guilt which many so-called 'housewives'
apparently feel at using such 'convenience' food products, and whether
such meals were comparable in quality and nutritional value to foods
prepared by the 'housewives' themselves. The manufacturers' spokesperson was at pains to further the claim that the processes and
techniques of freezing mean that the foods need simply to be cooked, and
need no extra preservatives and so on. The interviewer took him up on
this point, noting that many of the commercial frozen dishes he had
investigated contained monosodium glutamate. The spokesperson replied
that this was rather a reflection of poor cooking in the first place,
not an inherent limitation of the processing, as monosodium glutamate
was merely a flavour-enhancing additive. He went on to point out that
many Americans sprinkle it over their food, like salt and pepper.

Now it seems to me that this fragment of 'data' is potentially
interesting from a number of different, but related, points of view. In
the first place it highlights how the preparation and consumption of
foodstuffs reflects social attitudes and values: the presumed 'guilt'
of the housewife suggests that there are strong cultural assumptions
about the proper character of food and its production. It also
suggests that such values may depend on the extent to which food has
been 'processed' or 'tampered with' in ways which are disapproved or
viewed with suspicion. Finally, the implied objection to monosodium
glutamate reinforces these concerns. It would appear that the anomaly
here (if one is perceived) is the addition of a 'chemical' to foodstuffs.
The common terminology of 'artificial additives' seems to reflect this -
and the connotations of that phrase certainly do. Yet on the face of
it, there is little to choose between the addition of monosodium
glutamate and the sprinkling of sodium chloride (i.e. table salt).

This is not a question of gastronomics, nor of nutrition. My point
here is not based on whether salt or monosodium glutamate are equally
desirable flavourings, whether they are in the best traditions of
cordon-bleu cookery or whatever. Nor do I want to pursue the matter of
'taste' in the other sense - to spell out the issues of snobbery which
may underpin attitudes against 'convenience' foods (though my reference

9

to cordon-bleu is intended to resonate with such attitudes and pretensions). Rather, I want to pursue the issue of why the very notion of 'artificial' additives and so on should appear to carry the cultural connotations that it does. I want to argue that this relates to a more general issue, if how food and food mythology is available to convey meanings of what is more natural, what is proper and what is virtuous.

It has been widely remarked - particularly by structuralist observers - that food, and the activities of cooking and eating, furnish concrete realisations for the expression of implicit 'messages'. Food, drink and their associations provide 'codes': that is, terms for the working out of 'myth-logic', in which cultural oppositions, puzzles and paradoxes may be expressed, and may achieve a symbolic resolution.

Roland Barthes, for instance, found a place for food in his outline of systems of signification - along with others like clothing - which may be subjected to formal semiological analysis on lines derived from de Saussure's structural linguistics (Barthes, 1967). More recently Barthes has contributed a number of brief essays on food and drink, and their significance in French culture. In his essay on 'Wine and Milk', for example, he remarks that wine enters into every aspect of ceremonial in French everyday life, and indeed provides 'a foundation for a collective morality' (Barthes, 1973): it can accommodate a wide range of symbolism within French culture. Similarly, of milk he remarks (p.60):

> ...milk is cosmetic, it joins, covers, restores. Moreover, its purity, associated with the innocence of the child, is a token of strength, of strength which is not revulsive, not congestive, but calm, white, lucid, the equal of reality.

Barthes' remarks here are precisely paralleled in one of the recent advertising campaigns for milk in Great Britain. One of the advertisements appearing in magazines consisted of a strip of five photographs featuring a large balding man with a grizzled beard, and an infant girl. Both are wearing tee-shirts bearing pictures of cows. They each have a glass of milk. The 'story' is that the little girl's milk is spilled and she mops it up. The legend runs:

> Little Miss Moppitt and her dad
> Mister Moppit, dropped it all over the floor
> Oh dear, said Miss Moppitt,
> I'll mop it, flip flop it
> and Daisy will have to make more.

The final frame concludes with the assertion 'No drink can beat it. Milk is supreme'. No further claim for the value of milk is made in so many words. The wording of the advertisement has little, ostensibly, to do with any possible benefits or attractions for milk as a drink: the 'story' and the doggerel are, in one sense, of minimal referential value. But the advertisement does not rely solely on the text. The pictures convey a message all the stronger for being implicit. The imagery is powerful. Milk is 'about' big strong people, and small innocent children; it is 'about' pure innocence as well as grown-up understanding; it is 'about' caring, sharing and tenderness; it is 'about' a nostalgia for the simplicity of the nursery and the nursery rhyme. The presence of a large grizzled father, rather than a mother, recalls Barthes once more (1973, pp.60-1):

Some American films, in which the hero, strong and uncom-
promising, did not shrink from having a glass of milk before
drawing his avenging Colt, have paved the way for this new
and Parsifalian myth.

It would be invalid, however, to ascribe a single fixed 'mear..
milk, as if one could simply 'crack' a code and hence read off a
corresponding set of significations.   Other advertisements in the
campaign just referred to, for instance, stress different milk-related
meanings.   There is not a simple one to one correspondence between the
elements of such myth-logic or calculus and their value.   Particular
values depend on the contexts in which the various elements are placed.
There are, however, a number of symbolic or semantic spaces that seem
particularly well demarcated by the concrete representation of foodstuffs, even though the actual realisations will vary from cultural
setting to cultural setting, and within them, and from time to time.

Food and drink, then, would appear to be one appropriate mechanism
for the expression of meanings and values concerning the relationship
between Nature and Culture, between the spheres of Human and Animal
species, and concerning the boundaries of 'civilisation' (that is, 'our'
way of life, whoever 'we' may be).   In the milk advertisement referred
to earlier, it is one of a number of oppositions which are, as it were,
caught, suspended and glossed over: Innocence/Experience: Childhood/
Adulthood: Weakness/Strength: Nature/Culture.   Here, as Barthes
remarked, milk 'covers' and 'restores' by mediating these implied
oppositions.   It is a drink for the strong and weak alike - and indeed
it transforms the latter into the former.   At the same time it
reconciles the essentially human sphere of personal relationships with
the natural words of such 'nourishment'.

In a more general sense, milk is one of a number of foodstuffs which
do similar work in the context of Nature/Culture symbolism.   Like honey,
for instance, it has connotations of 'purity' (as well as 'plenty'),
possibly because they come in the form of 'naturally' occurring
'processed' foods.   They require no further processing by their human
consumers other than to render them even more 'pure' by the removal of
'foreign bodies' (cf. Atkinson, 1978).

Food and drink can operate in these symbolic environments by virtue
of both metaphor and metonymy.   Metaphorically, the transformation of
'natural' foodstuffs into the 'cultural' products of the table
parallels other general processes whereby the material world is worked
on and incorporated into the human domain.   It thus can stand for the
many different ways in which the world of culture - of meanings, values
and human work - is created and sustained in the face of an alien, non-
human universe (the jungle, the desert, 'the wild').   At the same time,
food furnishes a direct link - metonymically - between the human and
the natural, between the cultural and the biological: ingested and
processed, it thus spans the two spheres.   This is the observation
which is built on in Lévi-Strauss's exploration of the mythology, in
that 'we cook our food to demonstrate that we are civilized men and not
wild animals, and then...we discriminate types of cooking and food
preparation as markers of social occasions in accordance with a
systematic binary code' (Leach, 1976, p.60).

The 'binary oppositions' are of the form raw/cooked and elaborated/
non-elaborated, which together comprise the coordinates of Lévi-
Strauss's 'culinary triangle' (Lévi-Strauss, 1966). These oppositions
may be employed to construct myths (in the general sense of that term)
which can capture and appear to resolve the paradoxes implied by the
position of human beings who attempt to make sense of their own nature.
In our own culture, food and eating are used for the construction of
mythologies which express variations on the opposition between Nature
and Culture. Such oppositions and their symbolic resolution are used in
particular to express themes of 'health' and 'virtue', generally, by
means of a celebration of 'the natural'.

HEALTH AND THE NATURAL

Not all of the mythic use of food symbolism is necessarily quite as
grandiose as that outlined by Lévi-Strauss, although many of the same
sorts of issues recur in more restricted contexts. Elsewhere I have
argued at greater length (Atkinson, 1980), that contemporary views of
'health foods' and 'wholefoods' can be seen in precisely the same light
as that suggested by Barthes and Lévi-Strauss. Health foods and their
symbolism are, I have argued, remarkably consistent, and present a
coherent 'message'. I have suggested that the semantics of health
foods is based on a small number of stated or implied oppositions. These
oppositions in turn reflect a single underlying dimension of contrast.

In essence, my argument is this: the imagery of health foods -
particularly those which are commercially produced and distributed -
consistently reflect and trade off three fundamental themes or
dimensions. Each provides justification for the general superiority of
special categories of foodstuffs and the virtues of special products.
Put simply, these categories appeal to the 'natural', the 'traditional'
and the 'exotic'. Individually or in combination, these categories
are used to advertise, advocate and celebrate the use of 'natural'
health foods - and, indeed, their health-ful character. At root, I
argue, such imagery is not simply a way of 'packaging' health foods or
making them more attractive: rather, it is constitutive of their
supposed efficacy in the promotion of health and the remedy of disorders.

Let me summarise briefly and exemplify what this imagery consists of.
The 'traditional' and 'exotic' frames of reference are familiar enough
and they reappear consistently in other 'alternative' 'counter-culture'
and 'cultic' contexts - such as those associated with 'hidden wisdom'
and the occult. Thus they can make appeal to 'the wisdom of the
ancients', or of 'the East', to 'ancient' and 'traditional' remedies and
to the presumed qualities of 'primitive' and 'traditional' simplicity.
Herbs are, of course, one class of substances whose therapeutic value
is repeatedly warranted by appeals to their 'traditional' use. As one
promotional leaflet from Heath and Heather puts it, 'They've all been
tried and tested for hundreds of years'. Ginseng is one substance
whose value is often couched in such terms. It has, apparently, the
twin blessings of an 'exotic' provenance and a 'traditional' pedigree.
The following remarks are fairly typical of this sort of thing:

> Ginseng has been used in Eastern traditional medicine for
> centuries - it crops up in old prescriptions for all sorts of
> ills from dysentery to tuberculosis - but Western doctors have

12

largely ignored it in the past....Thousands of people are now
trying this ancient plant to combat the stresses of 20th
Century life.

As the above extract hints, there are overtones of opposition to
Western medicine and science, and undercurrents of 'mystery'. Ginseng
is frequently portrayed as a 'wonder' substance, the miracles of which
are lost in the mists of time:

Digging for the truth about this strange plant has always been
a bit like trying to do a complicated jigsaw puzzle in the dark.
Most of the old records from the East - going back at least to
the first century A.D. - are hard to substantiate.

The wonders which are embodied in this particular tradition include the
promise of youthful vigour and sexual potency:

There are some people who enjoy sex so much that they will spend
a small fortune consuming large quantities of a plant called
ginseng to make sure that lovemaking urges never desert them.
They obviously hope to emulate the emperors and wealthy nobles
of ancient China who found their strength and stamina so
enhanced from eating ginseng that they could spend hours a day
making love and conducting business with callers at the same
time.

This 'mysterious root from the East', then, exemplifies the appeal of
traditional non-Western therapeutic regimes. In some contexts, indeed,
it appears to be a major feature held in their favour that they are not
endorsed, or are even opposed by 'orthodox' Western science and
medicine. In the context of herbal remedies, for instance, one leaflet
remarks, 'However much progress science makes in the field of medicine,
people still come back to these simple, natural herbal remedies'. This
can be illustrated from the following extract from a magazine article
on the topic:

Graham Rudge, merchandising manager for Holland and Barrett, who
own 130 health food shops, agrees that few clinical trials have
been held to support the claims for many of the 1500 products
they offer in shops. 'On the other hand',he says, 'with many of
the herbal food supplements and remedies there are hundreds of
years of people's experience to call upon'.

Compare the preceding remarks with these, from a leaflet promoting
Vitamin C tablets:

The results of vitamin C deficiency have been known for
centuries. Scurvy was mentioned in the Old Testament and by
the Egyptians, and it is also well known how the fatal
consequences of scurvy which occurred on long sea voyages in
the Middle Ages, were overcome by giving sailors fresh lemon
or lime juice....

Thus even such relatively 'modern' discoveries as vitamins may be
linked with 'traditional' perspectives. In some contexts the two can be
combined. Healthcraft products, for example, market the GEB[6] combination - which combines the three 'magical substances' (as this
leaflet describes them) ginseng, vitamin E and vitamin B6.   This
dietary supplement of 'natural nutrients' is designed to 'combat
stress'. (In addition to the usual 'traditional appeals on behalf of
ginseng we are here informed that it was a compulsory part of the diet

an astronauts, and is used by Dr Henry Kissinger - in
ct, perhaps, not the best advertisement for the root's effects.)

ese vitamins, however, are redeemed from their 'modern' or
cientific' connotations, since - it is repeatedly emphasised - they
are 'natural' in origin rather than 'synthetic'. The literature and
promotional material go to considerable lengths to spell this out. For
instance:

Natural or synthetic vitamin E?

Natural vitamin E comes in two forms: d-Alpha tocopheryl
acetate, the oil, and d-Alpha tocopheryl succinate, a powder.
Synthetic vitamin E is known as d-Alpha tocopheryl acetate.
It's worth checking for the d-Alpha on the pack - natural
vitamin E has been found to be much more effective than
synthetic varieties.

This again is taken from a promotional leaflet.

This introduces the dominant appeal of 'health-food' imagery - that
it is all 'natural'. The appeal to nature as virtuous in itself is
frequently made. The products are variously referred to as 'natural
dietary supplements', 'food from nature' and so on. There is no need
to exemplify this at great length, since the 'natural' connotations of
health-foods are commonly known (cf. Atkinson, 1980).

The category of 'natural' carries with it overtones of 'purity',
which is also captured in the closely associated notion of 'whole' food.
As one magazine column devoted to this topic remarked:

It's simply choosing and using the best and healthiest
ingredients that haven't been 'messed about with' either in
the growing (chemicals and insecticides) or in the
processing (refining) that takes half the goodness out, as
with white flour and refined sugar, or preserving chemicals
that destroy vitamins and minerals.

This reflects one of the major components of the imagery - that most
contemporary foodstuffs, especially so-called 'convenience' foods have
been tampered with, adulterated, have had their 'natural' nutrients
destroyed, or have been otherwise impaired.

There is thus a contrast between the 'natural'/'healthy' on the one
hand, and 'unnatural'/'unhealthy' on the other. Poor food and poor
health are held up as both cause and symptom of much 'modern' malaise.
It is a cause in that poor or inappropriate eating is believed to
contribute to a lack of physical or mental wellbeing. It is a symptom,
insofar as modern living is unhealthy and stressful in general.

Health foods, then, can be thought of in the following way. They
offer a concrete solution to a particular conceptual 'problem'. They
provide a resolution - a reconciliation or mediation - between the
'natural' and the 'cultural' spheres, between the urban and the rural,
between the past and the present, between the pre-industrial and the
industrial, between the magical and the scientific. Health foods in
this fashion therefore provide for their consumers encapsulated
'harmony' and, indeed, virtue. As Carter (1976) perceptively remarks,
they suggest that 'you can chew your way back to a lost harmony with

14

nature: the way to the Kingdom of God lies directly down the gullet'.

It is clear, therefore, that the dominant appeal of health foods is a
mythological or symbolic one. It offers an embodiment of an urban/
suburban pastoral dream - of the 'good life'. It holds out the
promise of a lifestyle which is 'natural', and in such a return to
nature lies the promise of a simpler self-sufficiency: that is, a way
of life in which personal autonomy and control are celebrated. To
quote Carter again, it treats the person as a microcosm:

> He has poisoned his own system with meat, white sugar, refined
> flour, chemical additives. He has poisoned his ecological
> system, which is an image of himself. The self-sufficient
> farming unit...is a model of an environment over which he will
> be able to exert maximum control.

The point about health-foods as such, however, is that for the great
majority of people these ideas do not actually lead towards a 'natural'
or 'self-sufficient' way of life (whatever they might be in practice).
They lead in fact to minor adjustments in lifestyle. If anything,
they substitute for action. In that sense the purchase and consumption
of commercial health-foods is a ritual, or magical act. Health-foods
can substitute for any major changes in everyday life by allowing the
consumer to ingest virtue in a concrete form.

The categories of 'nature' and so on which are involved in such
contexts are not themselves culturally uncontaminated. They draw on a
wealth of imagery of rural and urban living, in which that contrast is
made to do service to convey moral messages: the contrast between rural
order and urban chaos, between natural virtue and degeneracy. The very
imagery of the adulteration of 'pure' food with synthetic additives is
pregnant with such associations. The pervasive imagery is of the
corruption of nature by artifice, or wholeness by impurity.

This mythology of food thus reproduces a more general and long
standing belief system. It is the contrast between the urban (the
'cultured') and the rural (the 'natural'): these also stand for the
'modern' and the 'traditional' respectively. These oppositions and
their potent connotations are entirely familiar to the sociologist.
They are part and parcel of that strand in sociology which rests on
versions of the selfsame dichotomy. As Newby (1977, p.96) says of one
tendency in the sociological tradition:

> Once the broad categories of characteristic rural social traits
> had been derived by Tonnies, it merely remained for a myriad of
> locality studies to establish how gemeinschaftlich was
> community X (equals 'good', 'healthy', 'natural') and how
> gesellschaftlich was community Y (equals 'bad', 'alienating',
> 'unnatural').

As Newby goes on to remark, many rural studies attempted to assess the
'health' of given 'communities' - an analytic metaphor which parallels
the present discussion of 'natural' health and health foods.

This mythology is potent. It is little wonder that it has been co-
opted by the manufacturers and advertisers of 'orthodox', 'unhealthy'
foods. The imagery here is redolent of the same themes that have
already been identified in the context of health foods. 'Nature' and

15

'tradition' abound. The 'country' and portrayals of a 'traditional' rural way of life are deployed repeatedly in advertisements for mass-produced foodstuffs.

The crusty 'farmhouse' loaf, 'farmhouse' cheddar cheese, 'farmer's wife' dairy products and so on all appeal to these image. They endow products with a supposed authenticity. Advertisements for brown bread, cakes and chocolates hark back to traditional craftmanships, for products which are mass produced. Cereal products, biscuits and the like, we are told, are full of 'natural goodness'. Butter advertisements on television feature rustic yokels, as do those for pots of meat paste.

The notion of factory farming is repugnant to many people. In large measure this derives from various sorts of revulsion at 'inhuman' treatment of the animals in question. There has recently been a flurry of interest in the moral philosophy of animals' rights, occasioned by such sentiments. Similarly, agribusiness is vilified - because it is regarded as wasteful of natural resources, relies on 'artificial' chemical fertilizers and so on. Such 'ecological' arguments are now familiar enough and have been widely disseminated. But I suspect that the repugnance may stem from an even more basic source, to be located at the symbolic or mythological level.

From this point of view the very term 'factory-farming' is a contradiction in terms. For the 'factory' is preeminently urban, modern, and a source of synthetic (manufactured) articles. Farming is preeminently rural, and is the home of natural categories. Their combination is thus a confusion of otherwise antithetical categories, and hence an 'abomination'. (See Douglas, 1966, for the abominations which are consequent upon the confusion of cultural categories). The pollution of the country by the city is, of course, reversed by the establishment of 'city farms', whereby the city is injected with rural virtue.

Mass produced goods which make their appeal to 'nature' and 'tradition' hence mask their actual production, and the 'abomination' they create. Rather, they invoke a mythological charter in which the categories are kept separate and pure. The 'old order' is maintained and the mythological contradictions of the new are thus glossed over. This resolution is the work of all mythology: and the systems of health foods and the promotion of 'ordinary' foods are alike in this respect. Both purvey the message that social order and personal virtue can be eaten. Just as in some belief systems one may be thought to consume the strength of one's prey, so in such food imagery one can ingest the mana of 'pure', 'natural' food. In this way can harmony be restored, and abominations abolished.

Both the marketing of modern 'health' foods, and that of many 'orthodox' mass produced food products draw on precisely the same stock of beliefs, myths and imagery. Indeed, it is remarkable how far advanced is the convergence between the two. Commercial products are themselves endowed with qualities of virtue. Their purchase and consumption is thus portrayed as a morally desirable act. In this way, therefore, eating does not appear to be a matter of self-indulgence, convenience or similar frivolity. It is itself virtuous. Manufacturers and advertisers can in this fashion offer the consumer a concrete manifestation of moral superiority.

The emphasis here upon 'natural' virtue and the corresponding connotations of 'tradition' and the 'primitive' or 'exotic', serve to highlight the pervasively moral nature of food and eating. Good taste is always simultaneously a question of aesthetics and of ethics. And eating what is 'good for you' is always more than a matter of mere nutritional value.

In this essay I have used the substantive topic of so-called health foods to illustrate that more general theme. But as I have gone on to suggest, the issues are much more thoroughly pervasive. In contemporary culture, 'eating virtue' is also congruent with other themes in health-related belief and action. These include the ever-growing significance of 'body-maintenance' through exercise, jogging and the like, notions that 'you are what you eat', associated with the search for food allergies, self-treatment varieties of 'alternative' therapy, the promotion of self-awareness and so on. These all have a number of common properties. There is a strong emphasis upon self-help and individualistic solutions to problems (including health and illness). They thus appeal to a mixture of self-reliant Protestant ethic and self-regarding narcissism.

Many of these 'alternative' approaches, and their popularised commercial versions, make appeal to the symbolic significance of 'natural' categories. They offer symbolic and concrete ways for members of contemporary society to formulate diffuse dissatisfactions with their culture, and express dissatisfaction with themselves, while simultaneously providing resolutions of personal problems and cultural paradoxes.

3 Vegetarianism and the Meanings of Meat

JULIA TWIGG

Animals bear a special and complex role in our relationship with nature. They are potent symbols. They are both in us, as our enduring biological heritage, and beyond us, as an extension of human society, as a parallel society and as a projection of what we are not. Eating, as has been commonly remarked, produces a particularly intimate identification with the consumed product: we are what we eat. It is therefore not surprising when we look cross culturally at food patterns that meat, and to a lesser extent animal products, are by far the most common focus of taboo, regulation and avoidance (Simoons, 1961). The eating of meat involves a literal incorporation of the animal, and as such presents us with the ambivalences and complexities of our own attitudes to animals and the animal, nature and the natural.

It is clear that food in the west is culturally patterned, and bears similar symbolic meanings to those familiar in the analyses of anthropologists (e.g. Douglas, 1972; Douglas and Nicod, 1974; Lévi-Strauss, 1966, 1970: Arnott, 1975; Robson, 1980) though these meanings tend to be more fragmentary and implicit. This is partly because of the more complex and highly differentiated nature of western industrial societies, which rest on different forms of integration from those of apparently simpler societies; though it arises also, erroneously, from the nature of our analyses, from the character of our accounting. Thus there is a tendency to treat western society in a privileged, over rationalistic way. We can be very sophisticated in our treatment of articulate areas of social knowledge like science or politics, but pass over unanalysed some of the most deeply embedded and fundamental of patterns within a culture. Too often our analyses unthinkingly accept the culture's own valuation of the daily, the domestic and the organic. Part of the purpose of a study such as that presented here is to show how seemingly trivial or mundane aspects of life, such as food and food patterns, touch at times on the most profound of issues.

Vegetarianism presents us in this context with the relatively rare example in the west of an explicit food ideology (c.f. Wellin, 1953) and as such it can offer us an entree into the much more pervasive, though largely implicit, ideology of dominant meat culture. (The expression dominant culture is used here as a shorthand standing in opposition to vegetarian culture, though it is of course itself complex and diverse).

Before turning to look at the meaning of meat in vegetarian and

18

dominant culture, I need to make one or two points concerning
vegetarianism and the scope of this chapter.

Here I shall confine myself to the modern western context, and
specifically to Britain (though there are parallels with America and
Germany, the two other significant centres of western vegetarianism).
Vegetarianism has, of course, had a much wider cultural ambit than this,
most notably in the classical and mediaeval worlds and in Indian
culture. In addition certain central ideas concerning meat have been
widely recurrent, particularly in its relationship to carnality,
spirituality and pollution, and to a series of images to do with
redness and inflaming. These have, however, been worked through
within very different cultural structures. Thus in the case of India,
vegetarianism is intimately bound up with caste. High caste Hindus do
not eat meat, and vegetarianism links with a series of other
prohibitions and taboos concerned with gradations of purity and status.
These act as divisions that define and separate the castes while at the
same time integrating them into the functionally interdependent
hierarchy that forms the basis of traditional Indian society (Dumont,
1970). In helping to underwrite this hierarchy vegetarianism is fully
part of the social structure. It is a culturally normative feature.
In the west, by contrast, vegetarianism is very much a product of
individual choice, and indeed, requiring one, as it does, to step
outside the culturally prescribed forms of eating, depends on the
development of a highly individuated sense of the self. Furthermore as
a cultural phenomenon it is strongly associated with an egalitarian,
anti-structural ethic that is in marked contrast to the Indian
experience. Western vegetarianism is also dominated by the imagery of
Eden and of its recovery, whereas such a return to a primordial
innocence of matter is essentially alien to Hindu thought. Cultural
contact with India since the nineteenth century has, of course,
influenced and reinforced western vegetarianism, particularly in its
spiritual connections. There remains, however, a fundamental
difference in social meaning between the two examples.

Again, modern vegetarianism contrasts with the case of mediaeval
'vegetarianism', the abstinence from red meat practised or at least
enjoined upon the monastic orders. The Rule of St Benedict, which
ultimately governs all western monasticism, was commonly interpreted as
forbidding all quadruped meat, and thus allowing poultry, fish and
animal products (see Butler, 1923; Knowles, 1940, 1948). Periods of
laxity resulted in the widespread evasion of this rule, though
reforming periods and orders often reinstated it more vigorously,
extending the prohibition to poultry and fish as well as at times of
fasting like Good Friday or Lent generally, to animal products
altogether. As we shall see these gradations of abstinence are
relevant also to modern vegetarianism. However, despite these and
other shared themes, mediaeval vegetarianism is contained within a
very different structure of meaning from that of its modern counterpart.
Mediaeval vegetarianism occurs in the context of virtuoso religion, of
the patterning of fast and feast days and of a straightforward denial
of the flesh that draws on manichaean conceptions. [1] The
predominant idea is negative, one of avoidance, and I can find no
sense of vegetarian food as being in any way 'better' or 'higher' food
or as having its own positive attributes - themes of great importance
in contemporary vegetarianism.

I shall therefore confine my comments in this chapter to what can very broadly be termed 'modern' vegetarianism. By this I mean the set of ideas and associations gathered around the eschewal of meat that begins tentatively to emerge in the late eighteenth century particularly in connection with the first romantic movement, and that gathers strength in the nineteenth, finding an institutional expression in the founding of the Vegetarian Society in 1847. Thereafter vegetarianism, though always very much a minority concern, expands in popularity, enjoying particular periods of success in the 1880s and 1890s, when it was associated with a wider progressivist milieu (embracing, among others, ethical socialism, Indian religion, anti-vaccination and anti-vivisection), or within a similar context, in the late 1920s and 1930s, nature cures, the sunshine movement and pacifism. The most recent period of upsurge was in the late 1960s and 1970s when vegetarianism was part of what can loosely be termed the counter culture and its wider cultural ramifications. While there are of course important historical differences in vegetarianism over this 'modern' period, there is enough of a unity to its ideas and concerns for it very broadly to be treated as a whole.

There is a second sense in which one can speak of modern vegetarianism as a cultural unity, and this concerns the unity of it as an ideology. Vegetarianism of course, like any other cultural phenomenon is very diverse, and the people who adopt it do so for many different reasons: however behind this diversity there is also a cohererence. For example there have traditionally been four major foci to the vegetarian argument - health, and animal welfare, and to a lesser extent, the economic/ecological and the spiritual. These are on the face of it very different types of argument that appeal to very different criteria of knowledge. However a closer examination in the context of the wider ideology shows them in fact to be interconnected and indeed to draw strength from one another. Thus the wrongness of exploiting animals relates also to the wrongness of exploiting the Third World. The ecological arguments concerning the devastation of nature and the destruction of animal species relate both to the rights of animals to exist and to essentially 'spiritual' conceptions of the whole and of the balance of Man within Nature. Natural balance is central in naturopathic ideas of health which are essentially concerned with either right living or natural ways of life. Health in vegetarianism means much more than just an absence of illness; it has a positive sense and includes wide ideas of mental and spiritual well-being. Spiritual wellbeing comes from right action in the world. There is a web of such cross connections, and the moral, the physical, the political and the spiritual merge into one another.

In addition to these interconnections, there is also a wider network of parallel causes that helps to make up the vegetarian milieu. It is one of the most characteristic features of vegetarianism that it rarely occurs alone, but comes in conjunction with a complex of other beliefs, attitudes and parallel movements. These associations are strong, but not necessary, both in the sense that they are not an inherent part of the definition of vegetarianism - thus neither an interest in communal living, nor a support for nuclear disarmament are themselves implied by an abstinence from meat - and that not all vegetarians need espouse them. However, what vegetarianism, as it were, 'goes with' is as important in an understanding of it as its more intrinsic features.

20

I have developed a general account of this vegetarian ideology, its
history and its wider associations elsewhere (Twigg, 1981). Here I
concentrate on just one aspect, namely the ways in which vegetarian
perceptions of meat endorse, mirror and disrupt those found in dominant
culture. In this way examination of a minority ideology can reveal
features of the wider, more pervasive set of ideas familiar to us all.

TABOO	Too strong	human beings carnivores uncastrated animals	Uncooked	raw meat
	DOMINANT CULTURE'S BOUNDARY			

MEAT	Strong
	    blood
	    powerful
		red meat	Cooking
			necessary
				roasted joints
				stewed meat

	non blood less powerful	poultry		roasted boiled
		fish		fried steamed
	VEGETARIAN BOUNDARY			
ANIMAL PRODUCTS	Less strong	eggs		fried boiled cooked as a dish
		cheese		raw, grated
	VEGAN BOUNDARY			
FRUIT & VEGETABLES	Too weak	fruit		
		leaf vegetables		
		root vegetables		
		cereals		

Figure 3.1 Hierarchy of foods

I would like to start by suggesting that the dominant culture contains
a hierarchy of foods represented in Figure 3.1. Meat is the most highly
prized of food. It is the centre around which a meal is arranged. It
stands in a sense for the very idea of food itself – a quality it
shares with bread, humbler and symbolically very different: our meat

21

and drink. At the top of the hierarchy, then, we find meat, and in particular red meat, for the status and meaning of meat is quintessentially found in red meat. Lower in status are the 'bloodless' meats - chicken and fish - and below these are the animal products - eggs and cheese. These are sufficiently high in the hierarchy to support a meal's being formed around them, though they are confined to the low status events - the omelette and cheese flan of light lunch or supper. Below these we have the vegetables, regarded in the dominant scheme as insufficient for the formation of a meal, and merely ancillary.

If we look at the top of the scale, we see that that which is highest in status approaches nearest the taboo. This is the familiar anthropological concept whereby that which is most highly prized, most sacred, can, by virtue of its power, be the most defiling. We have already noted how meat and to a lesser extent animal products are cross culturally the most circumscribed of foods, and there are muted aspects of this in the equivocation and ambivalence detectable in the dominant culture's attitude to meat. Thus animal derived foods have a potential for provoking unease that is not found in vegetable foods. Angyal (1941) in a study of disgust and related food aversions, found that the focus was always around meat or animal products. Similarly nearly every item in Macbeth's repulsively potent witch's brew is animal: little of such feeling can be made from vegetable substances. In the same way the rejected parts of animal food - gristle, blood vessels, eyes, in particular the distinguishable parts of the animal [2] - provoke revulsion while those of vegetable food - hard skins, cores etc. - do not: they are quite neutral. Vegetarians have long argued for an underlying unease, even guilt, within the dominant culture over meat eating evidenced in myths and legends. Thus Eden has for many centuries been characterised within dominant culture as vegetarian and similar ideas have been held about the Golden Age. In the same way utopian and futuristic novels, even when written by non vegetarians, have recurrently featured vegetarian communities.

And yet meat is at the same time the most highly regarded form of food. The answer lies in the qualities that meat is believed to promote, for eating meat involves the literal incorporation of animal flesh. Deeply embedded in dominant culture is the idea of animal food as containing certain qualities, a particular power. This power centres around the qualities of strength, aggression, passion, sexuality - all that culture has traditionally designated humankind's animal nature. Here we are faced with a certain ambivalence, for dominant culture prizes these qualities but in a qualified way; enough but not too much, as we shall see, is the essence of its attitude to this power.

Of central importance in this is blood. Blood has had a long history of symbolic significance. Three main foci are of relevance here. The first is as the living essence. Blood is traditionally the seat of the soul, the bearer of life - as it ebbs away in bleeding we die - and from this derives its sacred power and its ability to defile - blood will not wash off a guilty hand. Its vivid, violent redness has come to evoke deeds of violence. Spilt blood stands as an image of discordance, of the fracturing of harmony. It is the focus of powerful feelings, people faint at the sight of it.

The second focus is as the special and particular character of a person or group. Thus blood is commonly perceived - against biology - as the link in inheritance, and as the bearer of the characteristics of the group or individual - thus noble blood, tainted blood. A union in blood, whether biologically or ritually achieved - for example through blood brotherhood - is seen as producing a special unity, a mystical bond. Related to this set of ideas is the common use of the blood stream as an emblem of the self and of its state. In part this derives from fragmented survivals of the humoural system whereby blood is regarded as the paramount humour at the centre of an elaborate development of microcosm/macrocosm that links the states of the body and of the cosmos. These ideas survive most clearly in popular and folk medical ideas concerning the particular relevance of the state of the blood stream; though they are found also in more developed form in the theories of nature cure and of alternative medicine - movements with which vegetarianism is closely linked.

Finally blood is traditionally seen as the seat of the passions. The blood of the young and vigorous is conceived to be thick, hot and red, in comparison to the thin watery blood of old age. Hot blooded is angry and impulsive; cold blooded is cruel, lacking in proper emotions and passions.

These sets of meanings concerning blood generally, contribute. to the perception of the blood in meat. This view is thus associated with ideas of the living force, carrying aspects of energy and violence, of the arousal and stimulation of the passions and of the distillation of the particular essence of the animal and thus of animality itself.

Thus meat is associated with animal strength. Through the direct, though nutritionally incorrect, equation of muscle with muscle, it has been particularly associated with body building and athletic strength. Victorian training diets put an almost exclusive emphasis on meat, and this belief in its necessity is still widely held today, so much so that Wilf Paish in his Diet in Sport, feels he has to repudiate the misconception: 'Probably the most hallowed of the time honoured fads is the need for the pre-match steak or even the large emphasis on beef-steak in the diet of sportsmen'.[3] It is a perception that is judiciously encouraged by the meat industry who have sponsored athletes and sporting events. It also finds echoes in such practices as the ritual pre-flight steak of the astronaut.

Meat has also been traditionally perceived as a stimulant, something that feeds the passions. It makes men angry and fiery tempered, and there are a series of additional cross linkages here between the redness of meat and blood and that of fire - of enflaming and of the passions. Even today the belief in the stimulating qualities of meat recurs: 'I get aggressive if I eat meat', reported Keith Michel in Seed magazine.[4] A judicious amount of such qualities has traditionally been thought appropriate, for if meat made men aggressive it also made them brave and warrior like. Meat was traditionally seen as the food of freemen and not of slaves, and beef in the eighteenth and nineteenth centuries was popularly regarded as the very basis of English liberties.

This focus on the stimulation of the passions has always included a strong element of sexuality. Reinforced by the language of carnality - of the flesh and fleshlyness - meat has long been associated with the stimulation of lust. John Newton, the hymnographer, when a captain of a slave ship and experiencing the throes of evangelical conversion made a point of dropping all meat from his diet to prevent his lusting after the female slaves.[5] In a similar vein educationalists in the nineteenth century and into the twentieth often recommended a low meat diet for adolescent boys as a means of combating masturbation. (They also often recommended a diet that reduced the intake of hot and especially spicey foods - the word had by then taken on its dual connotations - and there were links once again with the idea of inflaming).[6] It should be noted that the sexuality meat is believed to stimulate is always linked to the ideas of animality. It is never eroticism, and meat does not feature as an aphrodisiac or as a specific against failing powers).

This image of sexuality that has a strongly masculine emphasis. The patterning of food has a sexual dimension. Thus red meat and men, white and women. This operates at the level of cultural stereotypes. There is no shame or taboo involved in women eating red meat or men white, and they do so happily. The symbolism is only at the level of associations, though these can influence eating patterns, as shown in the common expectation of waiters that the steak will be for the man and the fish for the woman.

Men in particular are thought in some sense to need meat, especially red meat, and a series of masculine qualities are encapsulated in the idea of redbloodness. It is part of the traditional image of John Bull, the beer quaffing, beef eating, fine figure of a man, and negative perceptions of vegetarianism within the dominant culture echo these ideas. Thus vegetarian food is commonly regarded as lacking: 'I don't think it's potent', remarked one man during a community experiment in the substitution of textured animal protein, 'there's blood in meat and there's none in this stuff'. In a similar style, anti-vegetarian prejudice presents vegetarians as pale faced and slightly feeble, and the condemnation of men is much heavier than of women. Vegetarian men are thought to lack the 'ruddy' good health, or 'red blooded virile' approach of the meat eater.

Meat in the dominant culture has never been taboo. However there has long been a tradition that has sought to reduce its consumption by certain categories of people, most commonly children, certain groups of women, the sick and those in bookish and sedentary occupations. Thus health manuals of the nineteenth and early twentieth century often suggested a reduction in meat intake for pregnant or lactating women, putting the emphasis instead on 'delicate', 'light' dishes like chicken, fish or eggs that both mirrored the women's own delicate 'feminine' condition and avoided any of the stimulation of those qualities of redbloodness that seemed inappropriate to those fulfilling the nurturing role. In a similar style the classic nursery diet was one of pale, bland food, devoid of strong tastes or rich sauces, and in which red meat was not a prominent feature. Where it did appear, the preference was for it in its 'weaker' boiled or stewed forms. Meat's stimulating effects were widely endorsed in the childrearing context; thus, for example, in Queen Victoria's nursery it was common practice to omit red meat from the diet of children - usually the youthful

Albert Edward - who were showing signs of temper or aggression.[7]

Invalids tended to suffer a similar fate, being fed on the classic 'low' diet of steamed fish, boiled chicken, poached eggs. Suggestions were also sometimes made that those in sedentary or physically restricting occupations would do well to cut down their intake of meat. Thus Andrew Ure, the apologist for the millowning class in the 1830s, castigated the wages of the cotton spinners that enabled them to: 'pamper themselves into nervous ailments by a diet too rich and exciting for their indoor occupations'.[8]   Similar comments were also made about scholarly pursuits. Thus meat was seen to lead to an undesirable stimulation, or where open outlet for such feelings was thwarted, to a nervous introversion of them. Red meat was felt to be 'too strong' for such vulnerable groups. Often this feeling was couched in the language of digestion; such food was hard to digest and would overtax the body through the demands it put upon it, and there is an underlying sense of eating as a form of taking over, even conquest, of the qualities residing in the food. Edward Carpenter writing as a vegetarian, made this aspect explicit: animal food 'containing as it does highly wrought organic forces, may liberate within our system powers we may find difficult or even impossible to dominate...which may insist on having their way, building up an animal body, not truly human'.[9]   Dominant culture to some degree shared these misgivings, and thus deemed it advisable that these vulnerable groups should eat down the hierarchy, away from the ambivalent animal power.

Bearing in mind the point concerning the ambivalences that mark dominant culture's attitude towards the power that resides in meat, we can return to the hierarchy and observe that items not eaten reiterate the significance of the hierarchical ordering. Thus in English culture, we do not eat carnivores. This is not nutritionally dictated, other cultures do. Rather I suggest that animals that eat animals are like a double dose, too much of a good thing. Similarly we do not, by and large, eat uncastrated beasts. The meat from boars and bulls has traditionally been regarded as tainted, though recent tests have shown it to be economic and wholesome. Both these groups fall into the category 'too strong'.

A second major variable in the hierarchy is cooking. Thus once again looking at the categories of the unacceptable, we find that they include raw meat. Tearing at raw flesh with one's teeth is an image of horror, suitable to monsters and the semi-human. It is an image of the bestial, as indeed in the narrow sense it is properly so, for animals do capture, tear at and devour their prey, sometimes half alive, whereas human beings first kill the animal, cook it and then eat it with implements. Cooking sets us apart from the beasts. Vegetarians have long pointed to these aspects and argued that the reason that meat, as it were, 'has' to be cooked is precisely to disguise its bloody taste, hide its true nature. Meat can also be stomached because in the process of cooking the 'power' in meat is to some extent tamed: 'cooked food is certainly safer - a certain grade of vitality being destroyed by cooking'.[10]   Thus the raw facts of nature are made into the acceptable ones of culture.

It is the nearness to animality that underlies the crowning status given to roasted joints. Roasting is a form of cooking that most preserves the blood within meat, giving it what Levi-Strauss (1966) has perceived as its semi-raw status, and joints resemble their animal origins more clearly than do the stewed forms of meat. (We have already noted how boiling and stewing are part of the 'low' diet of children and invalids). Throughout the dominant scheme cooking increases the status of food, and there are muted parallels both in dominant and vegetarian perceptions between cooking and meat.

Before going on to discuss the ways in which vegetarianism draws on and yet also disrupts this traditional imagery of meat, we need to touch briefly on one major historical dimension. As I mentioned at the start of this chapter I have chosen here to take a long historical period – from at least the early nineteenth century until now – compressing it in the context of the category 'modern' vegetarianism. One of the justifications for this – other, of course, than lack of space – is that perceptions at this level are slow moving, and it is important therefore not to miss, in a concentration upon change, the features of a culture that are more enduringly present. However, certain historical changes in the period are too important to be omitted. Traditionally the imagery of meat and blood was developed within the wider context of humankind's higher and lower natures. People's higher nature pertains to the rational, the spiritual and the moral spheres, whereas the lower relates to the bodily and to all that is designated their animal nature. This division into higher and lower has its counterpart in a profound series of oppositions between up and down, heaven and earth, and mind and guts/genitals.

Though this is an image of great longevity and power and one whose influence still contributes significantly to the meaning of meat, it is today a model that less clearly holds sway; other perceptions concerning bodily existence and the meaning of the animal have come into cultural prominence. The most important of these result from the accelerating growth from the eighteenth century of tendermindedness towards animals. This is a fundamental aspect in the development of vegetarianism, and it marks one of the features distinguishing 'modern' vegetarianism from the survival of earlier semi-manichaean influences. The causes of this major shift in consciousness are obscure, however one factor of undoubted significance is the growth in urbanisation. Town life breaks the organic contact with animals and drives a psychic wedge between animals as food and animals as pets. It is the bringing together of these otherwise separated aspects that in the context of modern consciousness provokes the unease on which vegetarian arguments can operate.

Returning to the question of vegetarianism's relationship to the dominant culture's perception of food, it is clear that vegetarianism shares many aspects of the hierarchy. Thus red meat, and particularly the blood in meat, has always been the main focus of vegetarian revulsion. 'Blood', reported the Vegetarian Messenger in the 1850s, 'is perhaps the most objectionable form of nutriment; flesh being principally composed of blood is next to it in its gross, stimulating and exciting qualities.[11] It is a commonplace in the process of becoming a vegetarian that you give up first the red meat, then the white, then the fish. People who eat no red meat, or only fish, are sometimes loosely referred to as vegetarians, and these distinctions have at times been given institutional expression in grades of member-

26

ship in the Vegetarian Society. (The older association with grades of abstinence within monasticism has already been noted). Those who adopt the most thoroughgoing of vegetarian diets - the vegan - eat, as it were, down the hierarchy, restricting themselves exclusively to the category furthest from the top. While it must be emphasised that the logic of veganism rests primarily on the perception of the inter-connectedness of the meat and dairy industries and thus of the exploitation and death that lies behind the provision of animal products, veganism is not devoid of some of the traditional themes concerning animality examined here in the context of meat. Thus the official five point declaration of the Vegan Society, after referring to 'the aspects of design in man and nature', to the 'reformed relationship of man to other living creatures', to the 'most efficient use of the fertile potential of the earth' and to an 'enlightened concept of health', turns to the way 'psychic properties of animal foods, reflecting the instinctual animal nature, probably tend to align themselves with the animal nature in man, and...cloud over the receptivity of the outward personality to the interior life of the spirit'. [12]

Thus vegetarianism can here be interpreted as a form of eating down the hierarchy away from the ambivalent animal power, and there are clear indications within vegetarianism's wider ideology and connections that fit such an interpretation. For vegetarianism has long been connected with various social purity movements that have sought to refine and desensualise human nature.[13] Lady Paget writing in the late nineteenth century expressed much of the predominating tone:

> Since I have adopted the diet, I have experienced a delightful sense of repose and freedom, a kind of superior elevation above things material...it has a decided effect on moral character, rendering people docile and more *spirituelle* and if spread among the masses would make them less coarse and brutal. It refines the lower instincts...and reduces sensuality. [14]

Thus vegetarianism can be interpreted as employing, though in more emphatic terms, an established social language. What dominant culture has treated with circumspection and cautious approval, vegetarianism, at least in some of its associations, has attempted to pull back from or rise above.

But vegetarianism has also been involved in more subtle redefinitions, for the meaning of meat is unfocussed, and the qualities it is believed to promote or embody can thus be given wide reinterpretation and revaluation. Take for example the traditional association with masculinity. Meat can here stand not for maleness in an approved sense, but for what is seen as a false, macho stereotype of masculinity. Thus 'strength' and 'power' becomes 'cruelty' and 'aggression'; masculine vigour and courage become violence and the forces of human destructive-ness. This perception is epitomised in the pacifist critique of war and of militaristic values, with which vegetarianism has close associations.

Vegetarian food is, as we have noted, female food in the grammar of conventional eating, and vegetarianism has had links with feminism from at least the 1880s. The links have been both with the movement for

27

women's rights and with the related wider critique that has been
concerned with the devaluation of 'female' qualities within
civilisation. Meat, both through the cruelty involved in its
production and the daily acquiescence to this involved in eating it, is
here seen to stand for egotism, selfishness and coldness of heart that
denies the natural empathy between human beings and beasts.
Vegetarianism from the late nineteenth century and before has been
linked with a growing ideology of intuition that has revolted against
what it sees as the coldness of rationality and the fragmented nature
of modern consciousness. This was quintessentially a theme of the
1970s, though it is in fact much older and represents the recurrent
return since the eighteenth century of an essentially romanticist
concept of being.

Vegetarianism, however, is not only a reflected version of the
hierarchy. It also challenges and disrupts the meaning contained in
the hierarchical arrangement. Thus it presents vegetarian food not
just negatively in terms of avoidance or abstinence from the undesire-
able, but in terms that stress its own positive and superior qualities.
It is something of itself and not just dominant food minus the meat
(Figure 3.2). This is extended into the way vegetarianism as a way of
life and a commitment is perceived. Vegetarian food is also wholefood
and as such links with a series of other positive images of wholeness -
moral, psychological, medical - that are part of this milieu.   This
revaluation can involve a revaluation of previously lowly foods, thus
rice, for example, from being a mere fattening fill you up, as it is in
the dominant scheme, becomes, especially for the vegan, a central source
of food value.   Seeds, nuts and grains are all indeed described in a
warmly vitalist language that stresses their special 'living' qualities,
and their high valuation in the vegetarian scheme is closely connected
with ideas of their containing in some sense the essence of the life
force.

'MOST FULL OF LIFE'   'LEAST KILLING TO PLANT'
        ↓   nut
                                 grains

                    FRUITARIAN BOUNDARY

                              leaf vegetables
                              root vegetables   ↑
'LEAST FULL OF LIFE'   'MOST KILLING TO PLANT'

Figure 3.2 Vegetarian version of the vegetable scheme

Vegetarianism constantly stresses eating as an ingestion of vitality.
It is a striking, almost paradoxical feature of vegetarianism that it
employs so strongly the language of alive and dead but in ways that
reverse the normal usage and indeed reverse the opposition on which its
explicit ideology rests: thus they do not eat living things and yet we
find vegetarians speaking of vegetarian food as 'alive' and meat as
'dead' (and this deadness is extended also to the deadness of over
refined processed foods).   The ways in which these oppositions are

worked through are complex. Put briefly, however, vegetarianism asserts the existence and importance of a different sort of 'power' and 'vigour' from that traditionally embodied in meat; the 'life' in vegetarian food is closely connected with images of lightness, sunshine and eternal youthfulness in conscious opposition to what is perceived as meat's embodiment of death, decay and corruption, and these opposing qualities underwrite a series of political, aesthetic and moral perceptions.

Vegetarianism also reverses the valuation traditionally given by the dominant culture to cooking. Vegetarianism praises the virtues of rawness. Certain vegetarians confine themselves to food that can be eaten raw, and the majority certainly put great stress upon food in that state. Explanations are largely couched in terms of the added vitamins and minerals thus absorbed, although the stress on raw food predates the scientific discovery of these factors and draws on notions of the 'goodness' of raw food that link with larger issues. Raw food is our 'natural' food - we can, as it were, pluck it from the trees - and no complex cultural mediation in cooking is required. In its freshness and newness it stands for an uncorrupted reality prior to the distortions and evasions of civilisation; and in this it relates to the Edenic or primitivist social myth that lies behind so much vegetarianism's utopianism. (c.f. Atkinson, 1980).

There has not been space in a chapter of this scope to do more than refer in passing to some of the ways in which vegetarianism uses food as a means to ponder and negotiate a series of major issues concerning the nature of human nature, the meaning and significance of a 'natural' way of life, the origins of illness and suffering, and human beings' moral place in the universe and among the beasts. In all of these the issue of meat is central. But in developing its ideas, vegetarianism has not operated in isolation, but has drawn on themes already present in the dominant culture's attitude to meat. What vegetarianism offers is an articulate body of ideas relating to meat. By understanding these ideas we can begin to get a purchase on some of the enduring symbolic relationships in the structure of dominant culture that otherwise remain largely implicit and only fleetingly observed.

NOTES

[1] Manichaeanism views flesh as totally evil, all nature as corruption and the cessation of physical being as the proper end. If one has to eat - and manichaeanism strictly implies starvation, and has at certain periods been pursued to that and through the 'endura' - vegetarian food is the nearest one can get to the rejection of all flesh in the rejection of flesh foods. Despite its heretical status, manichaean derived ideas have been influential in Christianity.

[2] See also Calvin W.Schwabe's aptly named cookbook Unmentionable Cuisine, University Press of Virginia, 1979.

[3] W.Paish, Diet in Sport, E.P., 1979, p.35.

[4] Seed (1974) 4, (11), p.5.

[5] D.Cecil, The Stricken Deer: or the Life of Cowper, Constable, London, 1929, p.118.

[6] See for example the vegetarian schoolmaster Eustace Miles, A Boy's
     Control and Self Expression, Cambridge, 1904; Cecil Reddie, not a
     vegetarian, held similar views, see Maurice Punch, Progressive
     Retreat: A Sociological Study of Dartington Hall School..., CUP,
     1977.
[7] Daphne Bennett, Queen Victoria's Children, Gollancz, London, 1980.
[8] Andrew Ure, The Philosophy of Manufactures, 1835, quoted by
     E.P.Thompson, The Making of the English Working Class, Gollancz,
     London, 1963.
[9] Edward Carpenter, Seed Time, April 1892, p.12.
[10] Ibid.
[11] Vegetarian Messenger, July 1850, appendix piii.
[12] The Vegan, Summer 1958, p.7.
[13] For an account of these and allied movements see Twigg, 1981.
[14] From The Nineteenth Century, quoted by C.W.Forward, Fifty Years of
     Food Reform: A History of the Vegetarian Movement in England,
     1847-1897, Vegetarian Society, Manchester, 1898, p.114.

4 Living from Hand to Mouth: the Farmworker, Food and Agribusiness

HOWARD NEWBY

Unlike the vast majority of the population, farm workers are concerned
with both the consumption and the production of food. An examination of
their experience thus reveals a great deal about how food production,
distribution and consumption is organised in a technologically advanced
and commercially sophisticated society like contemporary Britain. The
way in which food reaches the plate of the consumer is now a far cry
from the self-sufficient ideal of subsistence agriculture. The
production process is highly differentiated, with farming representing
merely one stage in the complex and frequently lengthy chain of
activities which stretch from 'seeds to supermarkets'. Somewhere in the
middle of this food production chain the farm worker performs an
essential role, but the farm worker only rarely and infrequently
consumes the food she or he produces - and even then it is mainly in a
fashion familiar to most suburban gardeners. For the products of a
farm worker's labour are no less alienated from him or her than those of
the average factory worker and the reality of food production and
consumption in the countryside barely corresponds to the prevailing
image possessed by the general public.

In order to overcome many of the stereotypes of rural patterns of food
consumption, this chapter begins with a description of the eating habits
of a farm worker's family with whom I lived while carrying out fieldwork
in Suffolk in the early 1970s (see Newby, 1977a, b). This is intended
to dispel many of the myths which surround the public perception of the
agricultural worker's access to vast amounts of food paid in kind and/or
to sources of food which are peculiarly wholesome and untainted by
'industrial' processes. In fact, as this paper will demonstrate, farm
workers obtain their food in much the same manner as the rest of the
population and demonstrates no distinctive dietary pattern. The second
part of the paper seeks to explain why this is so by examining, briefly
and schematically, the changing structure of food production in Britain
and the changing role of agriculture within it. Although only a brief
presentation of empirical detail is possible in a chapter of this length
this section will examine a number of the implications of the cliche
that British farming is moving 'from agriculture to agribusiness'. These
changes are incremental and often unrecognised, but they have far-
reaching consequences for patterns of food consumption for the
foreseeable future.

31

When I arrived in Suffolk in 1972 to conduct fieldwork and interviews
with local farm workers (described in detail in Newby, 1977b) I shared
most of the prevailing preconceptions about the rural population's easy
access to large quantities of cheap and wholesome food. This impression
was reinforced by my initial encounter with the tied cottage in which I
was to live during my sojourn in the field. It stood well back from the
lane at the end of a quarter-acre plot and was approached down a long
path which bisected a garden given over almost entirely to vegetable
production - apart from a miniscule lawn and flower border close to the
house, tolerated, as I was later to learn, 'for the wife'. To add to
the stereotype, the garden also contained some ramshackle sheds in the
modern Suffolk vernacular of creosoted timber and corrugated iron which
housed two pigs, two goats and a few 'bantam' chickens. It all seemed
appropriately bucolic.

I was to live in these surroundings for six months. The cottage was a
cramped, semi-detached 'two up, two down' with a recent extension. It
was to be both a haven from the stresses of fieldwork and the site of a
major element of that fieldwork. In it I shared and participantly
observed the everyday life of a farm worker, Jack Hector, his wife
Doreen and their two young children, Susan and Sally. (These names are
all pseudonyms). I have described elsewhere (Newby, 1977b) the
influence they were to have over my research and how they inducted me
into the realities of contemporary rural life. It was through them that
I was to learn at first hand of the actuality which lay behind the
superficially observed bucolic exterior.

The division of labour in the Hector household corresponded closely to
the ideal-typical traditional working-class family, as described, for
example, by Dennis, Henriques and Slaughter (1956). Doreen Hector
closely identified herself with the role of housewife and mother. She
accepted the fact that the home was primarily her sphere of activity
and she was exclusively responsible for cooking, washing, ironing and
cleaning. She explicitly recognised that it was her duty to ensure that
Jack Hector should be rested and well fed while at home and that the
house should be clean and comfortable. Jack Hector's domestic
responsibilities were limited to the garden, household repairs and
'mending' the fire. The fact that he helped with the washing up was
used by Doreen as an indication of his considerate nature. This rigidly
segregated domestic division of labour was entirely typical of the
Suffolk farm workers whom I encountered (see Newby, 1977a, pp.353-5).
Doreen Hector certainly regarded the situation as entirely normal and
even 'natural'. Her domestic role was a source of pride rather than
resentment (which is not to say that she did not, from time to time,
appreciate its drawbacks) and while all of her activities contributed in
various ways to her sense of achievement, it was undoubtedly the
preparation of meals which was central to her self-image as wife and
mother.

It is not an exaggeration to state that the daily life of the Hector
family was structured around its meals. The consumption of food was in
part an instrumental activity which Doreen Hector explicitly recognised
and she would frequently draw analogies between feeding her husband and
fuelling a machine. She provided the food which allowed her husband to

labour to obtain the wages which assured the continued wellbeing of the family: her role as cook was therefore pivotal. But the importance of mealtimes also lay in their social and symbolic role. During weekdays it was the only activity which the family performed collectively. The consumption of food thus reaffirmed the solidarity of the family. To miss or even be late for a meal without good cause was a cardinal sin; conversely a meal with a family member absent was not a 'proper' meal. The day was structured by its meals and the consumption of food was itself a relaxation, a break between instrumental activities, even though it was itself recognised as being partially instrumental. The consumption of food thus kept the body and some of the family together.

Devotees of Elizabeth David or The Good Food Guide would find the Hector's diet tedious in the extreme. In dietary terms it leaned heavily towards the more consciously instrumental aspects of the Hector's perception of the purposes of food consumption. Fats and carbohydrates were well represented. On a weekday Jack Hector would begin work at 7.30 am so Doreen Hector would be up an hour previously in order to prepare breakfast; cornflakes and milk, two rounds of bacon sandwiches and a mug of tea. Doreen and the children would normally have only cereals and tea, occasionally a boiled egg. Doreen would also pack Jack's 'nineses' (the rural equivalent of urban 'elevenses'): a flask of tea and two rounds of cheese or tomato sandwiches. This would sometimes be consumed at home if Jack was working adjacent to the cottage, but more often under a hedge or in a shed during a short break from work in the fields or farmyard. Jack would usually be home at noon for lunch, although during exceptionally busy periods, such as harvest, he might take a packed lunch out with him. Even if consumed at home lunch was considered a 'light' meal of bread rolls or sandwiches filled with cold meat or cheese, etc. or home-made cornish pasties or other meat pies. 'Dinner' was in the early evening – around 5.00 pm, immediately after Jack Hector returned from work. It was always 'meat and two vegetables' – or more precisely meat, mashed potatoes, dumplings and two or three other vegetables, the whole concoction sunk in thick gravy. This was followed by puddings – usually sponge or suet puddings of various kinds, fruit pies, rice pudding, etc. Supper was also served around 9.30 pm, tea or coffee, cake and/or biscuits. The portions were gargantuan. As a male I was expected to have a large appetite; indeed it was almost a token of masculinity. During six months of fieldwork I put on over a stone in weight.

Variations in this diet were minimal. The types and cuts of meat obviously varied from day to day; potatoes might be boiled, mashed or fried; toppings and fillings altered. But there was no 'ethnic' food – no pizzas, pastas, boiled rice, curries, etc. – and no changes in the culinary style. On Sundays, however, some variation was introduced to the weekday pattern. A more elaborate fried breakfast was prepared (mushrooms were a Sunday treat) for a later hour (9.00 am) with 'dinner' switched to lunchtime and invariably a Sunday roast. 'Tea' was cold meat and salad, jelly, trifle, cream cakes, etc. Casual observation of other farm workers' households suggested that the Hectors were by no means atypical in both the patterns and the content of their meals. It is also worth pointing out that there was nothing in this diet that was distinctively rural or agricultural. Indeed it was a regimen that was entirely familiar to me from my own upbringing in a Midlands city during the 1950s.

With this in mind it is important to examine the Hector's pattern of food consumption in more detail, this time emphasising not so much <u>what</u> is eaten, but <u>how</u> it is obtained. This is instructive, given Jack Hector's occupation in agriculture and many of the assumptions made about how the farming population obtains most of its food.

FROM HAND TO MOUTH

It is appropriate to begin this process by considering in more detail the superficially self-sufficient aspects of Jack Hector's domestic agricultural economy. As followers of the popular television series <u>The Good Life</u> were to learn there is much more to self-sufficiency than a large plot of vegetables and a few chickens. Certainly the Hectors did not even approach self-sufficiency: they did the bulk of their shopping in a supermarket like the majority of the rest of the population. The Hectors kept a pair of goats because their younger daughter suffered from eczema, which is relieved by drinking goat's milk. Cow's milk was also delivered to their doorstep in the usual manner - and at a price which Jack Hector calculated was well below his own cost of goat's milk production. Similar calculations applied to the pigs. Jack Hector, like most people who come into regular contact with them, had a great affection for pigs (cf. Harrison, 1982). He kept two pigs rather than one because the competition for food meant that they would eat more, and thus fatten more quickly. They consume most of the domestic food waste as swill, but this was supplemented by high-protein concentrated feedstuffs, which Jack Hector purchased from a local mill. Without the economies of scale available to most pig farmers Jack Hector could not produce pigmeat at a cost below the supermarket price. He was also constantly at the mercy of disease which had on more than one occasion eliminated many weeks' hard work and investment. Nevertheless Jack Hector kept the pigs as a hobby - and the quality of the final product was easily superior to the commercially-produced article. A year after my fieldwork ended, however, a severe outbreak of swine vesicular disease led to the introduction of much tighter MAFF regulations over hygiene and the use of swill. Jack Hector's employer also grew visibly more nervous about a possible source of disease on the doorstep of his own commercial herd. Consequently Jack abandoned his pigs.

While the pigs were present there was certainly no shortage of organic fertiliser for Jack Hector's vegetable garden. Even with the Hector family's high rate of consumption the garden provided them with the full complement of their vegetables for at least half of the year. This was supplemented from two other non-commercial sources. Jack Hector's employer set aside a small field each year in which potatoes were grown for the entire farm labour force. This was part of the employer's paternalistic managerial style (see Newby, 1977b) and was unique in the locality. It was to compensate for the fact that the farm, in common with most in East Anglia, produced little which could be directly consumed by its workers. Wheat, barley, sugar beet, etc. do not constitute suitable payments in kind. Elsewhere modern, mechanised, even automated, methods of production do not permit small quantities being diverted to the farm worker. However, they sometimes provide opportunities for the modern equivalent of gleaning. Thus in addition to the potatoes, the Hectors could obtain sufficient quantities of peas by gleaning the farm's pea fields in the wake of the pea vines which harvested for Bird's Eye. This partly accounted for an item of kitchen equipment which was uncommon in a working class household in the early 1970s, but which was ubiquitous in the Suffolk countryside: the deep freeze. Summer evenings were often spent in freezing the Hector's collection of domestically produced food, supplemented by their gleanings and occasional forays into 'pick-your own'.

The ubiquity of the deep freeze also becomes more understandable in the light of the Hectors' lack of accessibility to local shops and the latter's position in the overall pattern of food retailing. The Hectors lived two miles from the nearest shops, which were located in the nearby market town of Framlingham. At the top of the lane off which they lived there was a bus stop for a thrice-daily bus service to the town, but because of its irregularity and expense it was used by the Hectors only for major shopping expeditions when they 'stocked up' once a month. For daily or weekly purposes they used their bicycle - a pleasant enough experience on fine summer days, but disagreeable and sometimes impossible during the winter. Neighbours helped out with small 'errands' and a greengrocer's van called once a week (expensive and limited choice). So the deep freeze was an essential item to cover the long periods between major shopping trips.

The Hectors considered themselves fortunate to have a large number of shops in Framlingham available, complaints about the incidence of antique shops notwithstanding. Their physical location was certainly not as remote as many other farm workers' families in rural Suffolk and they were not dependent upon a single village shop. Nevertheless they were aware of the disadvantages of Framlingham as a shopping centre. At the time the town had only one 'supermarket' - little more than a slightly oversized family shop with the shelves arranged along aisles and a check-out at one end. It was a lonely outpost of Sir James Goldsmith's Cavenham Goods empire and in common with most such establishments its prices were 10-15 per cent above other, larger stores in the same chain located in urban areas. The Hectors were aware of this from their reading of advertising campaigns in the national and local press. But the 'High Street grocery war' of the 1970s passed them by. It was fought instead in the streets of Ipswich - only nineteen miles away, but requiring three bus trips in each direction and a journey lasting over three hours (six hours round trip). The equivalent for someone living in central London would be for the nearest Tesco's or Sainsbury's to be located in Darlington or Lancaster.

Most of the Hectors' shopping was therefore conducted in small, family run shops in Framlingham. Prices in these shops were 25-30 per cent above those prevailing in urban supermarkets and in one or two cases, 50-75 per cent above. This was not due to profiteering *per se* (although one particular example which involved a local monopoly over fresh meat appeared to this casual observer to come very close), but rather to the location of these enterprises in the chain of food processing, whole-saling, distribution and retailing. Family run shops do not have the volume of retail sales to deal directly with food manufacturers and processors. Instead they usually obtain their goods from 'cash 'n' carry' or similar trade distributors. The latter are usually (but not always) independent companies, who in turn obtain their goods from the major wholesalers - who usually are corporately owned. It is the wholesalers who deal with the processors, although often the wholesalers are the processors due to vertical integration along the food production

35

chain (see below). Although precise arrangements vary from area to area and item to item, the net result is the same. Each stage involves a mark-up of 25-33 per cent and a final retailer's mark-up of, usually 50 per cent. Major retail chains, of course, circumvent the whole process by dealing directly with the manufacturers on bulk-buy terms and establishing their own centralised distribution networks. As a result a small grocer in Framlingham pays more at the cash 'n carry for, say, a tin of baked beans, than a customer at one of the supermarkets in Ipswich. By the time the local grocer's mark-up is added, a considerable price disadvantage exists for customers like the Hectors.

The Hectors were therefore made acutely aware of a bizarre contradiction. Although Jack Hector was involved in producing food every day of his working life, he like most small town dwellers, had to pay considerably more for his food than those living in the centres of large cities far removed from the countryside and the business of food production. The Hectors noted this fact with bafflement rather than anger. To them it was another example of the insanity of the modern world, but they found it difficult to identify precisely the causes of such apparent irrationalities. This in turn was because most of the stages which constitute food production were invisible and unknown to them. Farming is no longer synonymous with the production of food and the Hectors were familiar with, and participated in, only two widely separated aspects of modern food production: farming and retailing. The irony was that while they occasionally poked fun at the ignorance of 'townies' about modern farming, they in turn had not realised that knowledge of farming is in itself of only limited help in understanding the modern organisation of food production.

FROM AGRICULTURE TO AGRIBUSINESS

The postwar period has witnessed a considerable transformation in the structure of food production whereby agriculture has been drawn into the embrace of a much wider complex of industrial companies involved in the provision of farm inputs (mainly machinery, processed feedstuffs and agri-chemicals) and the processing, distribution, marketing and retailing of farm inputs. Structural differentiation and segmentation of these and other functions into a 'food production chain' has been followed by vertical and horizontal forms of integration in order to create forms of unitary corporate control 'from seedling to supermarket' (Katz in Merrill, 1976, p.42). It is this rise of corporate agribusiness that has not only prompted the increasing rationalisation of agriculture, but the growth of a food production system, only a small proportion of which may actually take place on farms. As this has developed, so there has been a marked tendency for those engaged in farming to become virtually the twentieth century equivalents of outworkers for major agribusiness companies.

Some indication of this may be gained from Tables 4.1 and 4.2 which show the overall pattern of vertical integration of the major companies in the agro-input and food processing sectors respectively. It should be emphasised, however, that the direct involvement of these companies in agriculture in the United Kingdom is much less than it may seem from these tables. Most of their farming operations in Britain involve research stations and demonstration farms. Fully commercial involvement in agriculture almost entirely takes place overseas, particularly in the

Table 4.1

Extent of Integration by Corporations with Major Agri-input Interests

Company	Seeds	Agri-cultural machinery	Tractors	Pesti-cides	Ferti-lisers	Feed-stuffs	Agri-culture	Food Manu-facturing	Wholesaling & Retailing
ICI	x			x	x	x			
Fisons				x	x				
Shell	x			x	x	x	x		
Unilever	x					x	x	x	x
J. Bibby & Sons	x					x	x	x	
RHM	x			x		x	x	x	x
Dalgety/Spillers	x	x		x	x	x	x	x	x
Imperial Foods	x				x	x	x	x	
Massey-Ferguson		x	x						
Int. Harvester		x	x						
Ford			x						
New Holland (Sperry Rand)		x							

Table 4.2
Leading Food Processing Concerns with Subsidiaries in Agricultural
Production, Animal Feeds, Wholesaling, Retailing

	Agricultural production	Animal feeds	Wholesaling	Retailing
Unilever	x	x		
ABF				x
CWS	x		x	x
Cavenham		x		x
RHM	x	x	x	x
Tate and Lyle	x			
Unigate	x			
Union International	x		x	x
Cadbury-Schweppes	x			
Spillers	x	x	x	
Brooke Bond Liebig	x			
J. Lyons				x
Imperial Foods	x	x	x	x
Fitch Lovell	x		x	x
FMC	x		x	
United Biscuits				x
H.J. Heinz	x			
J. Bibby	x	x		
Booker McConnell	x		x	x

less developed countries (see Newby and Utting, forthcoming, for full details). Nevertheless farmers find that they have become drawn into the embrace of a highly concentrated agribusiness sector which controls both the supply of farming inputs and the disposal of farm outputs. It is a sector which is dominated by comparatively few, mostly multi-national companies and one which has seen rapid growth despite the volume of food expenditure having remained stable over recent decades.

The food processing industry has promoted, and prospered on the demand for, 'convenience' food - especially frozen food which increased by 250 per cent between 1968 and 1975. A two-part study by the Director-General of Competition of the Commission of the EEC (EEC, 1975) estimated that just 2.5 per cent of the companies involved in food processing, or 56 companies accounted for 78 per cent of the British food processing industry by output in 1968, and there has, since that date, been considerable merger activity in this sector leading to an even greater degree of concentration. The study also revealed that of the 22 industrial sectors covered by the report the food processing industry ranked seventh in terms of the number of mergers. Merger activity was particularly pronounced in the frozen food sector so that by 1973 three companies - Unilever (Bird's Eye), Nestle (Findus) and Imperial Tobacco (Ross) - controlled 90 per cent of the market. Bird's Eye alone accounts for 60 per cent of the British market, while Unilever and Nestle between them control 70 per cent of the market in Western Europe.

The frozen food sector is an example of merger activity having been accompanied by market growth. However, the tendency towards monopoly is

Table 4.3

Sales Concentration Ratios of Five Largest Enterprises in Food Product Groups, 1963 and 1968

	1963	1968
Trades showing an increase in concentration ratio		
Meal and flour (white flour for breadmaking)	79.2	80.8
Bread (loaves or rolls)	71.4	77.3
Flour confectionary	51.0	60.1
Biscuits	65.5	71.0
Bacon and ham	47.4	56.9
Sausages and sausage meat	52.2	56.2
Sugar confectionary	35.9	43.5
Marmalade and jams	72.9	75.6
Other preserved fruit	37.7	45.7
Vegetables preserved in airtight containers	65.3	66.7
Vegetables (quick frozen)	93.3	97.1
Pickles, sauces and relishes	68.0	71.5
Vegetable and seed oils	82.3	84.3
Self-raising flour	88.0	91.7
Condensed and evaporated milk	93.4	94.4
Cocoa products	82.3	83.3
Margarine	92.8	93.8
Sugar	98.6	99.3
Fish and marine oils	92.8	92.9
Trades showing a decrease in concentration ratio		
Fish and fish products (quick frozen)	91.7	91.1
Cheese and processed cheese	78.5	77.7
Meal and flour (excluding self-raising flour and semolina)	71.6	67.2
Cereal breakfast foods (for retail sale)	97.7	93.5
Butter	85.5	78.4
Milk powder	88.9	84.7
Ice-cream and lollies	93.1	91.2
Potato crisps	91.6	83.3
Soups	92.5	90.4
Compound fat	84.8	82.6
Coffee, coffee and chicory extracts and essence	98.4	93.7
Trades with concentration ratios for 1968 only		
Dressed poultry, carcase meat and poultry (quick frozen)	–	39.2
Heat treated milk	–	44.2
Tea, blended	–	82.9

Source: Census of Production, 1968

39

Table 4.4

Market Shares of Major Food Companies in Selected Products, 1972

Product	Size of Retail Market	Company	% Share
Breakfast cereals (ready to eat)	54m	Kellogs	56
		Weetabix	21
		National Biscuit Co.	10
Bread*	430m	ABF	26
		RHM	25
		Spillers	20
Biscuits	210m	United Biscuits	40
		Associated Biscuits	20
Frozen fish	96m	Unilever	63
		Nestle	18
		Imperial Group	7
Margarine	76m	Unilever	70
Sugar**	150m	Tate and Lyle	60
		British Sugar Corporation	25
		Manbre and Garton	11
Frozen vegetables	72m	Unilever	74
		Nestle	20
Tinned fruit	82m	Del Monte	36
		Libbys	33
Canned soup	60m	Heinz	63
		Cross and Blackwell	14
Ice cream	115m	Unilever	41
		Lyons Maid	43
Potato crisps, puffs	72m	Imperial Group	38
		General Mills	30
Tea	145m	Brooke Bond	41
		Typhoo (Cadbury-Schweppes)	18

*   In April, 1978 Spillers pulled out of the bread market

** Since 1972, Tate and Lyle have acquired Manbre and Garton. Also the
    relative market shares of Tate and Lyle and The British Sugar
    Corporation have altered considerably since Britain's entry into the
    EEC. Now these two companies have almost equal shares of
    approximately 98% of the total sugar market.

    Source: Wardle, 1977, p.25

equally apparent elsewhere in sectors where demand is static or
declining – as in the well publicised example of the bread industry.
After a series of mergers in the 1960s, three companies – Associated
British Foods, Rank-Hovis-MacDougall and Spillers – controlled 80 per
cent of flour used in the UK and after the recent withdrawal of Spillers
from baking, ABF and RHM now produce two-thirds of the bread we eat.
Initially all three companies entering baking in order to protect their
market for flour, but ABF and RHM integrated further into retailing –
ABF via its Fine Fare supermarket subsidiary and RHM by opening over
1,000 of its own bakery shops. Spillers' lack of a retail outlet was
eventually to prove its undoing, for ABF and RHM could, through the
device of transfer pricing, run at a loss on their baking activities
(for example, by offering high discounts to their own supermarkets but
not from their flour mills to their bakers) and force Spillers out of
the market. ABF is owned by the Weston family, is based in Canada and
owns 115 subsidiaries in the UK with 122 subsidiaries in 10 countries
elsewhere in the world. RHM owns 139 UK subsidiaries, sells seeds and
feedstuffs to farmers, has extensive milling and merchant interests and
produces a wide range of processed foods. Spillers' vulnerability was
emphasised by its takeover by Dalgety in 1979.

These examples can be placed in a broader context by examining Table
4.3, which shows the sales concentration ratios of the five largest
enterprises in each of 33 product ranges. Thus in 1968, 18 of the 33
product ranges recorded concentration ratios of 80 per cent or more.
However, Table 4.3 gives no indication of the size of the five largest
enterprises, so that this data must be combined with that in Table 4.4,
which gives the market shares of major food companies in selected
products, in order to obtain some idea of market power. The size, in

Table 4.5
Size and Growth in Turnover of Ten Largest Companies* in the Food
Processing Industry, 1972-1976**

Company	Rank	Turnover 1972	1976	Rank	% increase
Unilever	1	1539	6760	1	339
Associated British Foods	2	729	1301	3	78
Cavenham	3	462	1659	2	259
Rank Hovis MacDougall	4	441	921	5	99
Tate and Lyle	5	419	1274	4	204
Unigate	6	409	763	6	87
Union International	7	403	646	9	60
Cadbury Schweppes	8	349	667	7	91
Spillers	9	279	667	11	109
Brook Bond Liebig	10	263	591	10	125
J. Lyons	11	259	651	8	251

*The Co-operative Wholesale Society, not included in company analysis,
was the third largest food sector concern in 1972 with a turnover of
596m.
**T.O. figures for 1976 either apply to early 1976 or late 1975.
Source: 1972 figures – EOFI study
        1976 figures – Institute of Grocery Distribution, Research
        Services Division publication

terms of turnover, of the top ten food-processing companies in the UK is
also shown in Table 4.5.

This picture of concentration within the food processing industry is completed by considering the forward integration of these firms into wholesale and retail marketing. Here vertical integration has represented an alternative to merger activity as a means of protecting profit margins, minimising costs and securing an increased market share. Such forward integration has promoted, and been accompanied by, structural changes in the retail food trade since the 1950s, most notably the gradual decline of the small-scale, independent, family grocery shop and the rise of supermarkets and multiple chain stores. Seventy per cent of the grocery market is now controlled by the ten largest multiples, a development which has considerably altered the relationship between the food-processing and food-retailing sectors.

Table 4.6
Food Distribution Interests of Leading Food Processors

Food Processors	Food/Retail/Wholesale Interests	Type
ABF	Fine Fare (incl. Melias)	Grocers
	Allied Bakeries Group	Bakers
	Alliance Wholesale Grocers	Wholesale grocers
Cavenham Group	Allied Suppliers	Grocers
Union International	J.H. Dewhurst	Butchers
	T.W. Downs	Food Distributors
	British beef	Wholesale butchers
Brooke Bond Liebig	Baxters	Butchers
Fitch Lovell	Keymarkets (incl. D.Grieg)	Grocers
	West Layton	Meat
	Lovell and Christmas	Food wholesalers
Rank Hovis McDougall	British Bakeries	Bakers
Spillers	Mead-Lonsdale Group	Meat wholesalers
Associated Dairies	Asda	Superstores
Booker McConnell	Bugden	Grocers
	Holland and Barrett	Health food shops
	William Brothers	Butchers
	Booker Belmont	Food wholesaling
	James Harper & Son (Edinburgh)	Food wholesaling
Barker and Dobson	Oakeshotts	Grocers

Numerous food-processing companies have been forced to respond by securing marketing outlets, prompting a series of acquisitions and mergers, both offensive and defensive. Thus two of the five leading food retailers, Allied Suppliers and Fine Fare are owned by food processors (Cavenham and ABF respectively). The food distribution interests of leading food processors are set out in Table 4.6.

The extent of horizontal and vertical integration across large multinational conglomerates is striking. Unilever, for example, is integrated horizontally via its use of animal and vegetable fats, oils and solids in a range of products from margarine to deodorants. As far as vertical integration is concerned:

42

At the lower end there are plantations, purchasing boards and trawler fleets which between them harvest materials as diverse as herrings, groundnuts and timber. At the next level there are the oil mills, slaughterhouses, factory ships and timber mills. At the third, the manufacturing operations: detergents, soap and margarine and container manufacture, food processing, freezing and canning, etc. At the fourth level there is all the paraphernalia of selling, from market research, advertising agencies, distribution depots and retail outlets to fish restaurants, industrial caterers and cleaners and meat pie shops. (CIS, 1975)

The result is a vast range of products which include Bird's Eye frozen food, Vesta packaged meals, Bachelors tinned vegetables and soups, Walls ice cream and meat products, Blue Band, Stork, Summer County, Flora and Echo margarine, Spry and Cookeen lard, Crisp 'n' Dry cooking oil and detergent and toilet preparations such as Lux, Persil, Omo, Comfort, Sunlight, Rexona, Breeze, Vim, Sunsilk, Twink, Harmony, Sure, Shield, Gibbs toothpaste, Close-up, Signal and Pepsodent. Unilever also owns shipping lines (Norfolk Line, Palm Line), meat wholesalers and processors (Midland Poultry, Unox), paper mills (Thames Board Mills), and much, much more - 812 companies in 75 countries manufacturing over 1,000 products. Many of these products were purchased regularly by the Hectors in common with millions of other consumers up and down the country. The Hectors' rural location and close involvement with agriculture conferred on them no privileged awareness of how these products came into their hands; nor had they any means of relating their own everyday agricultural experience to the overall organisational characteristics of contemporary food production.

CONCLUSIONS

It is, in every possible sense, a long way from Jack Hector's vegetable patch to the corporate might of Unilever. One purpose of this paper has been to demonstrate that, even for the farm worker, the activities of the latter rather than the former are more relevant to an understanding of everyday food habits. Clearly the growth of agribusiness as described in the last section of this paper, raises important issues relating to dietary change, economic sovereignty, public accountability and the concentration of economic power in the production of a basic human need - food. A discussion of these issues would, however, extend far beyond the confines of this chapter. Suffice it to say that agri-business companies have become major agents in promoting economic and social changes in rural Britain since the war through their impact upon agricultural production and that they have had a profound effect on all of the population as food consumers.

The general public is, however, largely unaware of these trends - and, for that matter, rather uncaring. What counts primarily to the consumer is the price of food. Agribusiness companies themselves certainly believe that they are performing a public service by implementing the consumer demand for cheap food. The changing pattern of consumer demand for food is also encouraging the growth of agribusiness in Britain. More of the food that is purchased is processed food and, given current trends such as the increasing proportion of gainfully employed mothers, the demand for convenience food is likely to increase, quite aside from

the encouragement given by the agribusiness companies' own advertising
campaigns. Since the value added from processing food is much greater
than that which is accrued from growing it, agribusiness domination of
food production in Britain seems likely to increase for the foreseeable
future. As a result agriculture will continue to become organised
according to non-agricultural criteria, on the assumption that
agriculture is merely a disguised form of manufacture. This has
implications, not only for farming entrepreneurs, but also for farm
workers, the employees of food processors and ultimately all of us as
consumers.

5 The Hierarchy of Maintenance and the Maintenance of Hierarchy: Notes on Food and Industry

ERIC BATSTONE

At one level of analysis, the question of the provision of food in industry can be seen as one of diet: given the length of time which workers spend in the workplace, it may be seen as self-evident that they need to consume food and drink.   From this perspective, the approach to food in industry is essentially nutritional. However, what may seem self-evident today was by no means always so.   Accordingly, a full analysis of food in industry requires consideration of the way in which the recognition of what is now seen as self-evident has developed – and varied – over time. Some comments are made on this question in the concluding section of this paper. The bulk of discussion here deals with a series of related questions. For, even when the nutritional requirements of workers are recognised, the mode of recognition may vary considerably. Most obviously, the type of food and drink provided and by whom can vary; so also may the environments in which food and drink are consumed and the degree of discretion over when they are consumed. The first part of this chapter develops these themes by comparing the car assembly worker and the director.   The thrust of this comparison is that questions concerning food and drink reflect and reaffirm broader contrasts in the work situation.

The first contrast between food and drink provision for the car assembly worker and the director focusses around the question of the times at which they can eat and drink.   The company director can do so at any time. He may order tea or coffee as the whim takes him. He is not confined to set lunch breaks: he can have sandwiches brought to his room, and may leave the workplace at any time to eat.   The car assembly worker has little, if any, discretion as to when he eats and drinks. Times for eating and drinking are specified in detail. During an eight hour shift, three breaks are laid down: two tea breaks of ten minutes and a lunch break of less than an hour. Their occurrence is similarly specified. These breaks are the product of detailed negotiation between management and union.   Each side polices the agreement carefully; management stop and start the track exactly on time; a late stop or an early start is the subject of formal complaint by the steward.

Outside of these formal breaks, the car assembly worker does have some additional opportunities for eating and drinking.   In estimating the proper or 'normal' level of effort for each job, management include a limited but additional amount of time for 'personal needs'. Such needs include going to the toilet, and having a drink from one of the water fountains scattered about the assembly line. But these time allowances can scarcely be defined as generous and their use by workers is still further controlled: they are not allowed to use these allowances at the beginning or end of shifts, nor can they use them at will in the middle of a shift. They have to ensure that someone else, a 'floater', takes over their jobs while they are away. Hence, the number of 'floaters' and the number of others currently using their personal allowance time affect the degree of discretion which the car assembly worker has, even in getting a drink of water.

There is, then, a marked contrast between the company director and the car assembly worker in the discretion they have concerning when they eat and drink. The former has almost total freedom; this is a reflection of the high level of discretion found in such jobs and the related way in which the satisfaction of personal whims is seen as furthering the interests of the employer. The reverse is the case for the car worker; when he eats and drinks has to conform to the dictates of the assembly line. If the worker left the track without a 'floater' taking his place, severe disruption could well result: a car without wheels cannot leave the track, for example, and so forces a stoppage of the line. The presence of every worker on the line is therefore vital, in the same way that every component is. As a cog in the production of the car, the worker's presence must be closely controlled and timed. His personal needs for food and drink have to be controlled and specified in the same way as the delivery of components to the line.

This pattern of production in which the worker is paced by the machine and closely supervised embodies notions of 'time thrift'. 'Time thrift' indicates that time is money and that in order to achieve the basic goal of profit the employer has to transform the labour time for which he pays the worker into productive effort. From this perspective, the assembly line is a technical form of control whereby 'lost time' can be minimised. Similar conceptions serve to explain the level of supervision of breaks and the way in which the track is stopped and started for breaks.

If it is the case that the employer has an interest in minimising lost time attributable to eating and drinking in the car assembly shop, workers equally have an interest in expanding such times. The time allowed for personal needs and the timing and duration of tea breaks have both been the subject of negotiation and strikes. Workers were prepared to engage in strike action to prevent management introducing a new payment system, for example, which would have involved handing control of tea breaks over to management (see Batstone et al., 1978). One of the largest strikes in recent years in the car industry similarly centred upon the question of tea breaks.

Attempts by workers to expand their opportunities for eating and drinking are not, however, confined to set piece formal negotiations and major confrontations. Skilful bargaining leading to 'looser' times on particular jobs may make it easier for workers to move away from the line without the agreement of the foreman; workers may also re-arrange work on the line in such a way as to gain more 'free' time which can be shared by the group. In other areas, some workers are able to work up or down the line thereby gaining additional free time. Through these methods workers may gain additional breaks or extend the formal breaks.

In a few cases, worker accommodation goes beyond these marginal forms. Sometimes workers retreat to the pub at lunch time and decide to continue drinking rather than return to work; 'going over the fence' for a few drinks is a relatively common occurrence among those on the night shift.

The precise modes of food and drink provision also encourage various forms of worker accommodation. The employer's priority of minimising time spent in unproductive ways means that breaks for food and drink are short. Large numbers of workers may be expected to use the same source of hot water (for tea) or the same tea trolley in a matter of minutes. At the lunch break hundreds of men are expected to obtain meals from the same canteen and consume them in little more than half an hour. Queues are a feature of breaks; the worker who can avoid them by his early arrival at hot water point or canteen has more time to eat and drink. Consequently, those who are able to vary their workloads leave their job stations early and wait unobtrusively near the canteen, seeking to ensure both that they are at the head of the queue and that they avoid the watchful eye of the supervisor.

For the director there are no such pressures. His secretary, personal assistant, or even personal valet brings him tea and coffee as and when he wishes. The director eats in the directors' dining room. Rather than queuing, there is waitress service – the ratio of those serving to those eating is far higher than in the car workers' canteen. There is, then, no incentive to leave work early: the provision of food and drink is geared to the convenience of the director.

The logic of food provision is essentially the same in the case of both director and car worker. In both cases, they spend lengthy hours at the place of work which is frequently some considerable distance from home or even non-company sources of food. And yet the mode of provision is strikingly different.

Service in the directors' dining room reflects and reaffirms the status of director. The director sits at his traditional place and waitresses bring dishes of food from which he helps himself. The style is that of the restaurant. The waitresses are deferential, the food is laid out to please the eye, and the personal likes and dislikes of the directors are recognised in the menu.

The director may also choose to eat with 'guests' in a special dining room, reserved for the occasion, where discussion of business matters can continue in privacy and confidence. The overlap of work and eating – the conflation of hospitality and goal-oriented behaviour, the 'oiling' of commercial dealing through the rituals of commensality – lead to a domesticated organisation of eating for the director.

In the case of the car assembly worker, the mode of food provision by the employer reflects a tension between the productive necessity of nutritional provision on the one hand and considerations of cost and time thrift on the other. If breaks are to be kept short, the employer has to devise means by which several thousand workers can obtain food and drink within a short period of time. Hence a variety of tea and hot water points are provided; canteen staff have meals prepared at the appropriate time and they are served at the fastest possible pace. The mode of provision can therefore best be described as functional;

the pleasantries of the restaurant or home are rarely to be found in the works canteen. Men have to queue, take their food rapidly from those serving and find a space in which to consume it. The emphasis is upon meeting the nutritional requirements of a large number of workers in as short a time as possible. The queue constitutes a mode of regulation which shifts many of these problems onto the worker himself: it is a mode of regulation which permits the worker a degree of discretion, if only of a primitive nature, which the employer rarely permits in working time.

The functional nature of provision is reflected in other ways. Workers have little, if any, choice of what to eat if they use the canteen; the canteen staff ladle food on to plates with an emphasis upon speed rather than any quest for the artistry of *cuisine gourmande*.

In contrast to the style and luxury of the directors' dining room, the workers' canteen is basic: a large hall, with serried ranks of formica tables and steel framed chairs. Time pressure prevents the employer from permitting the majority of workers extra time to wash and change from oily overalls into clothes which would not ruin more comfortable and homely situations. The nature of the canteen, justified by the nature of the conditions in which they actually work, therefore confirms and extends those conditions.

The same point applies to tea breaks. Provision is not made by management for workers on the line to sit at tea breaks. They are expected to take their tea at or near their work stations: time precludes their going too far away. The cost of providing rest rooms for all workers, close to their stations, is seen by management to be prohibitive (in another plant – a foundry – management further claimed that workers would not want such provision).

Workers also seek to achieve some form of accommodation concerning the mode of food provision. Most obviously, many workers bring their own food and drink to work. Some are not overly impressed with the food provided by management; others prefer to maximise their rest periods, eating in relative peace, rather than racing to queue at the canteen. But perhaps the most striking feature of these forms of worker accommodation is the way in which they embody attempts at domesticity; this is so in two respects.

First, bringing one's own meal means bringing into the workplace food which is prepared within the worker's own domestic situation. It therefore provides a link with the home. It is yet another symbol of the central logic of work for the car worker: he endures the tedium of the line in order to maintain his family – this is his primary role in the domestic division of labour. The primary role of the wife – notwithstanding the fact that she may also work – is the provision of a 'home', an important feature of which is the preparation of food. The sandwich box prepared by the wife the evening before is, therefore, a symbol of the domestic relationship which constitutes the logic for the car worker's presence in the workplace (many car workers claim that they only went to work on the line when they were married and had domestic responsibilities; similarly, divorced and separated workers tended to have much higher rates of absenteeism and turnover than married men).

Moreover, by bringing his own food the worker can ensure that his particular tastes are met. In the works canteen he has little, if any, choice of menu. But his wife - as part of the fulfilment of her role in the domestic situation - ensures that the car worker's sandwich box contains those things of which he is particularly fond. This is the obverse of Murcott's (1983b) account of wives' deference to their husband's food preference as an expression of their domestic responsibility. The sandwich box therefore provides a link with the domestic situation and, in doing so, constitutes a form of 'personalisation' of eating, contrasting with the anonymity of the canteen.

The second form of domesticity is the way in which workers seek to carve out little 'homes' within the work situation itself. Around the track are stocks of components. The assembly workers rearrange these to provide areas in which they can sit, with stacks of equipment around them to provide some degree of privacy. They fashion chairs from components and boxes, each worker having his own jealously guarded seat. Pictures, graffiti and personal notes serve further to personalise these little 'homes'. In these ways, then, workers seek to deny, or at least modify, the stereotype of themselves which the workplace embodies - of a mass of undifferentiated appendages to the line. They seek to foster and provide their own personal identities in the workplace. In doing so they partially transform the locus of production to their own ends.

In contrast, the director has no such need to engage in 'informal' initiatives of this kind. The directors' dining room is more than functional; his office is more than a place of work. He may have been able to furnish it to his own taste at company expense. In any event, it contains the comforts of the domestic situation: armchairs, coffee tables, a drinks cupboard. Even the desk at which he works is a piece of carefully chosen furniture rather than a metal and formica construction.

The furnishing of the director's office reflects his status, and the high trust associated with it. But in addition it reflects the nature of his work: much of it involves contact with others, including persons from other companies. Hospitality and sociability are, therefore, part of the job. In contrast, the sociability of the car worker is strictly constrained in working hours. Stuck at his work station he has little opportunity to communicate with others and such social contacts as are possible during work are to a large degree managerially determined (although workers have successfully fought for the right to play a role in task allocation and hence who they work with). During tea and meal breaks workers have a greater range of choice: most workers belong to regular tea groups which reflect common interests and backgrounds. Such groups therefore serve to reaffirm affiliations and interests which cut across the identity fostered by the company.

The opportunities for sociability afforded by tea and meal breaks also figure importantly in more formal modes of worker accommodation to the work situation. These breaks provide the most convenient occasion for many workers to discuss grievances with their stewards; some of the convenors make a point of being in the canteen at lunch time (although not eating there) to provide an opportunity for workers and other stewards to discuss matters with them. It is common for groups of stewards to gather to work out tactics at lunch breaks, often retreating to their own secret places or to a pub to do so. Finally, tea and meal

breaks provide opportunities for the steward to 'educate' his members
(see Batstone et al., 1977, pp.104-112). For example, as we recorded
elsewhere, meal breaks were used by stewards to warn members against
accepting a change from piecework to measured day work in the car plant
(e.g. Batstone et al., 1978, pp.158-9). Commensality for the car
worker may, therefore, be important in attempts to block the ends of the
employer; for the director, in contrast, commensality is important in
promoting the employers' ends.

    Alcohol highlights the contrast between the car assembly worker and
the company directors. The latter is allowed to drink alcohol at any
time. It is the one form of food or drink which is actually stored in
the director's office, for alcohol is an important tool of the
director's trade: as a representative of the company he acts as host to
guests. As such it is 'polite' to engage in acts of hospitality such as
offering alcoholic drinks. And as a company representative the
directors' drinking is funded by the company.

    At the level of director, then, a good deal of work involves the
recognition of the norms of hospitality which properly belong to the
domestic situation. In an important sense, therefore, work is
domesticated and, at the same time, such domesticity means that the
employer trusts the director with alcoholic drink during working hours,
seeing it almost as part of the necessary equipment of work.

    No such trust is to be found in the case of the car assembly worker.
He is not allowed to have alcohol in the workplace. Notions of
hospitality do not apply in his position; and whereas the director is
seen as a person who can be trusted to control his drinking of alcohol,
the assembly worker is not seen to be capable of such control. While
the company provides the director with alcohol, the company disciplines
the assembly worker if he is found with his own alcohol in the workplace.

    The existence of such rules and regulations helps to explain some of
the practices noted above, such as 'going over the fence' and down to
the pub (such action by a director might be defined as a 'business
lunch'). In addition, groups of workers do drink on the line; through
'shift breaks', the extra time won by reorganising work, some workers
are able to retreat to the toilets or other 'private' areas where they
share bottles of beer or home made wine. In a few cases, assembly
workers are to be found drunk on the line; but generally the shop
stewards have been able to prevent management applying strict
disciplinary measures by arguing that drunkenness should be defined not
as an act of gross misbehaviour but as a sickness, in part brought on
by the very nature of assembly line work.

    The consumption of food and drink at work finds its origins in
nutritional requirements. But the recognition of these requirements for
the car assembly worker conflicts with the employers' aim of maximising
productive effort. In an attempt to achieve a balance the employer
seeks to control the timing and time of tea and meal breaks and to
ensure a service which precludes the 'stretching' of breaks. The mode
of provision reflects the nature of the work situation and the image of
the worker adopted, if only of necessity, by management. Food
provision, therefore, represents an expression of low trust and of the
worker as machine in the very process of recognising the nutritional

requirements of the worker as human being.

At the same time, workers attempt to challenge or amend this implicit mould of themselves proffered by management: the challenge the notions of 'time thrift', they seek to 'domesticate' their consumption of food and drink, and they use these breaks to foster their own non-work identities and to develop more general challenges to management.

Food provision for the car assembly worker and the director reflect and reaffirm contrasting models of different occupational groups. As one moves up the organisational hierarchy, not only status but also employer trust tends to increase. That is, the director occupies a position of high trust or discretion: he is not bound by detailed rules concerning food and drink, in the same way as he is not tightly bound by such rules as to what he should do or how he should do it. The car assembly worker, on the other hand, formally enjoys little discretion over his eating and drinking. This reflects the largely pre-planned minutely timed and closely supervised and controlled nature of his work more generally. Eating and drinking, therefore, reflect the funda-mental features of his low trust task in which 'the role occupant perceives superordinates as behaving as if they believe he cannot be trusted, of his own volition, to deliver a work performance which fully accords with the goals they wish to see pursued or the values which they wish to see observed' (Fox, 1974, p.26).

High and low trust work situations therefore embody very different conceptions of the worker. The high trust situation embodies an 'optimistic' model of the worker. It implies that by fostering and encouraging self development, by recognising the humanity of the worker, the employer can best achieve his own ends. In contrast, the low discretion or trust work situation adopts a 'pessimistic' conception of the worker: if he/she were permitted greater freedom 'irresponsible' behaviour would result, serving to subvert the ends of the employer. According to this model, the worker has to be constrained and controlled and 'humanity' given only limited recognition.

In the high trust situation, then, there is an emphasis upon the congruity between worker interests and corporate interests. The worker internalises the priorities of his/her employer and thereby the work role becomes an important part of the worker's more general identity. There is not, therefore, a sharp division between work and non-work roles. In the same way that work spreads into the domestic life of the high discretion worker, the reverse is equally the case. In this sense, the work situation is 'domesticated': it is structured in such a way that in a number of important respects the workplace is a second home, recognising the personal needs, comfort and tastes of the worker. This follows logically from the perceived congruity, indeed fusion, of worker and corporate interests.

In the low trust situation, the worker is denied elements of domesticity. He/she is treated rather as a factor of production, an appendage to a machine. There is, therefore, a sharp divide between work and non-work: work is experienced as a form of deprivation, in which personal needs, tastes and comforts are only minimally recognised. For many of these are seen to be incompatible with the corporate interest.

These contrasts are reflected in forms of food provision. For the company director, in a high trust situation, the provision of food and drink is seen as facilitating corporate goals; the mode of provision reflects the directors' discretion and can be seen to be of an essentially 'domestic' nature. On the other hand, for the car assembly worker food provision is much more comparable with the maintenance of a machine - a strictly regulated refuelling and lubrication function which bears little resemblance to the consumption of food and drink in the domestic situation.

Furthermore, in the high trust situation where the workers' needs are more fully recognised and where there is not the same structured conflict between corporate and personal interests, it is often difficult clearly and easily to identify situations in which the workers sabotage the employers' interests. The structure, predicated upon a congruence of interests, is simply not geared to the identification of such activities: its focus is upon achievement rather than upon the details of behaviour. The idea of worker accommodation is therefore less relevant, since the structure seeks to accommodate worker interests.

In the low trust situation, worker attempts to employ discretion, to make choices over the timing and modes of consuming food and drink, will often constitute challenges to the work structure within which he/she is located. Notions of worker accommodation attempts to evade, bend and manipulate organisational rules in order better to pursue his/her own interests, are therefore far more relevant. In short, in the low discretion work situation food and drink may constitute an arena of conflict and of worker attempts to change the work situation, albeit in somewhat marginal ways.

An awareness of the risks of conflict emanating from low trust situations has led some employers to adopt a number of strategies directed at reducing these possibilities. In recent years, for example, many employers have started to reduce discrimination in canteen provision between different occupational groups; that is, the modes of food provision are designed as a symbol of a unity of interest between employer and employee and to foster the notion of the good employer (e.g. Elliott, 1965, p.34; see also Wedderburn and Craig, 1974, p.146).

In the same way, an important stimulus to food provision in the first place has been the desire to increase managerial legitimacy in the eyes of the workforce. Joyce, for example, notes the use of works dinners in an attempt to discourage trade unionism (1980, p.149). Whereas in the early stages of the Industrial Revolution employers sought to deny their traditional responsibilities for feeding employees and argued the virtues of hunger as a form of work motivation (see e.g. Townsend cited in Bendix, 1963, p.74; and Braverman, 1974, pp.271-283), the growing power of the working class led to the adoption of a very different model of worker motivation and performance by the first world war. Under the influence of the welfare movement, it was formally accepted that a good diet was a precondition of productive efficiency (see e.g. Health of Munition Workers' Committee, 1916; Friedman, 1955, p.88; McKillop, 1917, pp.155-6; Mekle, 1980). These developments were further encouraged by the employment of persons who were seen to require special protection from the vagaries of industrial employment - women and children; this is seen in the Factories Acts and the sectors in which food was first, and widely, provided (e.g. Djang, 1942; Proud, 1916; Urwick and Brech, 1945; Nelson, 1980).

It is, indeed, possible to learn a great deal about changing labour relations strategies through the historical analysis of food provision in industry; unfortunately, such a task is beyond the scope of the present discussion (see Batstone, 1982). This chapter has, however, sought to show the way in which contrasting modes of food provision in industry reflect and reaffirm features of the more general work situation, thereby embodying different models of worker behaviour and encouraging quite different degrees and modes of worker conflict and accommodation.

SECTION II

FOOD, HEALTH AND GENERATION

6 The Management of Food in Pregnancy

SALLY MACINTYRE

INTRODUCTION

Most people are aware of the existence of food cravings - or of other
abnormalities of appetite, taste or digestion - in pregnancy. There is
evidence that such abnormalities are known in many 'primitive' societies
studied by ethnographers (Ford, 1964), stories about particularly
bizarre food fads are part of our society's folklore, and if a young
woman admits to nausea or perversities of appetite she is likely to
receive knowing looks from her peers (Murcott, 1981).

By and large, however, such abnormalities of eating are treated as
fairly unimportant features of pregnancy, involving only minimal impact
on the lives of women experiencing them, and as topics more for jokes
than for serious concern. Despite the prevalence of general knowledge
of food fads as being characteristic of pregnancy, remarkably little is
written about them either in textbooks for obstetricians or midwives, or
in antenatal advice literature for expectant mothers. The paucity of
material presented in such books perhaps reflects a lack of knowledge
about the incidence, etiology, and significance of such changes, a lack
in turn deriving perhaps from the assumption that they are trivial.

In both textbooks and advice manuals, changes in appetite and tastes
are mentioned, if at all, only briefly, and often only in the context of
lists of symptoms of pregnancy, in which they usually appear in a lowly
or residual position. Clayton and Newton, for example, complete their
list of the signs and symptoms of normal pregnancy with a category of
'other symptoms' which reads:

> Other symptoms which sometimes occur include vagaries of
> appetite, a dislike for smoking, constipation, tiredness,
> breathlessness towards term, etc. [1]

but do not mention these changes of appetite again. Similarly, the
Queen Charlotte's textbook[2] mentions 'excess salivation, waywardness
of appetite and cravings for unusual articles of diet' as symptoms of
early pregnancy, that is, up to 12 weeks, but does not mention these
conditions again, and does not even include them in the lists of
symptoms for mid- and late-pregnancy. In The Book of the Child, given
to every expectant mother in Scotland, number eight in the list of signs
of pregnancy is:

> Changing tastes.

Having a strange taste in your mouth, often described as
metallic.
Going off some foods, e.g. coffee, alcohol, spicy things. [3]

This is very similar to what Bourne says in his widely read guide for
expectant parents.

Alterations in taste may be among the earliest of pregnancy
symptoms. Some women will recognise a strange taste in
their mouth even before they miss their first period. Such
a taste is characteristic to each individual and is usually
described as metallic. Shortly after the first missed
period the majority of pregnant women start to 'go off'
certain things. [4]

Readers of such guides, although alerted to the fact that such
alterations in taste are common enough features of normal pregnancies to
merit mention as possible symptoms of pregnancy, are not given any more
information than this, and the impression presented is that, if
experienced at all, they are transient and of minor significance. This
impression is reinforced by the fact that some textbooks [5] and advice
manuals [6] make no mention at all of changes in appetite or tastes, and
that mention of them is often rather vague and tentative, suggesting
that little is actually known about the condition in question, e.g.:

A temporary craving for unusual foods or flavours *(pica)*
is not uncommon. The explanation is uncertain. These
whims may be met within reason but they should not be
allowed to offend against common sense. [7]

Even those advice manuals which mention aberrations in appetite or taste
in one context, for example, as a symptom of pregnancy, tend to ignore
them completely in other contexts, for example, when discussing
recommended eating habits. Advice given about diet usually focusses on
three themes: keeping down the overall weight gain during pregnancy,
providing the right sort of nutrition for the growing baby and the
pregnant women, and preventing or ameliorating certain common complaints
such as constipation, nausea, heartburn, dizziness, etc. [8] These
themes are nearly always discussed separately from each other and from
any mention of abnormalities of taste and appetite.

This separation tends to imply that the impact of pregnancy on
women's eating habits is trivial, and that the dietary measures
advocated are easy to accomplish. I wish to argue here that such
implications may be very misleading and that, in contrast, pregnancy may
exert a fairly overwhelming influence over the eating habits of pregnant
women. That is, I wish to suggest that issues such as what to eat, how
much to eat, when to eat, how often to eat, and the social and physical
consequences of eating - in short, all sorts of aspects of food and
eating which are normally relatively unquestioned, routine, and taken for
granted - for a variety of reasons, become problematic in pregnancy.
This happens both in the sense of coming to the forefront of attention
and consciousness and in the sense of leading to awkwardness or
unpleasantness.

I further want to suggest that because pregnancy exerts its impact in
a number of different ways it may sometimes be difficult for pregnant
women to reconcile competing injunctions or needs. For example, eating
sweets may stave off nausea or faintness, but it may also put on weight;

or one may develop an aversion to the very foods such as vegetables or milk one is supposed, for the health of mother and baby, to be eating more of. Exhortations to maintain normal social routines and relation-ships during pregnancy may be difficult to reconcile either with various other medical advice or with changes induced by pregnancy. For example, advice not to drink alcohol may lead to a curtailing of social life and contacts if these mainly revolve around pub or party going; nausea or vomiting may similarly render social occasions problematic as well as disrupting usual household routines such as preparing, or clearing up after, meals; feeling able only to eat little and often may create tensions if days are normally structured around mealtimes. And as I have pointed out previously (Macintyre, 1981) traditional views about the appropriate division of domestic labour within marriage may mean that it is more likely that the wife will get up earlier than necessitated by her job in order to prepare her husband's breakfast, than for the husband to bring her tea and a dry biscuit in bed to help reduce nausea, as advised in the antenatal leaflets.[9]

This chapter focusses upon the impact of pregnancy on eating and food habits, listing and illustrating the ways in which being pregnant can affect eating habits and the social implications of such changes. The data are taken from a prospective study of 50 married primigravidae undertaken in Aberdeen in 1977-78. This involved interviewing respondents three times during pregnancy - at booking for antenatal care and confinement (on average, at around 14 weeks gestation); at 24 weeks pregnant and at 34 weeks pregnant; and once after delivery. The interviews, which were tape recorded, were conducted in respondents' homes and focussed on their expectations, perceptions, and experiences of pregnancy. Further details can be found in Macintyre (1981).

THE IMPACT OF PREGNANCY

There are a number of ways in which pregnancy may alter eating habits. Although they are analytically distinct, and I here treat them in turn, it should be noted that in practice the divisions between the different types may become blurred. Thus it may be difficult for either the pregnant woman or the observer to determine the reasons for any specific change in eating patterns. The various effects of pregnancy on eating and drinking can be seen as originating in three main types of cause: physiological, social, and those relating to pregnant women's attempts to improve the outcome of the pregnancy.

Physiological

Physiological changes in pregnancy may affect eating and drinking in three main ways: appetite, tastes and digestive and related complaints.

Firstly, there may be changes in general appetite. Some women may find themselves very much more hungry, e.g.

SM: Have you noticed any change in your eating
                       habits?

Mrs Anderson:[10]   (first interview)...Yes! Eat, eat eat.
                       I'm always hungry.

Mrs Kerr: (first interview)...I was watching what I was

59

eating till I got pregnant and I (now) I want to
eat a lot more than I used to, 'cos every time
after a meal, maybe an hour after, I've got to
have something else to eat 'cos I'm starving.

Such feelings of hunger were not confined to the first trimester, e.g.

Mrs Ross: (third interview)...Eating too much,oh it's
                 terrible, I'd eat for ever, non stop. I mean,
                 I try to keep within my limits; y'know, if I
                 didn't I would eat any time. Just mention food
                 and that's it, I'm away!

Several women mentioned wanting to control their eating, but finding
their hunger compulsive, e.g.

Mrs Usher: (second interview)...Canna' stop eating. Just
                 eat all the time. I keep on, ken, after I've
                 just had my tea or that, I could just eat
                 another plate of the same things or rice
                 crispies or something. I try not to, but I
                 canna' help it.

Other women, in contrast, found themselves only able to eat very little,
e.g.

Mrs Mackenzie: (first interview)...I went completely off food
                 for about the first two months and if I did
                 eat a meal it was a very, very small portion.

Mrs Buchan: (second interview)...Now I'm pregnant I don't
                 eat nearly so much, you know. When I come
                 home at tea time I'm never hungry, it's just a
                 case of making tea for one, you know (i.e. for
                 husband). I do eat less at meals, yes, I used
                 to always finish my plate before, but I don't
                 now. A few meals I do skip because I just,
                 you know, I don't feel hungry.

One woman swung from one extreme to the other. At the first interview
she said:

Mrs Armstrong: I've been very off food lately. Off almost
                 everything.

and at the second interview she said:

Mrs Armstrong: I'm eating like a horse. I'm always hungry. I
                 have a big lunch and I eat again later...eating
                 everything I can. I think I over eat really,
                 you know, I'm always hungry, and I nibble as
                 well.

Other women said that they found that they could not eat big meals, but
felt hungry more often; that they no longer felt hungry at certain
times of the day; or that they felt very thirsty. These alterations in
appetite are included in the 'other' category in Table 6.1 which shows
the number of women reporting various changes in eating habits at each
interview.[11] This shows that at each interview over 70 per cent of the
sample reported some changes and that at the first interview 86 per cent
did so.

Table 6.1
Reported Changes in Eating Habits at Each Interview (Number of Women)

Eating Habits	Interview: Gestation (weeks)		
	c.14	c.24	c.34
Eating more	9	11	13
Eating less	16	6	12
Other	9	7	5
Deliberate changes	9	12	1
No change	5	9	14
Not stated	2	1	0
Total	50	46	45

Secondly, there may be changes in tastes for food and drink, with all sorts of foods previously liked now being strongly disliked, e.g.

Mrs Bennett: (first interview)...I used to like mince, an' beef an' that - but I can't eat that. And I used to like coffee, and I can't drink coffee now.

Mrs James: (first interview)...I dinna' eat a lot of chips like I used to. I used to be a lover of chips, but I canna' take them now.

Mrs Ross: (second interview)...I canna' eat cottage cheese, or corn on the cob.

Mrs Vincent: (third interview)...I went off tomato soup, and tomatoes and bacon.

Mrs Tait: (third interview)...Curries, and macaroni and cheese, I've gone off that.

There may also be sudden fancies or cravings for specific foods, e.g.:

Mrs Ritchie: (first interview)...It was corned beef and beans, and a type of sweets, sports mixture.

Mrs Nicholson: (second interview)...Pickles and bananas and grapes.

Mrs Noble: (third interview)...Ice cream. And advocaat, I've taken a right craving for that!

Mrs Webster: (third interview)...Ice cubes. I usually take a drink just to get the ice cubes. It's about 10 in an evening I ration myself to.

Mrs Cooper: (first interview)...Nestles white chocolate.

(third interview)...I'm going a lot for nuts now, peanuts and such.

Mrs Ogilvie: (second interview)...Custard. You know those big tins of Birds Custard? Well I went through one of those in less than a fortnight.

It is such cravings which are the mainstay of jokes about eating in pregnancy, although there were very few 'bizarre' cravings among this sample. Respondents obviously knew about the stereotypes of cravings and some told stories about other people's cravings, e.g.:

Table 6.2 Cravings and Aversions Reported at Each Interview

Interview at c.14 weeks gestation

Aversion only	Craving only
Fried food (esp. chips)	Cream buns
Boiled eggs and fried food	Primula cream cheese
Cooked meats and crisps	Ice cream
Tea and coffee	Oranges
Coffee and strong tea	Nestles white chocolate
Fried foods,pasta, sweets,tea and coffee	Pickles and tomatoes
Baked beans	Soup
Curry, macaroni, tea	Peaches and bananas
Coffee	Lucozade
Perfumed things (e.g. aerosol sprays)	
Cod roes	
Tea and coffee	
Coffee	
13 women	**9 women**

Both

Whisky	Oranges,liver,ice cream
Chips,coffee,oranges, vegetables	Ice cream,pickled onions
Vegetables	Corned beef,beans, sweets,fish and chips
Hot drinks, biscuits	Eggs
Boiled eggs	Beetroot
Chocolate	Bananas
Tea and coffee	Stuffed tomatoes
Chocolates, fried foods, mince	Ice cream
Eggs and cold meat	Fruit
Carbohydrates	Lucozade and liquids
Red meat	Tomato flavoured crisps
Coffee and fried dood	Fruit and tomatoes
Ice cream and milk	Mince and tatties
Cakes, fried food, chocolates	Curry and ice cream

14 women

Interview at c.24 weeks gestation

Aversion only	Cravings only
Coffee	Drinking chocolate
Liver and pork	Egg and tomato sandwiches
Oranges	Mince and tatties
Coffee	Rice Crispies
Coffee and steak	Liquorice
Fried foods	
Vegetables	
Apples, carrots, chocolate	
Fried eggs and chicken	
Coffee and fried foods	
10 women	**5 women**

Both

Meat	Fruit
Tea	Chicken curry and fruit
Tea	Pickles and bananas
Eggs and salad	Birds' custard and semolina
Boiled eggs	Beetroot and grapes
Peas	Crisps, sweets, lemonade
Cabbage	Tomatoes
Coffee, eggs, chicken	Occasional cravings

8 women

Interview at c.34 weeks gestation

Aversion only	Craving only
Coffee and white bread	Drinking chocolate
Fried eggs	Peanuts
Fried eggs	Pears
Coffee and peanuts	Ice cubes
Fried foods	Drinking chocolate
5 women	**5 women**

Both

Pork chops and liver	Ice cream
Milk	Grapes
Boiled eggs and bacon	Granny Smiths' apples
Mince	Ice cream and advocaat
Corn on the cob	Tomatoes and toast
Curry and macaroni cheese	Ice cream and ice lollies
Tomato soup, tomatoes, bacon	Eggs

7 women

Number unaffected throughout = 8

Number affected at some point in pregnancy 42/50 (84%)

Mrs Bennett: (second interview)...There was a lassie that stays at the top of the road, she's about 8 months pregnant, she's an awful craving for Galaxy milk chocolate she bought about 8 bars or something from the shop and she went back in the afternoon and he said, 'Oh, you've had the last of the Galaxy', and she said, 'Oh I dinna' think I'll survive through the night!' She canna' help it, she's got to have chocolate, you know. I've nothing like that.

Only one told a story about the embarrassment cravings had caused her:

Mrs Nicholson: (second interview)...I was sitting one night in my mother's friend's (house) and out she came with chocolate biscuits for our tea. (I said) 'I dinna' like chocolate biscuits. I fancy a banana'. So my mother's friend says, 'Oh, Ive got bananas'. I says, 'Have you got any pickles?' I sat and ate a whole jar of pickles and two bananas;...I've never been so embarrassed in my life.

Several mentioned that other people seemed to expect them to have cravings, usually for 'odd' foods, e.g.

Mrs Gordon: (second interview)...I've been quite lucky. Very lucky! One of my friends has got the coal and pickled onions looked out, but he's been quite disappointed so far.

As Table 6.2 shows, however, most of the cravings were for quite ordinary, mundane substances, rather than for the coal or newsprint of the folklore tales.

Hytten and Leitch (1964) suggest that such cravings may be due to a dulling of the sense of taste in pregnancy, which would imply that women crave more 'tasty' foods and lose interest in or develop aversions to more bland foods. Table 6.2 shows that the reported cravings and aversions did not fall into a pattern that would support this hypothesis.

As Table 2 shows, cravings and aversions declined in incidence between the interviews: at the first interview 74 per cent had a craving or an aversion or both, compared with 54 per cent at the second interview and 38 per cent at the third.[12] It is nevertheless clear that for this sample changes in tastes were not confined, as the literature sometimes asserts, to early pregnancy.

Thirdly, during pregnancy women may experience certain complaints which are either digestive (nausea and/or vomiting, heartburn) or otherwise related to food intake (e.g. constipation, dizziness, faintness): they may then be told, or find out for themselves, that varying what, how much, or when, they eat, helps to prevent the condition or to alleviate its worst effects. Women complaining of these ailments are usually advised to modify their diet in certain specified ways, e.g. to ingest lots of roughage and fluids to prevent constipation; to avoid fried foods to minimise heartburn; and to eat little and often to prevent the low blood sugar levels implicated in dizziness and nausea.[13] The eating habits recommended may differ considerably from those to which the women are accustomed, and be viewed as 'bad' habits by normal criteria, e.g.

Mrs Webster: (third interview)...I'm eating more sweet stuff. That doesn't altogether please me, because I feel it's habit forming. But obviously these dizzy turns have got something to do with blood sugar levels, so I feel I have to keep taking, say, a biscuit and a cup of coffee, and I carry a bar of chocolate, in fact, I was carrying sugar lumps because the doctor said, you know (to have) something instantly to give me energy. I tried sweeties, that was abominable, I was crunching my way through that many sweeties: I was worried about my teeth as well.

Mrs Armstrong: (third interview)...I started eating a lot of trashy foods, like chocolate or ice cream, which I didn't really have a taste for before, with the result that my skin was beginning to show it...I've been told to keep eating, even just to nibble anything, to keep the feeling of sickness away. I think it's more, for instance, Mars Bars, they've been very convenient to carry in a bag, so that's probably why I'm eating stuff like that (i.e. rather than a craving).

Table 3 shows the reported incidence of these four complaints at each interview. It can be seen from this that they were quite common, particularly at certain times in pregnancy: e.g. at the first interview 47 women reported nausea and/or vomiting, and at the third 43 out of 45 reported heartburn or indigestion.

Table 6.3
Incidence of Common Complaints at Each Interview (Number of Women)

Complaint	Interview: Gestation (weeks)		
	c.14	c.24	c.34
Dizziness/Faintness	8	17	14
Constipation	10	18	16
Heartburn/Indigestion	8	35	43
Nausea/Vomiting	47	12	2
Total	50	46	45

These complaints were significant not just because of their high incidence among the sample as a whole but also because for many of the women their impact was quite marked and for varying lengths of time dominated their lives. Some indeed resented the description of such problems as being 'minor complaints':

Mrs Simpson: (first interview)...There was one bit (in the BMA booklet 1977), the bit that said 'In your first 3 months you'll experience some mild disorders'. And I just thought to myself, leaning over the sink being sick as a dog, I thought, 'Well, if that's mild, God help us!'

Mrs Leslie: (first interview)...I dinna' think I would go
through all that. I thought it was, well,
they do say 'morning sickness', I thought it
was, you'd get up in the morning and you're
sick and then you're OK for the rest of the
day. My God, I never thought it would be all
day! When the time came it was murder.

One woman gave up her job when only a few weeks pregnant because she
could not cope with rushing out to the toilet to be sick; another was
admitted to hospital with hyperemesis; another lost 2.5 stone and went
to 5.5 stone. Even if not as extreme as that, many women found that
they had to be very conscious of what they ate and when, e.g.

Mrs Shearer: (first interview)...I find I'm better taking
something warmish, y'know, even warm milk, I
always take a cereal with warm milk...this
morning I got up late, I slept in, and I
didn't have time to have a cereal with warm
milk so I just took a cereal with cold milk,
and I was sick, y'know, I brought it all up
once I was at my work...You've to watch what
you eat, sort of thing. Before I could
almost eat anything, y'know, I've really got
a stomach that could stand anything, hot
curries and anything like that. I've really
got to watch it now.

Mrs Irvine: (third interview)...I sometimes do feel hungry
but I am sometimes scared to eat anything in
case the heartburn comes on.

Nausea was quite commonly associated with the sight or smells of food
preparation, cooking, or dirty plates. This meant that some women had
to alter their domestic habits as well as their eating habits, which
meant further disruption of normal routines, e.g.

Mrs Ogilvie: (first interview)...Occasionally he (husband)
has had to finish making a meal. Even though
I'm getting tablets from the doctor to stop me
being sick in the morning, I still feel sick
when I smell cooking.

Mrs Forbes: (first interview)...Sometimes, after you've had
the tea, the dishes, just the smell, ye canna'
look at them. He (husband) is good, he'll do
that for me.

Mrs Anderson: (second interview)...Anything fried, it just
puts me off. I dinna' enjoy nothing fried. I
used to give my husband bacon and eggs on a
Sunday but I just canna' do it now. Puts me
right off.

The effects of nausea in early pregnancy could extend over quite a long
time, some women saying later in pregnancy that they could still not
face foods which had earlier made them sick, e.g.

Mrs Baird: (second interview)...Oh, well, I think I just
got conditioned in the summer; some things,

65

you know, just the smell of them made me so sick
that now, although they wouldn't make me sick, I
can't face the thought of them.

Mrs Milne: (first interview)...I've really gone off pasta,
               since we were on holiday in Italy and I was
               feeling sick!

Social

In addition to the direct physiological effects of pregnancy on diet
there may be an indirect effect mediated by social factors. Two main
types can be distinguished: to do with social circumstances and with
legitimating unusual appetites.

Firstly, pregnancy, and particularly first pregnancy, may lead to
changes in social circumstances - such as leaving work, or ceasing
recreational activities - which in turn affect eating habits. Forty-
five of this sample of 50 were in paid employment at the beginning of
pregnancy: only one continued working throughout pregnancy, the others
stopping mainly around 28 weeks (although three stopped before 20 weeks
and six between 20 and 25 weeks). The main effect of stopping working
was that the women no longer had lunch (which had often been provided
for them at work); however, more of them now had breakfast because they
had the time to prepare it, e.g.

Mrs James: (third interview)...I sometimes dinna' have
               dinner now though, because I canna' be bothered
               cooking for one, but I always have a good
               supper and I always have breakfast when I get
               up.

Some women had lost weight since leaving work, e.g.

Mrs Ferguson: (third interview)...(had lost 6 lbs recently)
               ...You see, I knew I had a problem because of
               the food I was given at work. 'Cos I'd go in
               at ten o'clock and had hot rolls and then I had
               bacon and sausage or something like that. And
               then at lunch time we had a big three course
               meal and then at three o'clock you had tea and
               biscuits...and it was obviously the food that
               was doing it, but since I've stopped work we
               only have one meal a day, one good meal a day
               and I've been fine.

Those most affected by leaving work were women whose husbands worked
offshore, for periods ranging from a week at a time to a month at a
time, in the oil industry. While their husbands were away these women
had no source of routine external to themselves, and no one to cook for
or share meals with, and some of their diets and eating habits seemed to
'go haywire' in consequence, e.g.

Mrs Urquhart: (third interview)...I don't usually bother when
               he's away, just supper time. I don't bother
               with lunch or anything, just have cups of tea
               and coffee. I canna' be bothered cooking when
               he's not around. It's not the same, cooking
               for yourself I don't think, so I don't bother
               really. I just eat when I'm hungry, and

anything that just comes into my head, just what
I fancy.

Not all these women ate <u>less</u> while their husbands were away, e.g.

Mrs Armstrong: (second interview)...I'm on my own now, my
husband's away, and for instance, on Sunday
evening, I'd had my tea and then I was hungry,
maybe just because I was on my own, and I made
a cheesecake. Well, I ate the whole cheesecake
on Sunday evening, which was quite ridiculous.
That was terrible, you know, a whole tin of
cherry pie filling on the top, well, I mean it
was really ridiculous, I just had to eat it!

This same respondent mentioned another effect of having left work which
operated even when her husband was home:

Mrs Armstrong: (third interview)...(has put on too much
weight)...It might have been from not going to
work every day. I was filling in my time in
the kitchen more or less...I am accustomed to
being very busy, and I would spend a couple of
hours in the kitchen baking, just silly things
like chocolate eclairs which was quite
ridiculous. My husband would hardly eat any
of it because he likes to keep fit, so I found
I was eating most of it myself.

More common was the experience shared by many of the women of not having
anything in particular to do, and spending more time in the house just
sitting, and therefore of eating more snacks, e.g.

Mrs Webster: (third interview)...I get up now and have a
breakfast. And then, well, about half past
ten I'll have coffee and biscuits, then lunch,
then afternoon tea (laughing) and so it goes
on. All the things I laughed at my own mother
about.

Secondly, pregnancy may provide an 'excuse' for certain appetites or
tastes, since it is a condition seen as legitimating unusual desires, or
the consumption of nutritious food normally seen as luxurious, e.g.

Mrs Nicholson: (first interview)...My husband, he was just
goin' away to his bed, I says 'Would you like
to go for a curry for me?' He went, and I
really enjoyed it.

Mrs Davidson: (second interview)...Well, I'm not really sure
whether it's a craving or whether it's an
excuse. But strawberries and, you know, fruit
that's in season (August) like peaches.

SM: Have you had any particular cravings?

Mrs Ferguson: No, I haven't had any. Quite disappointed
there (laughing)

Deliberate attempts to enhance the outcome of pregnancy

In addition to finding that appetites, tastes and digestion have changed in pregnancy and that in consequence changes have been imposed, as it were, on eating habits, many women make deliberate attempts to improve the outcome of their pregnancies by altering what they ingest. Such efforts, which may involve not only manipulating diet but also cutting down on cigarettes and alcohol, are of course encouraged in the advice literature. A number of variants can be identified.

Minimising Weight Gain. Currently, guides for expectant mothers are firmly opposed to what they describe as the unhealthy old fashioned idea of 'eating for two', and advise women to try to keep their weight gain in pregnancy to a minimum. This recommended minimum varies between different authors, which is somewhat confusing to some women, e.g.

Mrs Gordon: (second interview)...I think I've put on a stone over the past 6 months. I'm not sure whether that's a lot or not. You know, some books say your ideal weight gain is about 22 pounds, some say 28, some say 32 or something.

The women in this sample were very conscious of the prescription that they should not put on too much weight; 22 of the women, nearly half the sample, reported that they thought they had been overweight anyway before they conceived and had already been trying to reduce weight prior to the pregnancy. Much of the conversation about food and eating in pregnancy therefore revolved around the problem of not putting on too much weight, which respondents sometimes found difficult to reconcile with other changes in pregnancy, e.g.

Mrs Irvine: (second interview)...Well, I'm always hungry. I always feel hungry, but I try not to stuff myself...I tend to eat more between meals but I stick to fruit as much as possible, trying not to put on too much weight.

Mrs Gordon: (third interview)...Lately I think I've been conscious of the fact that I've put on a lot of weight. But I think maybe actually it would be the milk,'cos you know, they tell you to drink a lot of milk, and I've been drinking a lot of milk.

Avoiding insufficient weight gain. While pregnant women are advised not to put on too much weight, failure to put on enough weight is seen by medical or midwifery attendants as a cause for worry. Six women in this sample lost considerable amounts of weight in early pregnancy; ten said at the second interview that they had been told they had not put on enough weight (including two who had lost weight); and seven said this at the third interview. These women were encouraged to gain weight, and for some of them the problem of putting on weight loomed large in their lives, e.g.

Mrs Vincent: (second interview)...(has lost 2.5 stone)...My mother's been coming up to make sure that I'm eating. She's actually cooking it and leaving it.

Mrs Edwards: (third interview)...He (the doctor) was askin' me what I was having to eat an' that. Well, I mean, I do have, I think I eat enough, you know. (But) the last time I went he says,

'Eat as much as you can next week', and that if
I don't put on any weight he'll ask questions.

Eating properly.   Pregnant women are exhorted to eat the right kind of
foods as well as the right amounts[14], and it was apparent that most of
this sample took these exhortations seriously, e.g.

Mrs Henderson: Well, I always make sure I have plenty of
protein and vitamins, I'm more conscious about
that.

Mrs Valentine: Well, I'm drinking milk. And vegetables, and
things like that. I feel I should eat them.

Mrs Owen: (first interview)...I suppose we eat more, well,
try to eat more vegetables. Fruit and vege-
tables, really, and drink more water. liquids,
and that's about it.

Mrs Young: (third interview)...I do watch, you know, I do
eat more vegetables and things like that now.

Mrs Ferguson: (third interview)...Just as long as I have
plenty of milk and fruit. As I say, the one
good meal is always, you know, plenty of veg.
anyway, so I feel I'm getting the right things.

Some women attempted to eat the recommended items even though they disliked them or found them sickening, e.g.

Mrs Noble: (first interview)...I eat liver, which I dinna'
normally eat. I bought cereal, which I dinna'
normally eat. But I've to drink, they said a
pint of milk a day, and I canna' drink milk
itself. I can drink hot milk and syrup...but
I canna' drink cold milk, I dinna' ken why;
it makes me sick.

Mrs Ritchie: (first interview)...You're supposed to drink a
pint of milk a day, well I don't think I could
drink a pint of milk a day. I wondered
whether I would get the things, y'know, like
to make a milk shake, y'know, and have it that
way.

Those women who had previously been on special diets of whatever sort
modified them when they became pregnant in order to follow the
recommended diet, e.g.

               (second interview)...My husband insists I eat
meat. I was trying to become a semi vegetarian,
sort of thing, but he insists that I eat meat
for protein. He's been reading these books
about how you should eat meats and things like
that.

Mrs Cooper: I was on a diet before I became pregnant but
as soon as I thought I was pregnant I stopped
dieting.

Smoking.   Pregnant women are, of course, recommended to stop, or cut
down on, smoking. In this sample, 23 women were cigarette smokers at

the beginning of pregnancy, of whom 12 stopped smoking. Several of them found this easier than they expected because they actually developed aversions to the smell and taste of cigarettes. However, some then complained that, having stopped smoking, they put on weight or ate more 'rubbish', e.g.

> Mrs Forbes: (second interview)...I think I'm eating more, 'cos I stopped smokin'. Well, I'll blame that; I was putting on too much weight (she put on 3 stone over the pregnancy).

> Mrs Paterson: (second interview)...I think it's probably with giving up cigarettes that I'm eating chocolates. I've been watching TV and that, and of course, not smoking I suppose you eat chocolates: substitute cigarettes.

Alcohol. Advice on alcohol consumption is more equivocal than that given about cigarette consumption. Some women, uncertain precisely how to interpret injunctions such as 'don't drink a lot of alcohol'[15], decided not to drink any alcohol at all. Others found that they developed an aversion to alcohol. Whatever the reason for their reduced alcohol intake, the reduction was often seen as having a marked effect on the women's social lives, e.g.

> Mrs Allan: (first interview)...I just don't like going to parties an' that. I was at a party on Saturday night and I was drinking water. Well, it wasn't fun seeing everybody else (drinking) when I wasn't drinking.

> SM: Has your pregnancy affected your social life at all?

> Mrs Baird: (first interview)...In a way it has, because I can't drink. Not that I've got any scruples about drinking, but because it makes me sick. Apart from that, it's very boring to go out in company and drink lemonade.

DISCUSSION

I have sought to demonstrate, by describing the above ways in which pregnancy may have an effect on eating patterns, that these effects may be quite important, in terms of their frequency and of the difficulties, disruptions to normal life, and unpleasantness they may cause expectant mothers. Although I have here dealt separately with each of these effects, it is obviously possible for an individual pregnant woman to be affected in more than one way, either simultaneously or sequentially. The cumulative repercussions on her daily life and social relationships can then be quite severe and long lasting, rather than trivial and transient as is often implied in the literature.

All the effects of pregnancy on eating that I have described are already well known; I have not presented any new findings about hitherto unknown changes in appetites, taste, digestion, or modifications to diet. Yet the impression I hope to have given - that for much of pregnancy and for many women, the issues of what to eat, when to eat, how much to eat, and the physical and social consequences of eating, may assume considerable prominence - is one that is rarely presented in the literature. Instead, various changes of taste or appetite are treated as matters of only passing interest to the diagnosis of pregnancy. Why this should be so is an interesting question, but is beyond the scope of this essay.

Whether the causes of the changes are physiological or social, they may have both physiological and social implications. That is, a woman may eat poorly and sporadically because her husband is offshore, i.e. for what I have called a social reason, but this may still have physical consequences for the health of the mother and baby. Conversely, persistent nausea may have repercussions on a woman's capacity to function normally at work or at home, or on her family relationships, and thus have social consequences. Disruptions in domestic or public social routines may draw attention to the pregnancy and underline the potentially ambiguous social status of pregnancy. However much one might wish to carry on as normal during pregnancy, one may be marked out as occupying a particular status by alterations in eating patterns.

Oddities of appetite can be welcomed precisely because of their symbolic value in confirming and signifying pregnancy. This can be illustrated by the one woman in the sample who did not experience any physical side effects of pregnancy (apart from amenhorrhea) or changes in taste or appetite, and who felt in consequence that she was not being 'properly' pregnant. The importance of the social meanings given to these symptoms is indicated by the fact that the ones she mentions are not normally thought of as pleasant or desirable at all, yet she is wishing them upon herself:

> Mrs Tulloch: (first interview)...Well, I just don't have any of the basic symptoms. I mean, I didn't expect to be smitten with everything but I though I'd have noticed a few changes so far. You know, I keep waiting for the day when I maybe start eating a chip or something and think, 'ooh, what on earth does that taste like!' Or to start fancying various things, strawberries or something like that. Or, ehm, to be sick, you know, 'please let me be sick, then I'll know'.

In fact, Mrs Tulloch had a miscarriage a few days after she said this, and may have been correct in associating lack of such symptoms of pregnancy with a poorly established or unstable pregnancy.[16]

The data on which this paper are based relate only to women pregnant for the first time, and I do not know whether the findings are generalisable to second or subsequent pregnancies. Despite the restricted nature of the sample I think, however, these findings merit attention, since they indicate that the management of food and of eating in pregnancy may assume considerable medical and social significance.

NOTES

[1] Clayton, S. and Newton, J.R. A Pocket Obstetrics 9th ed Churchill Livingstone, Edinburgh, 1979, p.13.
[2] Tomkinson, J.S.(ed) The Queen Charlotte's Textbook of Obstetrics

12th ed, J.&A. Churchill, London, 1970, p.64.

[3] Scottish Health Education Unit The Book of the Child: From Pregnancy to Four Years Old, 1st ed, HMSO, Edinburgh, 1979, p.4.

[4] Bourne, G. Pregnancy, Pan Books, London, 1975, p.95.

[5] e.g. Myles, M.F. Textbook for Midwives with Modern Concepts of Obstetrics and Neonatal Care, 8th ed, Churchill Livingstone, Edinburgh, 1975.

[6] e.g. Consumers Association Pregnancy Month by Month, 5th ed, A Consumer Publication, London, 1979.

[7] Passmore, R. and Robson, J.S. (eds-in-chief) A Companion to Medical Studies vol.3, Blackwell Scientific, Oxford, 1974, p.397.

[8] Bourne, 1975, op.cit. and BMA You and Your Baby Part 1: From Pregnancy to Birth, Family Doctor Publications, 1977.

[9] BMA, 1977, op.cit.

[10] Respondents are identified in this chapter by pseudonyms.

[11] Since not all of the initial sample of respondents were available for all the interviews there are some missing data and the totals vary between interviews.

[12] The incidence of cravings and/or aversions reported here is in line with that found by Taggart in Aberdeen in the early 1960s; two thirds of her sample of 800 pregnant women had cravings and/or aversions (Taggart, 1961).

[13] Bourne, 1975 and BMA, 1977, op.cit.

[14] e.g. SHEU, 1979 and BMA, 1977, op.cit.

[15] BMA, 1977, p.24, op.cit.

[16] Personal communication, Dr M. Hall.

7 A Question of Balance: Asian and British Women's Perceptions of Food During Pregnancy

HILARY HOMANS

The way in which people conceptualise food and its relationship to health and illness tends to reflect and reproduce dominant values of the society in which they live. This is most apparent at times of transition, such as pregnancy, when more attention is often paid to diet. Socially pregnancy may be seen as ambiguous (cf. Homans, 1982 and also Graham, 1977) and potentially polluting. Contradictions appear for instance in those sub-cultures where pregnancy raises a woman's status, but only temporarily, as the potential bearer of an heir (as in the British upper class) or a son who will be financially responsible for the parents in old age (as in Punjabi families, cf. Morpeth, 1979). Corresponding contradictions are found in perceptions of eating and distribution of food in pregnancy. There is an augmentation of some existing food restrictions and some new prohibitions are added. This occurs at the same time that pregnant women are allowed to eat certain foods normally forbidden, or regarded as extravagant or luxurious.

One of the reasons why pregnant women are able to argue for craved foods relates to the belief that there is a direct correlation between food ingested and the development of the foetus. For example some believe that all expectant mothers' desires for food should be fulfilled lest the baby be in some way deformed. A British woman in the study[1] on which this chapter[2] is based reflected this belief and shows how others in her social network had to go in search of craved food:

> My mother said if I ever fancied anything and I didn't get it,
> it'd have a birth mark looking like whatever it was I wanted.
> So if I've ever said 'Oh I fancy something' somebody's had to
> get it. (British working class woman, first pregnancy)

Other women, however, felt they were able to use cravings in pregnancy as an excuse for exercising control over their husbands (Homans, 1980, pp.288-9). Again, such ideas are sometimes extended to encompass ideas about food ingested and the sex of the child *in utero*. This may be most relevant when a child of a particular sex is desired. For example, an Indian mother of four girls expecting her fifth child said the following:

> Some say that if you are going to have a boy then you feel like
> having things that boys like....Take for example, vegetables
> and lentils and *karhi* (a dish made from gram flour and yoghourt)
> - if you are going to have a girl then you feel like having
> these things....Boys like mangoes and pomegranates (symbol of

73

fertility). Even in the dreams you can see these things....
(Sikh woman, fifth pregnancy)

This chapter will focus on the way that food is conceptualised in
India and in Britain and how traditional perceptions persist after
migration.   Additionally the role of significant others in managing or
instigating dietary changes will be examined in relation to lay or
traditional medicine and allopathic (scientific) medicine.

In the first section I concentrate on the relationship between
traditional medicine in India and health maintenance, and the role of
significant others in perpetuating traditional beliefs after migration.
This is followed by an examination of medical professional views
concerning diet not commonly shared by all pregnant women. The way that
British women perceive diet and its importance in health maintenance is
outlined in conjunction with social class variation.

ASIAN VIEWS: IN INDIA AND BRITAIN

The Asian women studied had migrated predominantly from rural areas of
the Punjab and subscribed to beliefs about food which were related to
Ayurvedic philosophy. (For a fuller account cf. Homans, 1980). Ayurveda
(which literally means the 'science of life') is the traditional Hindu
system of medicine and considers that 'the two main causes of disease
are faulty diet and faulty regimen, of which the former is held to be
the most important' (Tabor, 1981, p.442). Health is viewed as a state
of equilibrium and disease:

> as a state of disharmony in the body as a whole....Hence,
> according to it, treatment should aim at not only the finding
> of appropriate internal remedies but the employment of all
> available means to restore the normal balance or equilibrium.
> This comprehensiveness of Indian medicine is further evident
> from the attention it gives to diet - both in health and
> disease. (Report of Committee on Indigenous Systems of Medicine,
> 1948)

Ayurveda also considers a person's constitution to be made up of three
humours - *vata* (wind), *pitta* (bile) or *kapha* (phlegm). These three
humours are called the *tri-dosha* and when they are in a state of
balance the body is healthy. To maintain a balance between the *dosha*
people will pay particular attention to what they eat.

Foods are classified in the Ayurvedic tradition into the effect they
have on the body, or their after effect:

> Sets of bodily symptoms are associated with heating and cooling
> foods and subsidiary classifications have been assigned to
> foods causing specific symptoms such as wind or dizziness.
> (Nichter, 1977, p.149)

The classification of foods into hot and cold qualities is not
according to the temperature of the food, or the taste, but the effect
produced within the body.

Cooling foods include most dairy produce as they coat the alimentary
canal with a fat which slows the digestion process and which results in

74

a soothing and cooling feeling. Thus the prescription for heartburn is to eat butter (a cold food) to relieve the burning sensation. Excessive consumption of cooling foods can have a contrary effect and leads to constipation, headache and chills. Illness may be caused by eating foods at the wrong time of year or the wrong time of day. For instance, drinking buttermilk cool on a hot afternoon is seen as the cause of a headache (Nichter, 1977, p.150).

The other kind of foods in this classification are heating foods; these are usually digested much quicker than cold foods but this does not mean that they are more digestible:

> The over-eating of heating foods may cause dry hard faeces, heartburn, diarrhoea, back pain, burning eyes, mouth sores, rashes and a specific burning sensation in the body.
> (Nichter, 1977, p.150)

Three criteria are used to classify heating foods. 1) hot to taste: for example, chillies, radish; 2) hot in the effect on the stomach and digestive system: for example, ginger; 3) foods which cause a hot reaction in the stomach because of their extreme coldness: for example, ice. Ice is so cold it is said to cause a burning sensation in the stomach. This burning is due to the body's reaction of heat to the extreme cold nature of ice. Thus 'cold is qualitative and a substance which is too cold will cause the body to react in an opposite manner' (Nichter, 1977, p.151).

Although most followers of the vedic tradition agree that the essence of a good diet is a proper balance between hot and cold foods this does not mean most people consciously select their foods in order to balance their everyday diet. There are times, however, when people are more aware of the foods they are eating, for example during illness and pregnancy.

Asian women in Britain were found to observe these traditional dietary prescriptions during pregnancy, particularly the prohibition on 'hot' foods. This was most marked in the early months when it was considered that the foetus is easily dislodged by excessive heat in the body:

> I've had everything except 'hot' things. In the beginning I didn't even have egg for two or three months, I also left fish and *sundh* (dry ginger)   (Christian woman, first pregnancy)

> Q: Why don't you eat 'hot' foods?

> A: Because they want to make sure that the child stays there. As you know our Indian women have so many complications and very often have miscarriages after two or three months.
> (Sikh woman, first pregnancy)

Nichter (1977) provides us with an explanation for the accumulation of heat in the body during pregnancy in terms of the Ayurvedic tradition. He says

> During pregnancy, a woman's womb is full of blood and heat. A woman's body should not become too hot or cold during this time or she will abort. For this reason, she is not allowed to eat extremely heating, cooling or gaseous foods. (p.94)

A Brahmin woman in the sample whose grandfather had been a *vaid* (a practitioner of Ayurvedic medicine) religiously followed the traditional Ayurvedic prescriptions instructed by her mother:

> My mother said not to have 'hot' things, not to sit in front of the heater, and not to have coca cola...the body acquires too much heat and causes miscarriage. And not to go out in the cold, if it's raining not to go out.
>
> Q: Why can't you have coca cola?
>
> A: Because of the gas in it. In the beginning when the baby is not very secure it can cause miscarriage.
>
> (Hindu woman Brahmin, first pregnancy)

Other beliefs women held were that 'hot' foods would burn the baby inside, while water and extremely 'cold' things were avoided in the belief that:

> the inside will clear out and become clean. They (older women) say don't give water because it will flow into their veins and their stomach will get bloated.
>
> (Sikh woman, first pregnancy)

After delivery the woman's body is considered to be excessively cool and cold foods and substances must be avoided to the extent that cold water is not even used to wash hands:

> If you touch cold water after birth you may have permanent aches, so you have to be careful.
>
> (Hindu woman, first pregnancy)

A special 'hot' food called *punjeeri* is given to women in India after delivery (sometimes it is also given to the woman immediately before delivery to give the woman strength). This food is prescribed for the parturient woman by her mother or mother-in-law. Gideon (1962) describes it as given to strengthen the newly-developed woman in the rural Punjab in India:

> *Punjeeri* is made by browning *atta* (whole wheat flour) in a large amount of melted butter, then adding sugar, raisins, almonds and tiny crystals of *gur* (crude sugar)...*Punjeeri* has the reputation of giving great strength; almost every woman had a handful of it every day after her confinement. (p.1230)

A variation of this food women in the research were familiar with (and seventeen (65%) were going to eat) is *dabra*. This has the same basic ingredients as *punjeeri* and is made in the same way, but additionally it contains *sundh* (dry ginger), *juan* (barley), *saunf* (aniseed), ground *khaskhas* (poppy seed) and the *magaz* (kernels of seeds of water melon, sweet melon, cucumber and pumpkin) are ground along with *pista* (pistachio nuts) and almonds. The ingredients tend to vary according to individual taste and their availability in Britain. Some women have their own variations and one ate *bajay*:

> In that we put *ghee* (clarified butter), almonds and all the *magaz* (kernels of water melon, sweet melon, cucumber and the pumpkin seeds), *pista* (pistachio nuts), *sougi* (raisins) - all this...I'll buy all the stuff myself, my auntie says it gives strength. (Sikh woman, second pregnancy)

In addition to giving strength, *dabra* is also renowned for curing the backaches and headaches which often follow birth:

76

It's good for your health after that! For your back, when you
work you don't complain about your back.
(Hindu woman, second pregnancy)

Yes, *dabra* must be eaten. The backache and headache get
better with it. It's good to have these things in milk as well.
(Sikh woman, second pregnancy)

Dabra is considered a special treat as it is made out of nuts and sweet
foods not normally eaten. It is very expensive to make and other family
members often like to taste it.

Another dietary prescription women were familiar with was the taking
of oil orally in the month before delivery. This is believed to
lubricate the birth passages and aid the expulsion of the foetus and
afterbirth. Five (19%) women said they would take either almond oil or
ghee (clarified butter) in milk in the weeks prior to delivery:

If there's more grease inside it's easier for the birth...
almond oil keeps everything soft inside.
(Hindu woman, first pregnancy)

They (older women) say have oily food otherwise it will be hard
for you. Have this and have that - have more *ghee* in your milk.
(Sikh woman, fourth pregnancy)

However, one woman feared the lubricating powers of oily food thinking
it may cause a premature birth:

I've heard of taking almond oil and *ghee*, but I've never done
it because I think the baby might slip out.
(Hindu woman, first pregnancy)

These traditional dietary prescriptions were widely known among the
women studied and are consistent with their indigenous system of
medicine and lay concepts of bodily change during pregnancy. Although
the prescriptions can be closely correlated with the Ayurvedic
philosophy, the changes in diet were recommended by significant others
within the woman's social network.

Within Asian culture it is the responsibility of older relatives to
provide traditional advice about diet to pregnant women in an attempt to
secure a healthy baby for the social group. Twenty three (88%) Asian
women said they had been given specific instructions about diet in their
current pregnancy. The main sources of information were the mother or
mother-in-law; in their absence a *būa* (father's sister) or sister-in-
law would give advice.

Older female relatives therefore played an essential role in
reproducing traditional beliefs about the foods to be eaten during
pregnancy. Additionally, these same women were often in a position of
power to ensure that traditional prescriptions were followed. This was
most noticeable for women living in extended families[3] or those women
whose mother or mother-in-law intended to stay with them for forty days
after the delivery (as is the custom). For instance, women living with
their mother or mother-in-law will almost certainly be given *dabra*, or
one of its variations to eat. The preparation and consumption of food
is closely related to notions of reciprocity which are well defined in
the traditional Indian family. In the case of *dabra*, the pregnant
daughter-in-law is obliged to eat the food which her elders have

prescribed for her and which they believe is beneficial to her. A
woman who does not like *dabra* and lives in an extended family is likely
to experience some tension between herself and her mother or mother-in-
law, who has prepared the costly food:

> Well I <u>have</u> to eat it - not yet (after the delivery). The last
> time before birth, but I didn't feel like it much. But this
> time they were forcing me. I say 'No, I don't want it at all,
> if you give it, it will only be wasted'. My mum told me this
> time, I said 'I will waste it. I don't want it'...and I said
> 'Well I won't eat it because I don't like it at all. It's
> alright afterwards, but I don't feel like eating it yet.
> (Emphasis in original)
> (Hindu woman, second pregnancy, living in an extended family)

> After the delivery my mother-in-law and everyone on her side
> <u>insisted</u> I eat some semolina pudding with much healthy stuff in
> it. But I didn't take it because I don't like the greasy food.
> (Emphasis in original)
> (Sikh woman, fourth pregnancy living in an extended family)

Women living in nuclear families who do not like *dabra* because of its
sweetness or greasiness, are advised by older female relatives to eat
almonds, either whole or crushed in flour or milk:

> No I told her (mother) I don't want it (*dabra*). I don't like
> it...She said I should eat almonds, she said I should crush
> them and have them in my milk if I don't like them in flour.
> (Sikh woman, second pregnancy living in nuclear family)

Even women with no female relatives in this country may receive advice
from relatives in India or Pakistan:

> My mother wrote to me and she said you should eat almonds
> and things like that.
> (Muslim woman, fourth pregnancy no relatives in Britain)

Women living in nuclear families were more likely to exercise autonomy
over what they ate. However, the actual presence of the mother-in-law
in the household was not the determining factor, as some women lived
adjacent to their mother-in-law. These women had less autonomy over
what they ate and how they behaved in pregnancy than those women whose
mother or mother-in-law lived in another city, or was still in India.

The close proximity of significant others within the Asian community
provides a certain immunity against adopting a British diet. Furthermore there are very few alternative sources of information on diet
available to Asian women in Britain. The Parentcraft classes (which
only two (8%) English speaking Asian women in this pregnancy attended)
considered diet in terms of traditional British diet, while only seven
(27%) Asian women said their GP had spoken to them about diet. Some
foods recommended by doctors trained in allopathic medicine contravened
the Ayurvedic restriction on hot foods during pregnancy. Eggs are one
such example. The main foods the GPs advised women to eat were meat,
milk, eggs, fruit and vegetables. Vegetarian women were not given
special advice on what foods to eat:

> Well he knows (that I'm a vegetarian) I told him the last time
> anyway. He never told me about diet nor did they at the

hospital. They haven't told me anything.
(Vegetarian Hindu woman, second pregnancy)

The Ayurvedic philosophy of regulating the balance between 'hot' and
'cold' foods ingested during pregnancy is observed by Asian women on
migration to Britain. The presence of significant others (within the
family setting) who subscribe to and perpetuate these beliefs means
that Asian pregnant women in Britain have as yet little knowledge of
how British people conceptualise diet. In contrast, the British women
were not familiar with such a coordinated system of traditional beliefs
about the importance of diet during pregnancy and they were more
dependent on advice located within a western scientific philosophy often
propounded by health care professionals.

BRITISH VIEWS

Earlier it was stated that within Ayurvedic medicine the most important
cause of disease is 'faulty diet' and health is restored by a change of
diet. In allopathic medicine disease is seen to be caused by external
agents and chemotherapy is most commonly used to restore health.
Changes in diet may be recommended in the case of certain illnesses,
but these changes are derived from nutritional theory rather than being
an integral part of allopathic philosophy. Moreover, whilst the
Ayurvedic philosophy has remained stable over a long period of time,
British nutritional theories change rapidly and are largely concerned
with what constitutes a well balanced diet and the relative merits of
certain foodstuffs, for example, sugar and fibre.

In industrial societies with a well established medical profession it
is often assumed that health care workers will deal with all aspects of
the pregnant woman's health within the clinical setting. As a result,
women may receive contradictory information from health care workers
and those members of their own social network who also feel qualified
to speak on these matters. Tensions may therefore arise between a
theory of diet located in the science of nutrition and lay beliefs
about which foods should be prescribed or prohibited. The classification of foods into groups (for example, fats, proteins,
carbohydrates) and the quantification of foods in terms of calories, is
often at variance with lay conceptualisations of foods in terms of
'platefuls' (Murcott, 1982b) colour (Weymes, 1981) or the effect the
food has on the body, for instance, 'heating' or 'cooling' (Nichter,
1977).

The British women's knowledge of diet during pregnancy was nonetheless largely founded on a belief in the science of nutrition, although
this was class-based. The British middle class women believed that the
concept of a 'well balanced diet' was fundamental to maintaining health
in pregnancy. Knowledge of what constituted such a diet was often
learnt at school as part of biology or domestic science. The British
working class women, on the other hand, were more likely to focus on
which foods should be avoided during pregnancy, information which was
usually provided by older women.

The sources of information about diet for British women were varied
and the advice given was more fragmented than for the Asian women,

coming from school, GPs, Parentcraft classes, books, relatives or friends. The dominant response to questions about diet was that it was up to the individual to eat the 'correct' foods and it was assumed she would <u>know</u> what they were. This attitude is different from that held by the Asian women who saw diet much more in terms of a collective responsibility based on a coordinated system of traditional beliefs.

Like the Asian women the British women did not find their GP particularly forthcoming about diet. Only four (15%) British women mentioned their GP as a source of information on diet. Parentcraft classes included information on diet, but most women did not attend these until they were seven months pregnant. The advice given at classes was to eat 'a good well balanced diet' consisting of meat or fish, eggs and cheese at least once a day. They were also told not to eat for two, and to try and cut down on the amount of starchy foods eaten. The importance of foods containing iron, or fresh vegetables and of milk, was also stressed. Some Health Visitors who taught these classes, assumed however that the women who attended do not need to know about diet in pregnancy as they are already well informed (cf. Homans, 1980, p.340). Women who went to the Parentcraft class on diet reflected this same assumption:

> They told us about it (diet) when we went down to the re-
> laxation, what things to eat. But she (Health Visitor) says
> – there's about eleven of us that go down there – she says
> we're alright because we're about the right build anyway.
> (British working class woman, first pregnancy)

Middle class women who had not been given any advice about diet by a health professional in their current pregnancy also reflected the view that 'everyone knows' about these things; 'it's taken for granted that you should drink milk' or 'it's one of those things that one knows about really'.

> I did buy one or two books and I did go to the library and
> read what I could (about diet). I thought that if I just
> went along eating <u>what I thought</u> was a fairly healthy diet
> um...and a <u>balanced diet</u> then I would be alright. And I do
> drink a lot of milk. (Emphasis added)
> (British middle class woman, second pregnancy)

> You more or less <u>know</u> what you've got to eat, you've got to
> try and eat plenty of vegetables, drink plenty, perhaps
> plenty of water...I think you <u>know</u> anyway...I do try and eat
> plenty of nourishing foods if <u>I</u> can...It's up to you yourself
> – <u>if you're responsible.</u> (Emphasis added)
> (British middle class woman, second pregnancy)

These women also considered that they ate well when they were not pregnant:

> I eat a very varied diet anyway. I've always drunk milk and
> I eat an awful lot of cheese.
> (British middle class woman, first pregnancy)

> We eat a good well <u>balanced diet</u> anyway. (Emphasis added)
> (British middle class woman, second pregnancy)

The working class women, on the other hand, were less likely to have read books other than the clinic leaflets on diet, and they were also less likely to have an adequate diet when not pregnant. One of the pregnant women whose husband was unemployed said that she often went all day without eating:

> Like Wednesday when I go out (to the clinic) - I never have much when I go out - I never bother eating or drinking...I never bother having anything till when I come back here about ten at night. That's when I really start eating.
> (British working class woman, third pregnancy)

The working class and unmarried women were far more likely to rely on advice given to them by their mother, than to obtain information on diet from any other source. The advice given to these women by their mother was most often in terms of the amount of food to be eaten, and specific kinds of food to be eaten or avoided:

> She (mother) says 'Oh you'll have to keep off anything like the stuff which you know affects you, like fresh tomatoes'... The skin on fresh tomatoes does. Well I mean I really get it bad (indigestion) at the best of times, that's without being pregnant, you know. (British working class woman, second pregnancy)

Lay advice was more acceptable to working class women than the clinic literature which tends to deal with the question of diet in more 'scientific' terms, and assumes a certain amount of knowledge:

> Do eat sensibly. This means eating iron-containing and high protein foods. It means eating little carbohydrate....[4]

Although the middle class women tended to gain their information about diet from books and independent sources, while the working class women tended to rely more upon traditional advice from their mother, there is a sense in which both groups of women were either beginning to question traditional knowledge about diet or incorporating ostensibly scientific knowledge into lay theories of health maintenance. Seven (27%) British women mentioned that iron, calcium, vitamins and protein were needed by the pregnant woman. This change in attitude to diet reflects a greater dependency upon the doctor, who administers the prescription for the iron tablets, and the drug companies who manufacture the iron and vitamin pills. These pills were seen by four (16%) women as the panacea for all dietary deficiencies:

> I have taken multi-vitamin tablets as well, on my own initiative, especially when I thought I hadn't had a very good diet that week. Then I took a few multi-vitamin tablets.
> (British middle class woman, second pregnancy)

> You see you have iron tablets now, everybody has them, don't they? They fill you full of vitamins. If they (doctors) think you're lacking in anything they'll find out, through your water tests and things like that.
> (British middle class woman, second pregnancy)

Iron and vitamin pills were viewed by some British women as essential in ensuring a 'good well balanced diet' in terms of nutritional theory.

This discussion of the importance of diet in maintaining health and the contrasting scientific view which sees diet as something to be controlled and regulated during pregnancy, illustrates some of the tensions pregnant women experience. On the one hand, there is folk knowledge about diet, which in the case of Asian women is closely related to the Ayurvedic theory of medicine. This folk knowledge is contained within the family and passed down through generations of women. The health of the individual is seen as a matter of collective concern and several female relatives may be involved in preparing dietary prescriptions. On the other hand, scientific knowledge about diet is primarily concerned with quantifying food, counting calories or specifying weights. The scientific model presupposes individual responsibility for health - it is up to the individual woman to know that she should eat a balanced diet and to know what that consists of.

CONCLUSIONS

This chapter has illustrated factors which influence the food eaten during pregnancy and the extent to which they are socially determined. Asian women conceptualise food and its relationship with health maintenance according to the Ayurvedic philosophy. These traditional principles are learnt from significant others who also are often in a position to exercise control of what is eaten. British women on the other hand, do not possess knowledge of such a coordinated belief system relating to diet, rather their knowledge is more fragmented and derived from changing theories in nutritional science of from lay ` beliefs passed on from older women.

Additionally during pregnancy there may be a tension between the way that members of the medical profession view diet and lay advice given by significant others within the social network. The woman's social class and ethnic background are seen to play a large part in determining access to knowledge about traditional recipes and medical prescriptions.

NOTES

[1] The data refer to a study (Homans, 1980) funded by the SSRC conducted while in the Department of Sociology, University of Warwick, of Asian and British women's experience of pregnancy in Britain. In this study 39 British and 39 immigrant women from the Indian sub-continent were interviewed at their first visit to a consultant ante-natal clinic. Twenty-six of the Asian and 26 of the British women were given a second long structured interview in their own homes at eight months pregnant, using an interpreter as necessary. Questions about diet were included in both interviews.

[2] The use of an interpreter was made possible by a grant from the Health Education Council. I would like to thank Bhupinder Dhesi for her interpreting services and insight into Asian culture, especially in relation to food. The Birmingham Interpreting and Translating Service worked hard translating and transcribing seemingly endless tapes. Margaret Stacey and Anne Murcott made useful comments on earlier drafts of the paper. Finally, thanks to all the women involved in the study.

[3] In India it is the custom for women to move from their natal home to the home of their husband on marriage. Normally the woman is married to a man from another village, but they are married within

the same caste or sub-caste.
Eleven (42%) Asian women were living in an extended family at the
time of the second interview. Two (8%) were staying with their
in-laws for the duration of their pregnancy and returning to their
own home after the birth and forty day lying in period.   Three
(11.5%) British women were living in an extended family household,
one was unmarried and living with her parents, one was separated
from her husband and living with her widowed mother and the other
one lived with her husband's parents.

[4]   You and Your Baby Part One: From Pregnancy to Birth BMA A Family
      Doctor Publication, London, 1976.

8 Food for Equilibrium: the Dietary Principles and Practice of Chinese Families in London

ERICA WHEELER AND TAN SWEE POH

INTRODUCTION

Food must be eaten in order to maintain the body as a functioning system: foods are also sought out for their aesthetic and sensory qualities. To the physiologist, food is a source of disturbance to the human system, calling regulatory mechanisms into play, and also a means of stabilising and maintaining that system. Food has qualities in itself, and it also enhances or alters the qualities of the eater.

It might be supposed that since food does interact with the body's regulatory mechanisms, popular explanations of its functions would incorporate some idea of regulation. This is seen, for example, in the common classification of foods by the British as 'fattening' or 'non fattening' (descriptions of effect, by no means equivalent to the qualitative description, 'fatty' and 'non fatty'). Various traditional systems of medicine and health care have invoked regulatory aspects of food. We here discuss the conceptualisation of food, eating and health found among the Chinese community in London, which yields both explanations of the qualities of food, and a set of principles upon which these qualities may be employed to support and reinforce the body's regulatory systems.

The study and the sample from which we derive our conclusions are fully described in Tan & Wheeler (1982) and Tan (1982). Briefly, the sample consisted of 50 families living in Greater London. All the adults originated from Hong Kong (mainly from the New Territories) and their length of stay in London ranged from 0.5 to 20 years. The study consisted of serial interviews, between 3 and 5 in number, conducted over a period of 18 months with the women of the families. Interviews were initially structured around a questionnaire, and progressed to informal and wide ranging discussions. The general subject area was food, cooking, the feeding of the family and of children in particular, and health care. Regular anthropometric measurements were made of the young children. The interviews were conducted in Cantonese. A short subsidiary study consisted of the administration of a questionnaire on food to Chinese teenagers in London schools: these were not members of the 50 families in the main survey.

Three main conclusions emerged from this study, which we shall discuss in turn. Firstly, all but one of the Chinese women were practising a pragmatic version of the traditional system [1] which has

84

dominated Chinese medicine and health care for centuries, central to which is the concept that 'harmony' or 'equilibrium' is the desirable condition at all levels of the perceived world: in the individual, in society, and in the universe. Secondly, it was clear that their choice of food for themselves and their children was genuinely influenced by this system, and that they were incorporating into it some of the English foods which they had encountered in London. Finally, the teenagers were not learning the 'Chinese system' [2] in the same depth as their mothers had done.

PRINCIPLES OF EATING AND HEALTH

In the 'Chinese system', health is perceived as a condition of bodily equilibrium somewhere between two extremes called 'cold' and 'hot'. This equilibrium is not described as a single fixed point, but rather as a continuum of acceptable states. Thus, one of two individuals could be 'hotter' than the other, and yet both could be healthy.

The terms 'hot', 'cold', and 'equilibrium' apply to a person's 'body base': their own personal, characteristic physiology, determined partly by inheritance and partly by age and sex. If 'body base' shifts in the range of equilibrium, towards one of the two extremes, one perceives first of all a sense of physiological change. An individual may say "I feel hot", indicating a feeling not of actual illness but of disturbance, or potential ill health. (In rather the same way, an Englishwoman on one day might say "I don't feel too good" or "I feel as if I might have caught a chill", and on the next day feel "quite well" again). At or near the two extremes, one is actually ill, and there is a categorisation of 'hot diseases' (e.g. fever) and 'cold diseases' (e.g. diarrhoea). Being at, or near, the extremes, also predisposes one to invasion by external agents of disease such as bacteria. Thus, disease may arise from internal disequilibrium itself or from disequilibrium plus an 'attack' from outside.

State of the Body Base	cold		equilibrium		hot
Individual Positions	A(1)	A	(B_1) B	C	
Subjective Experience	disease		health		disease

Figure 8.1 Conceptualisation of individual experience of health and disease

This conceptualisation of the body and its state is illustrated in Figure 8.1, where A, B and C are three healthy adults, each with their own unique 'body base'. All are 'in equilibrium' but B is furthest from the undesirable extremes of 'hot' and 'cold'. This means that B is the least vulnerable to the external influences which might push him to one extreme or the other: his equilibrium is more secure. Also, he is less vulnerable to the agents of disease. Should A, B and C all

experience something (such as eating a particular food) which has the
effect of shifting their 'body base' further towards 'cold', it is A
(now at point A1) who is the most likely to feel unwell. 'Body base'
is characteristic of each person, but it shifts during the lifecycle.
Essentially, the younger one is, the 'hotter' is the 'body base'.
Elderly people are 'cold', pregnant women become 'hotter' as pregnancy
progresses because of the 'hotness' of the growing foetus within. The
adult male is nearest to the most desirable equilibrium state, and he
has the broadest 'tolerance': that is, he can cope with the greatest
extremes of 'hot' and 'cold' in his diet and surroundings. Figure 8.2
shows the relative positions of adult and children in this regard.

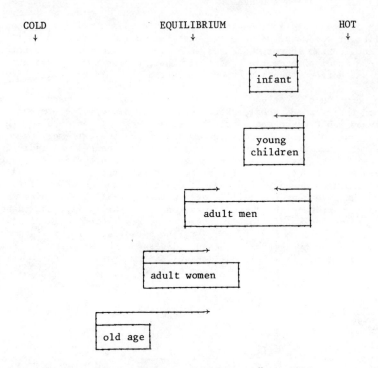

Figure 8.2 "Body Base" and "Degree of Tolerance" at different stages of
         life

   An important feature of the Chinese system is that it is not only
people and illnesses, but also inputs to the body, such as foods and
medicinal substances, which are characterised as 'hot' and 'cold' [3].
A 'hot' food or medicine 'makes one's body base hotter', a 'neutral'
one does not affect it, a 'cold' item 'cools the body base'. It
follows logically that children should have mainly 'cold' and 'neutral'
foods, that adults, especially men, can eat most foods without
experiencing feelings of illness, and that the elderly should have
increasing amounts of 'hot' foods. A 'cold' illness will be treated
with 'hot' foods. Cooking methods, and mixtures of foods and
medicines, interact so that cooked dishes have differing properties

from those of the original ingredients.   The Chinese woman knows how
to prepare foods and drinks which are 'heating', 'cooling' or 'neutral'.
Tables 8.1 and 8.2 show the categorisation of one food group
(vegetables), and of cooking methods.   The expression *beng yau hau yap*
"an illness caused by the mouth" was frequently used by the mothers,
and underlined the close association between illness and eating.

Table 8.1
Classification of Vegetables according to the Chinese Women

Neutral	Cold	Wet – Hot
cucumber	watercress	cauliflower
spinach	bamboo-shoot	Chinese leaves
lettuce	radish	cabbage
brocolli		brussel sprouts
potatoes		bean sprouts
choi sam		
baak choi		

Besides categorising foods as 'hot' and 'cold', the women used four
other main terms.   These were:

repairing (*bo*)
basic or essential (*gei boon*)
beneficial, good for the body (*yau yik, diu san tai ho*)
poisonous (*duk*)

The 'basic and essential' foods are the cornerstones of the Chinese
diet: tea, rice oil and salt.   Indeed, they were so much taken for
granted that mothers would not mention them unless asked specifically,
and then would say "Oh yes, rice, of course we eat it every day.
Without rice, I go soft".   These foods are in a sense too essential to
be ruled out of anyone's diet except under special circumstances.
However, rice is a 'strong' food and as such cannot be given to young
infants except as the watery gruel known as *congee*.   By about six
months, the baby's digestion is considered mature enough to take
soft-boiled rice, and from then on it is a daily item.

Table 8.2
Categorisation of Cooking Methods

	Ordinary	Repairing
COLD	boiling	
	stir-frying	
through	steaming	
NEUTRAL	stewing	
to	grilling	
	roasting	simmering
HOT	deep-frying	double-steaming

The concept of 'repairing' (*bo*) foods is elusive but important.   *Bo* means something that mends, patches or repairs, or even, as one woman described it, a 'lubricant' to facilitate the body's workings. *Bo* preparations are good when the body has been stressed in some way (e.g. by childbirth) and are always good for the elderly. *Bo* helps to restore vitality to the body, and children, who are full of vitality, do not need it unless they are weak and sickly. Ingredients for *bo* include pork, offal, herbs, and a miscellaneous array of substances such as fungi, bird's nest, seaweed, gingseng, ginger and a host of others. All these could be obtained in Chinese supermarkets in Central London. A few *bo* preparations (subclassified as 'purifying') could be given to ill children, but others ('strong') were only for older people.

'Beneficial' foods are those that generally build up and nourish the body: they include fish, meats and vegetables. 'Poisonous' foods are not necessarily toxic, but are considered to be dangerous to people who have been stressed in some way (by illness, trauma or childbirth). Shellfish are poisonous, and so are duck and goose: they may be eaten by strong adults but not by children.

The more positively valuable a food, the more carefully it should be cooked in order to conserve its properties. Good quality fish is cooked very lightly: poor quality ones are deep fried or boiled. *Bo* preparations are carefully prepared in small quantities, to meet the special needs of the elderly, the sick, and women after childbirth. One way is to cook by double steaming, the ingredients being placed in a small china jar with a double lid, which then itself stands in boiling water. In this way all the essential qualities of the ingredients are mingled and conserved.

The main objective of the Chinese strategy of foods, eating and health care is to maintain a healthy, stable state right through life, and particularly in old age. The Chinese woman, planning her family's meals, is not only averting 'hot' and 'cold' illness now but also preventing the development later of some illnesses which she regards as especially characteristic of the elderly.

The 'ideal' individual has a 'body base' which is in equilibrium, and can consequently repel many of the external agents of disease. The 'real' individual, by use of suitable foods and medicinal substances, is constantly attempting to get as close as possible to this 'ideal'. Some agents of disease, if they invade the body, can cause illness at any time, but there is also an influence generally described as 'wind' which may cause unpleasant effects in the long term. 'Wind' is neither flatus nor an inefective organism, but a vaguely defined agency associated with (thermal) coldness, damp, and chill. Indeed, there seems to be a close correspondence between the English terms 'cold in the head', 'chill on the stomach', 'chill on the womb/bladder' and so on, and the Chinese concept that 'wind' accumulates in various parts of the body and causes pain. 'Wind' attacks the individual who is in disequilibrium, and is a danger to anyone who becomes physically cold and wet, but it is an especial threat to women after childbirth.

Summarising, the 'Chinese system' turns on the presumption that body constituents need to be in equilibrium with one another if health is to be positively maintained and disease resisted. Implicit in it is an idea of homeostasis, with the further presumption that the regulatory system within the body can be actively supported - or thrown off balance – by various inputs, of which food is an important example.

PRACTICAL APPLICATIONS

The Chinese mothers easily handled the concept of maintaining body base in a desirable equilibrium state. Indeed, they gave practical advice on occasion to the investigator:

> While you are young, it is good that you observe food regulations, lest you regret too late when you become a sickly old lady.

Their application of the system can be illustrated by their strategies for looking after school age children, and for maintaining their own health after childbirth.

Most of the children who attended school would eat school meals, the constituents of which were outside the mother's control. The women perceived the typical school meal as being rather 'hot', since it tended to contain deep fried foods, which are regarded as 'heating'. For this reason, several mothers prepare special 'cooling drinks' for children on return from school: these infusions of herbs and other substances would counteract, or counterbalance, the 'hotness' of the British school food. Then for the evening meal there was a tendency to cook steamed or boiled foods, since these again were regarded as 'cooling'. In this way the 'hotness' characteristics of younger children, plus the 'hotness' induced by the school food, were dealt with to the mother's satisfaction. One mother said

> I prepare cooling drinks three times a week. The children get too hot after eating all that deep fried food at school. So I tend to prepare them steamed food in the evenings.

Several women gave cooling drinks at a meal called 'tea time', which was additional to the Hong Kong pattern of breakfast, midday and evening meals. It was prepared for children on their return from school around 4 p.m. The mothers felt that the school meals, as well as being 'heating', were not substantial enough, so they produced buns and cakes, and drinks, for the children. This was one meal at which the women might use non-Chinese food. They would never do so for an evening meal, because then the family would eat together and the food would be purely Chinese. But at breakfast, lunch and 'tea time' they might use 'English' food such as breakfast cereals, bread, pasta, hamburgers, bacon, crisps and ice cream. Several of these were incorporated because they filled the gap left by some Chinese foods which are not easy to get in London: breakfast cereals were an example of this. Others were used because the children enjoyed them: these were the hamburgers, sausages and crisps. Others, such as pasta, were sufficiently similar to Chinese foods, such as noodles, to be used as a substitute.

In feeding their school age children, the mothers followed a definite strategy. They realised that their children were growing up in the English culture and needed to be familiar with it, hence the school meals and the use of some favourite 'English' foods in the home. At the same time they felt responsible for the children's health, so they counteracted the English food with a choice of Chinese dishes and preparations which they perceived as equilibrating. Further, when the family ate together they provided full scale traditional Chinese cooking: for their own and their husbands' benefit, of course, as well as for the children. The mothers did not continue to follow the 'Chinese system' quite uncritically: they were well aware that most people did not follow it in Britain, and that its efficacy could be questioned. Where the children were concerned, however, they felt that the mother is primarily responsible for the child's health, and: "I'm not quite sure, but if I have a weak child, I shall be blamed". By using food to build their childrens' health, they were also averting criticism from husbands and relatives.

After childbirth, there are important practices to follow. One is 'sit for a month' (*joh yuet*) to avoid 'wind'; another is eating foods which will help to repair the damage and stresses of childbirth, and finally there is the need to eat correctly for lactation. In Hong Kong, a mother would be cared for by a female relative after childbirth, and for a month she would not be expected to do housework, or to go out of doors at all, and she would be given a suitable diet. This would include *bo* for repairing the body, and a special preparation of pork, eggs, ginger and vinegar. The 'body base' post partum is 'cold' and therefore the mother should avoid 'cold' foods. On the other hand, since the baby is 'hot', she should not eat foods which will make her milk 'hot'. Suitable foods therefore are 'neutral' to slightly 'hot', such as chicken, pork, eggs, offal, some fish, cooked suitably, with the 'basic and essential' rice. Some 'neutral' fruits and vegetables may be added.

This is the ideal, but in practice the London mothers found it difficult to follow, because they lacked the support of female relatives. Living in nuclear families, they had to go out to shop and collect children from school, and did not always have time to prepare special foods for themselves. In hospital for the delivery, they were unable to get *bo* unless husbands or friends brought it to them. A number of the practices in the traditional system are directed to evading 'wind': these include the staying indoors for a month, avoiding hair washing, bathing in water in which ginger (a 'hot' item) has been boiled, not drinking cold unboiled water, and many others. In London, the Chinese women found some of these practices impossible to follow and they are worried about attacks from 'wind'. The significance is that 'wind' is considered to accumulate and cause problems in the elderly: thus old women who did not take proper precautions post partum are considerely likely to suffer, for example, from arthritis, pneumonia/bronchitis, and swollen painful feet and legs.

The women felt themselves forced to practise a rather truncated version of the 'traditional system', and they expressed foreboding about the bad effects this might have on their health in old age. One woman claimed that she could feel herself becoming gradually 'weaker'. 'If you simply eat anything' said another 'you will probably not get bad consequences immediately, but what if it is manifested in old age?' Whereas others would blame her if her children were ill or 'sickly', she would blame herself for the illnesses of later life. One way of avoiding blame was not to breast feed the children. Most of the women bottle fed their infants, and two classes of reason were given for this. First, there was the 'inconvenience' and slight social stigma which

90

they perceived as attached to breast feeding in Western society. Secondly, there was the argument that if they bottle fed, they knew that cows' milk preparations were always 'hot' and could simply counteract them by giving the baby 'cooling' drinks. If they breast fed, however, the nature of the milk was uncertain, depending on their own diet, and illness in the baby might be attributed to this. One mother said

> When I first came to this country, I breast fed my baby...
> only when I was later instructed by friends in the
> preparation of 'cooling' drinks, I became confident to
> give powdered milk, which is a more convenient form of
> feeding.

THE YOUNGER GENERATION

At school, the Chinese teenagers studied biology and (in some cases) home economics and cookery. Of course, they are taught in English. Have they encountered the Western concepts of nutrients, calories, a 'balanced diet', and so on? In response to a short questionnaire (in English), they displayed some knowledge of simple 'scientific' nutrition. At the same time, they were being cared for by mothers who operated the 'hot'/'cold' system and who would be communicating with them exclusively in Cantonese. It seems that the teenagers had some knowledge of the 'hot'/'cold' system, but that it was not as complete as their parents' and they tended to confuse 'thermal heat' with 'heat in the Chinese sense'. For example, some described ice cream as a 'cold' food, yet in the Chinese system ice cream is 'hot', because it is made from cows' milk.

When asked to comment on their preference for Chinese food vis-a-vis English, and on the food which they would wish to give their own children, their responses were mixed. Most expressed a preference for the flavour, taste, and variety of Chinese food, though there were certain English foods which they specially enjoyed. Several, however, stated that English foods were 'more nutritious' or 'better balanced', or 'more healthy' than Chinese. We are not clear whether this is because the teaching in school simply did not mention the nutritious values of traditionally Chinese foods, or whether they had gained the impression that certain typically English (or at least non-Chinese) food items such as raw salads, milk, and wholemeal bread, conferred extra 'healthiness' to the English food pattern.

VIEWS ON ENGLISH DIET AND HEALTH

It may also be (although we do not have specific information) that some Chinese mothers gave their children the impression that the English diet was in some respects safer than the Chinese.

The Chinese women have observed the majority Caucasian English population and have reflected on the differences between the Western and Chinese system. They are aware that English women do not take the same care over diet and maintenance of body balance as they do, and their comment runs along three general lines. One is, that there are genetic differences among peoples and therefore that what is necessary

91

for one ethnic group is not so for another. "They have a different body base" and "They are different in colour and size, and their body mechanisms are different" are two comments given by the women. This explanation, therefore, says that care in maintaining equilibrium is only necessary for certain people.

The second explanation is that the regular English diet is 'balanced' anyway, so that no special care is required. "They always eat 'hot' meat dishes with 'cold' desserts and vegetables: and their large consumption of beer cools them" was one comment. Another woman said that the English dietary does not include very 'hot' or very 'cold' foods, and that therefore food selection is not a problem. This reflects a general view of the English diet; that although there is a wide variety of processed products available, these all derive from a relatively narrow range of basic foods, and that the choice of fresh food, in particular, was much wider in Hong Kong. Western dietary is perceived as adequate but rather limited and uninteresting. However, just because it is less wide ranging in its scope, some of the mothers perceived it as better balanced and 'healthier'.

The third line of comment is that the English do suffer from their neglect of health care.

> The old English people don't look as healthy as the Chinese. Look at old English women: their feet and legs are swollen with 'wind'. This is because they don't take proper care when they are young, so the 'wind' accumulates in old age.

The women are aware that young English people aim to keep slim:

> The girls don't eat well: this is unhealthy, and they will be weak when they are old.

These three lines of explanation are mutually contradictory and indicate quite different attitudes to the majority population. One woman in our sample, who was unusually well educated (she had studied to 'A' level in an English school) had abandoned most of the traditional concepts. She ate freely what and when she liked, and did not take any 'special' care with her children's diet. The remainder of the women, however, saw the English either as people who were 'different' in kind, or as people of the same kind who behave differently and who may or may not suffer as a result.

GENERAL CONSIDERATION

The Chinese system demands a considerable amount of planning by the food preparer, with forethought, knowledge of the qualities of foods, and practical application of that knowledge. In return, it offers the satisfaction of feeling that she is making positive contributions to family health, and of reinforcing the body's constant efforts to maintain itself in a stable and healthy state in the face of the challenges and damage inflicted by the environment. It is also guilt inducing, however: the Chinese mother is liable to blame herself, or to be blamed, if ill health in the family coincides with some failure of correct practice. Can she regard herself as free from blame if she has taken the correct actions? It seems likely, in view of the complexity of the system, that she would always be able to recollect, or suspect, some 'failure' on her own part.

The Chinese system seems to be enunciating a principle which Western science also recognises: that of homeostasis, the body's capacity to return to conditions of 'normality' after disturbance and change, and to repel and destroy invasive organisms. Where it parts company from Western science is in stating very precisely how the homeostatic and immune processes can be actively assisted by a scheme of diet and life style, and in relating this to the unidentifiable and unquantifiable qualities of 'hotness' and 'coldness', which appear to be a way of describing individual perceptions of well being. In the Chinese system, 'nature' is not 'left to do her work' (a common metaphor in the West for the process of healing, and restoration of bodily function), but 'nature' needs active support and encouragement.

There is a conceptual gap here between the Western scientists' perceptions of homeostasis, as a process which the body will carry out unaided, under a wide range of conditions, and the Chinese view that it needs active help. The popular Western view of 'looking after yourself' does include protecting the body from infection and damage, and exercising it (but not overworking it) but this is a view of the body as a tool or machine, rather than as a vulnerable and manipulable homeostatic system. It may include dietary precautions ("don't clog up your arteries", "don't get too fat", "don't get constipated") but the metaphors are those of one caring for a mechanism, and guarding it from damage. Western science says that the body's regulatory processes do not need to be assisted: implicit in the conception of homeostasis is the notion that its wonderfully complex interlocking system will run itself, adapting to a wide range of inputs. This is particularly so in the case of diet. Westerners perceive the body as able to cope successfully with diets as diverse as those of the Eskimo and the Brahmin, extracting the same nutrients from both. Western science has no place for the 'fine tuning' of homeostasis by, say, eating stewed meat instead of roast. Indeed, even 'coarse tuning' is only regarded as necessary when the system begins to fail: by low salt diets in hypertension, carbohydrate regulation in diabetes, caloric restriction in obesity. For the Chinese, such measures would come as the last resort, when a long process of adjustment of balance had failed.

The concept of eating in such a way as to help the body to balance and adjust itself is of course a widespread one, not exclusive to Chinese culture. 'Hotness' and 'coldness' are attributed to food in countries as far apart as Latin America and South East Asia. It is perhaps only in cultures dominated by Western medical science that food supposedly is no longer seen as having quasi medical and purifying properties, and becomes simply something that gives pleasure and nourishes the body. It is, however, interesting that in Western countries the vitamins have come to occupy an intermediate place between 'nutrient' and 'medicine' in the popular mind, and that people who wish to make positive contributions to their own healthfulness tend to take vitamin preparations as well as choosing foods and cooking methods which should result in a vitamin rich diet [4]. Vitamins are advertised as preventing 'tiredness' or 'feeling run down': concepts as well understood by their users, and as difficult to define to people outside the culture, as 'hotness' and 'coldness'. Vitamins are also advertised as a kind of protection for children against illness, and a maintainer of top level health. It is tempting to speculate that although the idea of 'eating for bodily equilibrium' is muted or absent in our culture people resort to vitamins in the belief that they protect health and vitality. As some sort of charm they assuage feelings of guilt or responsibility which may overcome mothers if their children become ill. There is not, however, an obvious Western equivalent for the Chinese concept of 'eating to ensure a healthy old age'.

The Chinese women still operate a system which may (for they are not completely convinced about it) give them the feeling that they have successfully assisted their families and themselves to be healthy. In doing so they face some practical problems. Obtaining the correct items is not difficult, because of the proliferation of Chinese food shops in London and elsewhere. But being in nuclear families, they lack the advice and support of other women; a whole generation of mothers, aunts and grandmothers has been left behind in Hong Kong. In addition, it is harder to maintain correct practice when one is the only woman cooking and caring for a husband and several children. A further difficulty is that English health and education services give no help to the Chinese women if they wish to practise their own system, apart from permitting food to be brought into hospital for the use of patients. It would perhaps be difficult for this to be done but since no attempt is made, the extent of the difficulty cannot be assessed.

What will be the attitudes and practices of the next generation of young Chinese when they grow up and establish their families? It is most unlikely that they will have taken in all the information which their mothers now hold, or that they will operate the Chinese system as a means to bodily balance. We may predict that they will use Chinese food and cooking methods, but without consciously basing their practice on the rationale of the traditional system. Will they, then, begin to increase their consumption of vitamin preparations?

NOTES

[1] We use 'Chinese system' to denote the practices and opinions which we found in our London sample, and 'traditional system' to denote the fuller account of health and healthy practices which derive from a philosophy originating in mainland China (see, for example, Fung, 1963).
[2] See note [1].
[3] The characterisation of foods in this way is of course not unique to the Chinese but is found in many Asian and Latin American societies. See, for example, Molony, 1975; Cosminsky, 1977.
[4] Dietary fibre is also taking an intermediate position, and the popular interpretation of 'regulation' is 'the maintenance of a regular bowel habit'.

9 The Goodness is Out of It: the Meaning of Food to Two Generations

MILDRED BLAXTER AND ELIZABETH PATERSON

> You got baked rice. It was made wi' eggs and there wis currants
> in it, and this wis a luxury, mind. Nowadays they get a tin and
> there's nae eggs in it and the goodness is out of it. The thing
> nowadays - the richt good is out of them.

It was this quotation, embedded in a series of long transcripts from a
study of health attitudes and behaviour among two generations of working
class women, [1] that was the genesis of these speculations about the
historical and moral meaning of food. For the purposes of the study, we
had been interested in food only peripherally and for quite practical
reasons. Was the health of the children in the sample families
affected by poor nutrition? Did their young mothers have much knowledge
of nutrition? Were their ideas on this and other topics which were
relevant to health derived from an older generation? This woman's words
however, alerting us to the existence of many similar statements by
other respondents, suggested a different analysis. Many of the women
had talked of food at length. They frequently used the word 'good' and
others which seemed to mean more than simply nutritionally sound. What
did they mean by 'good'? Why were the older generation so nostalgic,
when there was a great deal of evidence that the 'old days' that they
were talking about were a time, for them, of great deprivation? Was the
difference between them and their adult daughters a historical
difference, or simply related to a stage of life? Where did the ideas
that they expressed come from? In short, what was the real meaning of
this concept and commodity called food?

The sample for this study consisted of 58 three-generation families
living in a Scottish city. The major focus was upon the health care of
children. The possibility was being explored that less efficient care,
perhaps associated with particular attitudes to health and sickness,
might be repeated through generations of families in poor economic
circumstances, resulting in continuity of disadvantage for the children.
Because of this emphasis, the sample was specifically chosen as one in
which continuity would be likely: the older generation (women in their
late 40s or 50s) had lived in the city for most of their married lives
and remained there, in close contact with their married daughters.
These younger women in their 20s or early 30s now had children of their
own. Both generations had, at the time of their childbearing, been in
semiskilled or unskilled working class families.

The study was longitudinal, recording the health and the service use
of the young families over a period of six months. The data used here

are, however, primarily derived from semi-structured, tape recorded
interviews with the women of each generation, exploring their social and
health histories and attempting to elicit their ideas and attitudes on a
wide range of health related topics. On diet and nutrition, each woman
was asked a rather general question: 'What do you think keeps children
healthy?' In their reply they frequently mentioned food. If they did
not mention it spontaneously, a follow up question was asked: 'What
about food, are there any things which you think are specially good for
children?' For most of the older generation, this was a sufficient
stimulus to set into motion an enthusiastic account. For the younger
generation it often brought forth a discussion of their problems in
catering for their families. During the series of interviews in each
family there might be additional comments about food, and all these
were extracted and taken into account in the following descriptions.

THE OLDER GENERATION

The foods most frequently mentioned by the grandmothers as 'good' for
children were (in order of frequency) meat, soup, potatoes and other
vegetables, porridge, fish and fruit. Eggs, cheese, cereals, milk, and
puddings of various sorts were offered by smaller numbers of women.
These individual foods were less important, however, than their
combination into a 'good' or 'proper' meal:

A cooked, solid meal - she should cook a right meal for them

Plenty o' good food, solid meals

We always had a cooked meal at teatime, with potatoes and veg.
and beef and whatever....

We just had our usual meals like most families, I mean, your
soups, your potatoes, your meat and your pudding....

The 'goodness' which these meals epitomised was to be found in simple
and natural foods, in foods which although they were always cooked (raw
or salad foods were rarely mentioned) were prepared in basic ways, by
boiling or baking, and never in tinned or highly processed foods:

Plenty soup, made wi' good stock. Plenty o' vitamins in that.
Not so much steak and things like that, your basic down to
earth foods

Now we were brought up on country stuff, a bowl o' brose and a
plate o' chappit tatties, an' whatever

Good food, wholesome food. Home-made. Nae goin' in for this
tinned soup. I couldnae afford it! In those days, you know,
you didnae get all that much money to keep them...the like o'
tattie soup, pea soup, broth, rice, semolina - you know, you
used to make it out the packets. It's a' tinned now

We lived off the land, more or less, there wasn't so much
tinned stuff and things like that, it was more like rabbits
and fish, and more vegetables, plenty of fresh vegetables.
I think this has got an awful lot to do wi' being healthy.
Well, my grandfather died when he was 92. (This respondent
had previously described how her own mother 'had ten
altogether, and six of us survived', and how at 13 years old
she had looked after her mother who died from scarlet fever).

Referring to the straitened days of the past, the fact that simple
food might be cheaper was often emphasised, but this went only to prove
that relative affluence had its dangers; that which was plain and
inexpensive was by definition full of virtue. Indeed, the diets
described as 'good' were often spartan:

> You didnae get a plate o' stew beef or anything. Maybe tatties
> an' white sauce, or tatties an' mustard sauce, cabbage, a plate
> o' kale. Stuff like that. We enjoyed it. We had bowls of
> porridge. Nae necessarily expensive things – lentil soup, wi'
> tatties – corned beef. (This was described as 'plenty o' good,
> solid food').

The place of 'meat' as the most frequently mentioned requirement
represented, in fact, a more complex set of ideas than might appear at
first. In the aphorism repeated by more than one woman, in different
forms:

> My father aye said if you've got a fire and a diet o' meat
> you'll aye be a' right

'a diet of meat' is not necessarily to be taken literally. 'Meat' was
still, in these women's vocabulary, sometimes a synonym for 'food'. A
'diet of meat' meant primarily 'sufficient food', with overtones of
'good nourishing food'; only secondarily and by association was animal
protein implied. Again, 'beef' was sometimes used for all fresh meat,
whatever animal it derived from. The meat dishes most frequently
mentioned here were in fact those in which a relatively small amount of
cheaper meat went a long way – mince, 'stovies' (mince, potatoes and
onions) or 'bradies' (meat and vegetable pasty). Milk was surprisingly
rarely mentioned. Vegetables aroused enthusiasm, and so did fruit: 'An
apple a day for rosy cheeks!' though many of these older women said that
they had not actually given their children fruit, because it was too
expensive:

> They only had fruit at New Year, 'cos I couldn't afford it

The greatest 'goodness', however, was to be found in the soup or broth
that the women lauded so universally. This represented the most
economical use of the approved foods:

> A plate o' soup, or a plate o' stovies, a good diet, that's the
> only thing that keeps them healthy. They were cheap at that
> time, cheap to make a plate o' soup. Maybe a bittie beef or a
> marrow bone an' that. Sometimes we lived on soup. It wis the
> only way to heat them up

> ...Basic down to earth foods, which can be made quite cheaply,
> you know. Get a bone, get the stock off that

And somehow a long cooking, boiling up the meat and the vegetables,
distilled the essence of goodness:

> Nae tinned soup. There's nae nourishment in that. You're
> better wi' your own. A bone – you're getting the goodness off
> a bone. The marrow oot o' a bone

The opposite of 'good' food was, of course, that which was processed
or prepared, or substituted for a 'proper' meal – 'all this snackery',
'that snackery that they get, sweets and things'. Sweets, buns and
biscuits were 'rubbish'. Indeed, almost anything except perhaps fruit

which was eaten outside the framework of a 'proper' meal was rubbish, as if the timing and manner of its consumption deprived it of all nutritive value. The fact that 'they're feeding bairns a' this rubbish nowadays' was the most prominent criticism of their daughters' child care:

> Good food, that's the main thing wi' bairns. Cooked food. Nae all this fancy muck they're advertising on the TV today, that's nae use to folk. A decent pot o' broth....

It has to be added that - as one might expect - it was often in fact the grandparents who were observed to be particularly generous with biscuits and sweets for their grandchildren.

THE YOUNGER GENERATION

The young mothers were rather less likely than the older generation to mention food spontaneously when asked 'What keeps children healthy?' About two-fifths did so, but some others had to be pressed to talk about it, and a few said specifically and definitely that 'what you eat makes no difference'. The foods that they did mention as 'good' were, again in order of frequency, milk, eggs, fruit and vegetables, with minorities mentioning meat, cheese, fish, soup and cereals.

Amongst this generation there was rather more diversity than amongst their mothers. A few did express similar, but perhaps less enthusiastic, views about 'cooked meals', usually explicitly connecting them with an older generation's teaching:

> My mother always made meals, and so do I, they like a' things home made. My husband's like that, too, no' one for tins - quick meals. I cook meat, and (toddler) gets the gravy. Maybe it doesn't make any difference to their health, mind you. I only do it probably because my granny aye did. And my husband's mother she's a great cook, she wouldna buy pies and that. I have to keep up!

Several echoed the disparagement of 'tins', though they admitted that they used a great many:

> It's that tinned food that makes them fat!

> I never buy tinned stuff hardly. I mean, you like to make good food. Tinned soup and that - though I do buy it....

> My husband wouldn't eat my mince so I have to buy tinned

'Baby tins' were especially scorned, but this was less a criticism of their nutritiousness than an expression of the very common feeling that infants should be eating 'ordinary' food, simply what the rest of the family ate, at the earliest possible moment:

> I dinna believe in a' this baby tins. I've never bothered wi' them, I think they're a waste of time. Well, to me - if they get the same as you - tatties wi' mashed up mince, wi' the gravy oot o' the mince an' that, that's how they should eat. The same as they're going to get when they grow up

> I just put what we've having into the liquidiser. She has all sorts of things - I like to let her taste lots of

different things   (referring to a baby of 6 weeks).

Expense may also have been a factor, but it appeared that the idea of 'proper meals' as 'good' was applied very soon after birth. Where the feeding of infants was concerned, this was of course a source of continual conflict with health visitors (Graham, 1979).

A difference from the older generation was the lack of a universal emphasis on meat. There was some suggestion that 'made meals', with cooked meat and potatoes, were necessary for men, but not for women and children;   as one single handed mother said:

> It's difficult, when it's just you and the kids. You haven't
> got to make meat and that, so you don't - you get like them,
> eating rubbish all the time. My mum's always on about soups
> and that, but they don't like soup

Several said specifically that their children never ate meat, and even if they did, they admitted that a high proportion of it was in the form of pies or other processed foods. Vegetables were very frequently mentioned as 'good', but at the same time they were the most common thing which children were said to dislike and never eat;   it appeared that few except potatoes were ever used. Sometimes it was the husband's tastes which were said to prevail:

> Their father eats no vegetables at all, so neither do they

Like their mothers, the young women frequently mentioned fruit, and those who wished to present themselves as taking special care of their children's nutrition often claimed proudly that 'I like to give them fruit'. Some still perceived it as too expensive to give children, however:

> An apple a day keeps the doctor away is a stupid saying.
> Anyway, the things that are supposed to be good for you are
> too expensive and you can't really afford it

Only a few of the young women made the soup recommended so vehemently by their mothers, very few mentioned cereals or porridge, and bread seemed almost to be seen as something which had to be apologised for, though the children were often observed eating it. One mother was ashamed because her child liked to eat bread

> ...with nothing on it. I'm affronted in case anyone sees
> her. She doesn't even fold it over   '

and another demonstrated how unfussy her children were by saying

> It doesn't <u>have</u> to be biscuits. They'll eat a slice of
> bread and butter

Perhaps the greatest difference between the generations, however, was the young women's emphasis on milk. It was milk, rather than the 'pot o' soup', which represented for them the child's basic nourishment, and only the destitute or the completely feckless would fail,they suggested, to ensure that their children drank sufficient. Fruit was perhaps the symbol of prosperity, but milk was the symbol of fundamental well being:

> If you have a family to help you...they would never refuse you
> milk. I know my family wouldn't. If I went to my mother and
> she had only half a pint of milk, she'd give it to me for the
> bairn and I'd get a cup of tea. Even if you don't have a

> family there is always a chum or a neighbour you could go to
> for milk for your bairn

Indeed, all the children appeared to drink very adequate amounts of
milk.

Whatever the women might describe as 'good' food, the actual diets of
the majority of the children, they very freely admitted, were full of
'rubbish', the word which like their mothers they used to describe buns
and cakes from travelling vans, constant sweets, crisps and icecream,
tinned beans and spaghetti, pies and 'convenience' foods. The sort of
meal observed at lunchtime, typical of some (though certainly not all)
families, consisted of a tin of soup, icecream and a tin of fruit,
supplemented by a cake and sweets from the baker's van. A child had
been sent to buy these things, and had chosen a tin of strawberries.
Though the mothers did not claim that this was 'good' food, and indeed
many did talk at length of the difficulty of restricting children's
sweets, they did not on the whole appear to feel that they should be
defensive about this sort of diet:

> I used to make a meal with potatoes at lunchtime, but I stopped
> because they wouldn't take it...they won't eat   (The father of
> these children interrupted at this point to describe their diet
> as 'Crisps and Smarties!').

The mothers perceived their children as 'normally' healthy and strong.
With the exception of milk and perhaps fruit, they did not make any
clear connection between nutrition and illnesses. Fussing about food,
or taking positive steps, was quite unnecessary:

> I just thought I would try vitamin drops on her - she was on
> them for two months and to me it never made a particle o'
> difference

The young women were of course subjected to more intensive media and
commercial pressures, particularly on television, than their mothers had
been. They might also, however, have had more exposure to health
education, especially as they were at a stage of life when they were all
in touch with health visitors or child health clinics (or had been in
the relatively recent past). The vocabularies of both generations were
examined to see whether ideas appeared to derive from advertisements, or
media information, or specific teaching by health service professionals.
In fact, the young women, even more than their mothers, demonstrated a
sturdy scepticism about commercial claims, and there was little
evidence of influence from advertising or health education publicity -
though this is not the same, of course, as saying that their purchasing
habits had not been affected. The older women had appeared to exempt a
few wellknown and long advertised products (Oxo cubes, Bovril, packeted
infant foods) from the general embargo on processed foods, and spoke of
them as though they, too, contained concentrated 'goodness', but the
young women did not mention even these so frequently. Their emphasis
upon milk, and perhaps upon eggs, may have echoed health education or
other publicity. They spoke often of 'vitamins', to be found in milk,
fruit and vegetables. In many cases their comments about vitamins were
confused, however, and it did not seem that much had been remembered
from the teaching (if any) that they had received.

100

PRINCIPLE AND PRACTICE

It must be emphasised that we have no independent data on what was actually fed to children, either in the 1950s or now, nor on the children's nutritional status. Our own observation over the six months survey tallied well with the accounts of the food that was eaten in the young families. However, from medical records and histories, it can certainly be judged that the third generation (although there were certain aspects of their health and health care which might give rise to some concern) were generally healthier and better developed than their mothers had been as children. The reasons for this might be various, of course: a major factor was the disappearance of many diseases – mostly infectious – which had been relatively common in this social group and this area only thirty years ago. The tuberculosis, scarlet fever and diphtheria which had run through whole families in the grandmothers' young days had by no means vanished by the 1950s, for several of the young mothers had suffered from them as children. Conditions such as pleurisy, pneumonia and gastro-enteritis did occur among the third generation children, but they were much rarer than they had been a generation before.

The generally well developed state of the children, and their clinical records and assessments, must however suggest that growth and health were not only affected by the disappearance of diseases: they were in fact better nourished than their mothers had been. One quotation may illustrate this, and at the same time demonstrate the rather poor knowledge of nutrition that was typical of the younger generation of mothers:

> I took rickets as a child – nobody else in the family took rickets, I don't know why I took it, nobody seemed to have any idea. I could have been playing with someone who had it and passed it on

THE ROOTS OF CHANGE

There are, we suggest, several questions raised by the attitudes to 'good' food which have been described. Why did the older generation select the foods they did? Why did they present the past as being so much better than the present, when the evidence suggests that it was not? Is the difference between the generations in their attitude to food simply a function of age and place in the life cycle, or does it represent a general change over time?

Some of the reasons for the older women's presentations are obvious. Many of them had rural backgrounds, and they were, like many migrants to cities, remembering a golden age of their country youth. It was not only in relation to their ideas about food that continuity was a very salient value: in their discussion of the cause of illness, and family patterns of disease, it seemed that they could make sense of their lives only by stressing the importance of heredity, and their conviction that their family experience offered explanations for contemporary events, their feeling that the past was relevant to the present. The fact that their past had often been, in terms of social and economic history, very deprived only made it more important to stress those positive aspects which they felt they could sustain. The plain, simple and

natural were 'good': this was all that they could offer from their own
experience to the more prosperous, better educated younger generation:

> An' if they're getting proper meals, and a good home and a
> clean bed, then there's nothing coming over them. Everybody
> canna have grandeur. Bit I think that's the main rudiments....

Also, it must be remembered that these women had grown up during war
years. Those things which had been severely rationed were necessities,
and those which had been unavailable were indulgences. They belonged to
the generation who, as Margaret Drabble has noted in her novel The Ice
Age 'had always been astonished at their own purchasing power each time
they bought a pound of bananas or a small pot of double cream'. To
them, as to many housewives of their age, meat, butter, cheese and
cream would always be 'good' foods at an emotional level whether or not
they were aware at a cognitive level of what nutritionists might say
about them. Fruit would always be good for you, but a luxury.

Thus some of their presentations derived from a particular social
history. There were strands, too, from more general social change.
Food and meals have symbolic and social meanings, and it has been noted
before that the idea of the 'proper' meal has much to do with the idea
of 'proper' family life. The 'cooked dinners' of the young mothers in
South Wales described by Murcott (1982a) and the 'solid' or 'proper'
meals of our respondents alike represented an ideal of family life as
much as an ideal of nutritious eating.

Neither of our two generations saw this in terms of roast Sunday
joints, for they did not belong to a social group where these had ever
been very common. Symbolically, however, the meal was the same - a
cooked meal, prepared lovingly by the mother, and served by her to a
family all seated at one table. The fact that many (though certainly
not all) of the older generation had belonged to sadly broken families
through the untimely death of parents or husbands, desertion and
divorce, with children in care, being fostered, or living with grandparents - all this was irrelevant to the idea of family. In the family
eating its 'proper meal', the father was provider, mother the nourisher,
and the group was united around the family table.

To the younger generation, the idea of a 'family meal' was not always
appropriate. Many children had school meals or meals at day nurseries.
Many mothers were working, sometimes in the evening so that the father
could look after infants at home. Some fathers were unemployed, and in
fact taking care of the children while the mothers worked. In these
families, different members might be having their main meal at different
times of the day, and there were few times when a formal assembly for a
meal was possible. Our respondents' 'proper meal' is similar to the
'good meal' which Nicod (1979) has described as structured, in contrast
to unstructured snacks which lack the complex and symbolic rules of the
meal. This author, considering dietary change, has concluded that

> Cheap labour-saving substitutes or additions to a diet can be
> introduced in the unstructured parts of the system without
> much difficulty. Thus...in children's food, at breakfast,
> and for women eating alone cereals and snacks are admitted.
> In these areas the diet has seen great changes in the last 20
> years, but these are changes which have no effect on the

dietary system as such.

This appears to imply that it is only men's meals which constitute the dietary system. For some of our families this was true; as has been noted, they spoke of 'making meals' specifically for their husbands. For others, however, it appeared that 'women's and children's meals' had become the family norm.

The idea of family life, and women's roles, expressed in the concept of the 'proper meal' had some connection with another concept, that of the 'store cupboard' from which the meal was produced. Again, this idea (or the vegetable garden, which served a similar function for those of the older generation with rural backgrounds) with its suggestion of family security, long term planning, and a bulwark against hunger, was not always practically appropriate for the younger urban generation. Working mothers, or those tied to the house by small children, or those living in housing estates where only 'corner shops' or visiting vans were easily accessible, naturally tended towards a pattern of piecemeal shopping, buying things to eat immediately. Only a few appeared to do 'weekly shopping' at supermarkets, for this probably involved the use of a car, and certainly implied the laying out of larger sums of money at one time.

There were other practicalities of the situation. Like all children, these had very pronounced and often peculiar tastes. The general dislike of vegetables has been mentioned, but there were also children who would eat no cheese, or no eggs, or who went through phases of eating 'nothing but' tinned spaghetti or sausages. Both time tables and the differing tastes of fathers and children meant that, even if the young mother prided herself on making 'a proper meal' for her husband, the children's meals might be different. We cannot know, of course, whether children were less 'fussy' or less indulged in the grandmothers' time, though the majority of the older women suggested that this was so. On the other hand, some recognised that children had not changed, and new norms about catering to their fads did not necessarily mean that mothers were careless:

> It was a job getting them to eat sometimes - I used to stand
> beside them and you'd have made all the different bonny shapes
> an' things just to get them to eat. It was stupid when you
> think about it. Cos my daughter, now, she disnae bother if
> they dinna eat - which is the best way, don't you think so?

The older generation's view of this 'new' family life tended to have warring elements. On the one hand, they were forced to admit that their daughters led lives which were on the whole 'better' because they were more economically secure; the extreme deprivations of the past were over. They recognised that 'things had changed' and life was different now:

> The kids are a' healthier nowadays, are [aren't] they? In one
> way, they're a' healthy. They're even bigger, are they? Even
> in size they're bigger - oh, aye, they're healthier...they're
> getting a' things nowadays, you ken, mair money in their hand.

> They can do a lot more for children now than what we could
> ever do. We had to go to jumble sales for clothes and a'
> thing, but they can buy them now.

103

It must not be implied that the majority were critical of their daughters, for most had a proud, admiring, and in some cases almost humble attitude to the younger generation, whom they described as more competent, more sure of themselves, than they had been at the same stage of life:

> I think she's more capable, actually, than I was, I think she's more mature for her age...she'll maybe ask if I think she's doing the right thing. But she's more or less made up her mind before she comes

> They don't worry the same - but it's a good thing in a way, because it does make them stand on their own feet, I suppose, that bit quicker, you know. I don't know - they seem more advanced in everything nowadays than in our day

On the other hand, their daughters' lives frequently violated their ideal of family life, and in other parts of the interviews they were likely to condemn what they saw as new norms:

> Things are so different nowadays - see how they a' sit an' watch that thing (TV)....

> We got up and got their breakfast ready an' their claes ready, got their bath, got their breakfast, washed, changed, fed, doon. Get on wi' your work. We used to play a lot wi' our kids at night. They were bedded at half past seven. You had to work it like that, you had to get some time to yoursel'. But nowadays, the kids get up wi' the family, they ging to bed wi' the family, so there's nae routine

The view which they presented of the days when they themselves had young children tended, of course, to be romanticised:

> It's mair o' a ratrace now, it's a' working mothers....I think it was much better in them days. You'd less money an' everything, but I think you were happier

> I aye say to them, 'the two of you's out working, going out gallivanting, you've mair need to bide in the hoose', things like that...when we wis young, you see, we didnae hae that kind o' money, so we sorta contented oursels, ken? Like, I used to say to mysel' when the dark nights come in, 'Oh that's fine, that, I like the dark nights', cos the kids were a' in the hoose an', well, they were a' in the hoose an' it was fine, ken

It is not of course surprising that this distrust of the new, and the appeal to continuity represented an idealising of the 'natural, simple' days of the past, was found in an older generation rather than a younger. It may be noted, however, that this concept of naturalness, purity and simplicity has been re-erected in sophisticated form, as Atkinson (1979) has shown, in the 'health food' movement, where contemporary industrial society is seen as over-cultured, cut off from its natural roots, and therefore suffering from stress and ill health. This movement is perhaps most prominent in the younger, and the more privileged, sections of society. It had certainly touched few of our younger working class women. In cyclical processes generally, it is usually the more prosperous classes who are pace setters, with the fashions diffusing downwards: tonsillectomy becomes a popular treatment for children in lower social classes just as the higher classes are turning against it. If the young women of our sample return, when they become middle-aged, to the ideas of simplicity and purity in food of their mothers, will this be due to the diffusion process? Or will they, like their mothers, present the essence of 'goodness' as being the food that they eat now, while they are young, somehow finding a particular moral virtue in a tin of baked beans?

NOTES

[1] This study was funded by the DHSS/SSRC Joint Working Party on Transmitted Deprivation, and is published under the title Mothers and Daughters: A three-generational study of Health Attitudes and Behaviour, Heinemann Educational Books, Studies in Deprivation and Disadvantage, 1982.

10 The Salt of the Earth: Ideas Linking Diet, Exercise and Virtue among Elderly Aberdonians

RORY WILLIAMS

When the attempt is made to capture that elusive phenomenon 'style of life', it is sometimes described as a particular kind of relation between consuming and producing, between the food, homes, clothes and possessions which are swallowed up by members of a society, and the skills, work, interests and activities which they generate from these resources. That relation often underlines what is thought of as health in the broadest sense. Those who grow fat by consuming too much for what they produce, for instance, are criticised for their unhealthiness as well as for their greed.

> I've always been light, never been over ten stone; it's the heavy ones have the trouble....People ask me how I do it - I say moderation.

> Moderation in what - in food, or drink, or other things?

> In everything.

Correspondingly, those who grow thin by producing too much in relation to what they consume are attributed, amongst their other misfortunes, with an analogous unhealthiness:

> My mother died when I was just a toddler.

> What did she die of?

> Och, well if I was left tae guess, I would say hard work. A big family, you know.

This equilibrium between intake and output, with its implications for health, virtue and happiness, is moreover by no means merely a folk belief. It is underwritten, for instance, by the Health Departments in a recent consultative document on prevention and health.[1] In that part of the document which is concerned with 'life-style', proper diet and exercise feature as universal essentials for health, the lack of exercise being indeed quoted as 'one of the besetting sins of modern man'.[2] The complementary error of excessive hard work is not, however, so greatly stressed in this governmental review of public sins, as it is in some popular thinking.

In choosing, therefore, to explore what older people see as the relationships between food, activity and health, a researcher plunges into matters with deep moral, as well as medical, implications. The moral and medical theories which support people's beliefs in this area are my main concern, but the contradictions which are generated when these theories collide in experience are illustrated in an additional case study.

The older people who provided the material for this analysis were two groups of Aberdonians who lived in a middle class area and a working class estate respectively. There were seventy of them, all over sixty years of age, and they were sampled by the use of quotas for age, sex, marital status, social class, family support and club membership, proportionate to these characteristics as found in the elderly population as a whole. This form of sampling was used because the aim was to select informants who were mutually acquainted, at least at the minimum level of being introduced by one other person in the sample, this person being one of several through whom all other members of the same social class network would be 'reachable' (Mitchell, 1969) by further links of acquaintanceship. This feature of the research design may give a little insight into the way in which beliefs are criticised, reinforced, or made the property of households, cliques and other groupings.

The questions asked of these informants centred on attitudes to health and illness, against a background of health history and residential, familial and occupational history. Issues concerned with food and exercise arose mainly in connection with a question on whether informants did anything in the way of keeping healthy; but after the first part of the first interview, concerned with the informant's general history and current situation, evaluative comments already made were taken up and their implications explored, and some of these spontaneous comments also concerned the importance of food or activity. These first interviews were tape recorded, and later interviews, which have occurred in nearly half the cases, were recorded in field notes.

It is interesting to compare with these elderly informants the grand-mothers described by Blaxter and Paterson (1982 and in this volume), and it may be useful at this point if I summarise what is similar and different in the two samples. The essential differences are that my informants are older, and from all social classes, and they are talking about their own health, not that of their children and grandchildren. Nevertheless it will be evident that they have much in common with the working class grandmothers of the next generation - not least being the experiences of war and hard times in the cold shoulder of Scotland. The relevance of food to growing children, and to the task of caring for them, is more evident than its relevance to old age, and to the less admirable task of looking after oneself. In talking about children, most of the grandmothers described by Blaxter and Paterson seized upon the subject of food; but in talking about their own health only a little over a third of my sample developed the subject. One who did have much to say on it recognised that she was unusual:

Lots'll say, just the two o' you - and you make soup!

And I says, Aye, I make soup.

Soup, in this instance, stood not only for the meaty broth which had been handed down from her mother, but also for the fact that the meal which, her husband said, they had 'every day o' the week' was made, by the presence of the soup, into three courses. That this trouble should be taken when there were only two of them, their children having left home was remarkable to their acquaintances.

Food is thus bound up with the relation of parent and child, with the giving and receiving of nurture; and when children are away some of the significance of meals is lost. Another aspect of that significance is, however, marriage; and so, although very few of my informants had children still living with them, their inclinations or disinclinations to eat sometimes became a subject associated with marriage and widow-hood, and I return later to this subject in considering at more length the contexts in which food and health become important together.

FOOD AND HEALTH

Having indicated briefly, then, the overall context of this study - that of old age and the empty nest - I begin by describing the detailed kinds of connection which people make between food and health. These connections are by no means uniform and there is at least one major distinction which is very striking: the distinction between health food and illness food.

The term 'health food' generally conjures up a vision of muesli and brown rice; but though these connotations are relevant in the English middle class, they remain something of a late arrival in Aberdeen, and my intention is to draw attention to an idea quite similar in concept but very different in content. This idea, like that of the 'health food' movement, hinges on a notion of health which is quite separate from the mere absence of illness, but it is an idea which has a certain sturdy independence of holistic theorising.

Herzlich (1973) has pointed out that health may be conceived of not merely as the absence of illness, but also, and distinctively, as a reserve of strength, which provides resources both for health activity and, where necessary, for engaging in combat with disease. A similar conception was apparent among elderly Aberdonians. They referred to people as 'healthy' because they had the strength to survive a critical illness where they were expected to die; and this health was unimpaired by the experience of continuing locally specific chronic conditions. Correspondingly they referred to people as 'unhealthy' or as having 'a weakness' not necessarily because they had chronic diseases (in certain cases these unhealthy people had no current disease) but because they were seen to be vulnerable on the evidence of a past pattern of disease, or on the evidence of being easily tired.

This notion of health was thus logically independent of the notion of disease and illness; and while some discussions of food were related to a particular illness condition currently being experienced, others were related unmistakably to the notion of health as strength.

Illness foods (17 cases) were advocated to deal with a variety of familiar complaints - most commonly digestive problems, especially stomach or duodenal ulcers, and circulatory problems like angina and hypertension; but diet was also used as a means of treating diabetes, of alleviating chest conditions or arthritis of the hip (reducing the strain placed on physical function by obesity), and - more recherché - as an attempt to control glaucoma (by means of fresh fruit) and multiple sclerosis (by means of sunflower oil). In most cases these prescriptions were attributed to doctors or, in the case of the sunflower oil, to research disseminated by the Multiple Sclerosis Society; only in the case of digestive problems were fried foods avoided as a folk nostrum with little reference to medical authority.

Health foods (11 cases), by contrast, were very seldom defined with reference to doctors or medical research, and less orthodox form of naturopathic research and so forth were wholly unrepresented. Such diets might include doing without sugar (not because of its medical connotations, but because it was a good habit from the war years) and tended to place heavy reliance on 'plain' ethnic or locally grown ingredients, namely kale, oatmeal, peasemeal (peas ground to a meal), brose (oatmeal and water midway between porridge and gruel), skink soup (soup made from shin of beef), neeps (turnips), tatties (potatoes), jam made from home grown rasps (raspberries) and rhubarb, and 'baking' - not bread, for oatmeal was the traditional staple in Scotland, but scones, bannocks, oatcakes and biscuits.

Only one person advocated what was more recognisably 'health food' in the different sense associated with medical or nutritional principles, and even then her advocacy was cautious, and acknowledged certain residual 'Aberdonian' traits:

> I'm not faddy with food, except that you know when you're on your own you're apt to not cook a lot, but I do see that I get the right things to eat. I suppose I'm intelligent enough to know what's the right things to eat, and eat what's the right things to eat. Balanced diet, just say. I don't eat a lot of meat, because cooking meat for one person is not an economical thing to do - that's the Aberdonian in me coming out. Eat a lot of fish...Not a lot of bread - whole-meal biscuits and things; fruit; vegetables. I get protein - eat a lot of eggs, but take them raw. Eggs and milk...There's still plenty protein and calcium and everything in what I'm taking.

If this diet is compared with that previously described, it becomes apparent that there are at least two notions of health food available in Aberdeen, both of which are to be distinguished from illness food; moreover there is already a hint that these different conceptions may be advocated by different social groups, and may depend on different sorts of moral belief. These themes will shortly be explored in more detail, but in the meantime I turn to consider the relationships which Aberdonians suggest between health and activity.

ACTIVITY AND HEALTH

Just as there is illness food, so there is illness activity; but this is too large and ramifying a subject for the space here available. Rather I concentrate on health activity, which supplies some important points of contrast with health food.

Health activity was a little more popular than health food amongst my informants - nearly a quarter of them (16 cases) advocated some form of activity as a way of building up health, in the sense of strength, leaving aside those who were concerned with it as an antidote to illness.

These strength building forms of activity were defined in different
ways, not so much because their physiological components differed
(nearly all consisted primarily in walking), but because these physiological components were framed within social settings which gave them
their enjoyment, attraction and meaning. The attraction was often, for
instance, use of a physical skill in competitive games - golf especially
(a pursuit which in Scotland does not necessarily carry the connotation
of wealth or status found elsewhere); or it was an identification of
'being on your feet', 'getting out', and 'keeping going' with 'work',
'hard work' which brought reputation and the sense of duty done.
Walking, rather than using a bus or car, also had some virtue, for
though it was seldom an end in itself, it was a means of doing, for
example, the shopping which enabled one to look at favourite sights or
make casual meetings on the way. Least favoured, however, as one would
expect from these preceding instances, were exercises performed as a
drill. Conversion to exercises sometimes occurred after a drastic
illness, but conversion it was: one man, after a double amputation,
said that if they'd told him twenty years ago that exercises were good
for you, he'd have replied 'Awa wi' ye'.

For these elderly Aberdonians, then, the performance of health
activities abstracted from a 'natural' social context, in the manner
prescribed by the literature on keeping fit, was, in all but a few
cases, anathema. As with health food, there was an implicit understanding that their activity was healthy because it was a normal part of
their way of life. But explicit linkages were also made, between
health, food, activity and moral beliefs, and it is time now to consider
these.

MORAL BELIEFS AND SOCIAL STRUCTURE

Most of my informants assumed that their way of life was healthy, and
did not argue specifically for health food or health activity; what
follows is concerned with the structures of though available to the
remaining two fifths or so who did put forward such arguments in the
way I have described. How far these arguments matched the practice of
these informants is, of course, debatable; it was reasonably easy to
check whether some of the recommended foods were taken, or some of the
recommended activities practised, but I did not pursue the more
exhaustive details necessary in particular to assess the balance of
recommended foods in the total diet. It is at least possible, though,
to explore how food beliefs which have medical authority fare against
food beliefs which have none.

There were two sets of beliefs, yielding prescriptions concerned with
healthy diet or with healthy exercise, as the context dictated, which
offered relatively comprehensive pictures of a way of life: one set of
beliefs may provisionally be characterised as the Scottish rural
tradition, and the other, linked with it, as the Scottish Communist
tradition. In addition to these relatively explicit and coherent bodies
of ideas, though, there were other ideas specific either to diet or to
activity, which had, however, some inexplicit linkages with one another,
and were propounded by members of a particular social circle. Thus both
logical linkages of ideas and social linkages of membership can be
usefully explored in accounting for attitudes to diet and exercise.

The Scottish rural tradition, as one would expect, involved the
advocacy of plenty of home grown, and characteristically Scottish,
foods, and the commendation of being 'out', 'out in all weathers',
'keeping going' and 'hard work'. Those who invoked this tradition were
usually concerned with only one side of the equation - the consumption
side or the production side, whichever was for them the more difficult
to maintain - but they coincided in deriving their values from the
'country', the 'fisher folk', and the idea of home production, from
parents, grandparents and the 'auld tradition'. Associated with these
ideas, in some more elaborate accounts, was religion - not necessarily
the Kirk, for theological quarrels have been endemic in Scottish
history - but the broader notion of shared bonds in a common faith:

> I was brought up with my grandmother who was very food
> conscious, no tinsel. I mean everything was clean, and aye,
> she wasn't a religious person but she believed in a higher
> hand; and so brought us up the same way, you know, to
> respect everybody, and just spread your helping hand in
> every way you could.

Correspondingly, there was a protest involved in this way of thinking
against a diet and a way of life which had usurped its place. The
protest, as expressed in the previous quotation, was against 'this
tinsel', against food that was packaged or tinned, or even merely sold
in shops. One old man had tasted 'shop jam' once in his life, and spat
it out (he presented a graphic re-enactment). It was not so much that
he objected to shops as such - he was content, when the home made jam
ran out, to take his 'Lyle Syrup' - but he was offended by shops
attempting to emulate what people should grow and make for themselves.

I suggested earlier that, within this broad context of shared mores,
'moderation' was a concept used to regulate the relation of consuming
to producing. There was also one other expression which nicely caught
that relationship in the rural past to which these Aberdonians were
appealing. This was the notion of being 'starved'. In the North East,
the word 'starve' still retains a historic connotation of suffering
from cold, as well as the notion of suffering from hunger; thus to
starve can either imply lack of proper food, or it can indicate, as it
did to one man, deprivation of proper exercise; when horses were used,
he explained, it was fine working with them, you were always warm,
keeping going, out in all weathers; but when tractors came in you were
starved with the cold, sitting in the cab. The cold, in fact, was the
great adversary of Scottish country life, and it was only through
plenty of plain home produced food on the one hand, and through being
out working and keeping going, that strength to resist the cold was
maintained.

Those who explicitly referred these characteristic beliefs about diet
and exercise to this kind of 'auld tradition' (six cases) were mostly
in the working class network, and beliefs about food and activity which
were similar, although not referred specifically to this tradition, were
only expressed by working class informants (five additional cases). The
performance of warming physical tasks as part of one's daily 'work', the
emphasis on being 'out', the addiction to 'plain' foods acquired in lean
years and to 'moderation' with a religious sanction, seemed, indeed,
especially intelligible in a working class community with a strong rural
background; and since they were beliefs often related to preceding

generations, one might also expect them to owe more to earlier experiences than to current discussion and criticism. In this context it is interesting to note that these were beliefs expressed very much by individuals, being as likely to be contested as accepted within their own households, and being favourite topics among people who had little direct acquaintance with one another.

The Scottish Communist tradition is interesting in part as a reaction to this rural inheritance, but it will receive only brief mention here since it was linked to diet or exercise by only two people, both working class men who had read Marx and Lenin, but who were otherwise unacquainted with one another. To this way of thinking the rural diet had been poor enough, just 'kale, neeps and tatties' - there had been little money for other things, and although food was still more expensive than it need be, because of the profits taken by farmers and middlemen, it was possible now to buy more of what was 'good'. This 'good' food, notably, was not much different from the ideal rural diet as described by protagonists of country life - there was simply more of those items which were additional to 'kale, neeps and tatties'. Because these items had been scarce in the actual diet of farm labourers, the work sometimes overtaxed their strength. But exercise was important, nevertheless; prevention was better than cure. People should learn physical drill when they were young, as was done in the army, and have monthly examinations by their doctors 'as they do in Russia'.

In this sketch of what these two men had to say, it is easy to see some of the characteristic positions of interwar Communism: the indictment of profits, the martial discipline, the emphasis on prevention, the appeal to the Soviet model. Less obvious, perhaps, was the way in which the dietary conservatism of the rural tradition was grafted on to the experience of army drill in the aim to 'mak better' the way of life which they had inherited.

The last cluster of moral beliefs about healthy food and activity which I will discuss (eight cases) was united by a less specific notion - that of a 'discipline' or 'balance' whose constituents were implicit and taken for granted, emerging only in the context of their social setting. It is appropriate to the idea of balance that diet and exercise were advocated by people in social positions which were, in a sense, opposite and complementary: exercise was the concern of retired men, diet of women living alone. Both the men and the women concerned were, moreover, mainly in the middle class network; and, at least in the men's case, there were logical reasons why this should be so.

The retired men had, by definition, finished with their previous main activity at work, and they had replaced it with the notion of com- petitive games which would maintain a physical skill into old age. In this way they reaffirmed the 'balance' of their way of life, thus maintaining, by the same token, their health and strength. By way of illustrating this proposition, they frequently went back to the experience of their schooldays or early manhood:

> I had everything, you know, every children's disease under the
> sun...but then I think it was going to Gilbert's and mixing
> with the rest of the boys - and of course apart from the
> educational side Gilbert's is a very prominent athletic school
> too, and I became interested and started playing games of all

> sorts...and from about twelve onwards I became very fit and
> robust.
>
> I was very, very keen on tennis, but then after the war there
> was that gap of about six years in your life – you're getting
> older, and I decided that probably the best thing to do from
> the long term point of view was to take up golf....It's
> taking you out for three or four hours on a golf course in
> the country, walking and exercise. I do look upon it as
> being a form of exercise.

Three of these men went to the same fee paying school and were linked
by direct acquaintance, and a fourth, though originally from a skilled
manual occupation, belonged to one of the exclusive golf clubs much
patronised by the old boys of the school. It was a background which
had bred a life long respect for competitive games and a strong belief
in their beneficial effects, not only on health and strength, but also
on other aspects of moral character.

The women who placed an emphasis on health diet resembled the men in
that they were concerned about failing to perform a function when they
were no longer called on to do so by the needs of others – in their
case, the function of making 'proper' meals. Three were from the
middle class network, and a fourth was a local notable, but there was
less associational basis for connecting them than there was with the
men; essentially, their emphasis on diet was one which could be
expected of any woman living alone who placed a strong and explicit
value on 'discipline' and being 'sensible':

> Discipline with food – in that I'm awfully tempted sometimes
> not to make any lunch, you see; and I say to myself, 'Good
> for you, now go on, you make your lunch'. Just to try to
> eat sensibly.

Discipline was entailed primarily by the deviant position of these
women; it was mainly a protection against eating too little, and only
in one case, already quoted, was it a routine aimed at eating the
'right things' in terms of nutritional recommendations.

Discipline, being sensible, a balanced life, competition with one's
equals, these were all values which were alike in appealing to an
unwritten code, a way of life which, in being 'obvious' to its mainly
middle class adherents, needed no expression. A profession of faith in
healthy diet or healthy exercise was, in these circumstances, only
elicited from those who were deprived of what was considered the normal
basis for meals or activity. Such professions were carefully designed
to do no more than reassert that the normal was being maintained, that
the code was intact; for if this was so, health followed. Health
could not be pursued at the cost of what was normal; a tart old lady
in the middle class network summed matters up by explaining that she
walked a good deal in the ordinary course of events, 'but not for that
purpose', and did not bother about her weight, although the doctor said
she ought to; and she wound up with a scornful reference to a public
figure who was 'cranky about his food'. Crankiness, or, as in an
earlier quotation, faddiness, was in a sense health unhealthily
acquired.

The middle class code, then, or alternatively the Scottish rural tradition or its Communist critique, provided premises which lay behind most beliefs which linked food or activity to health and strength. A few such beliefs had no background of this kind - mainly those concerned with the virtues of walking - and formal isolated premises with only a single application; but in general, beliefs about health food and health activity had a deep structure which contrasted sharply with beliefs about illness food.

Illness food differed strikingly in that beliefs about what was appropriate very seldom had the reinforcement of more fundamental premises; they usually involved one specific *ad hoc* application which was referred to medical authority. In these circumstances, such diets ran a chance of contradicting beliefs about health food, and the outcome of such contradictions is clearly of some interest.

In conclusion, therefore, I present a brief case study of a collision occurring between beliefs about illness food and beliefs about health food.

ILLNESS FOOD AND HEALTH FOOD: A CASE STUDY OF CONFLICT

Scotland has a notoriously high rate of death from ischaemic heart disease (Information Services Division, 1979) amongst other conditions, and the Scottish diet is one factor which has been indicted (Wynn and Wynn, 1979). It is of some interest, therefore, to follow the career of a believer in that diet, who suffers from coronary heart disease. Though there remains considerable controversy among researchers about the most important effects of diet on heart disease, there is an orthodoxy often found in medical textbooks, which advises reduced con- sumption of sugar and animal fats; and this particular belief is important in the present case.

When I first met Mrs Nigg, she mentioned food spontaneously, early on while discussing her present house which she and her husband found expensive. The cost of good food - 'and I know what foods one needs to be well' - was, she said, becoming prohibitive. People's complaints would be halved if they ate proper things, and had the money to buy the proper foods; 'but everything's packaged - there's no food value in it'. There was, she concluded, nothing like a pot of home made soup (made from beef); and amongst other valuable foods of the ethnic kind described earlier she listed milk and butter.

Asked how she became conscious of the importance of food for health, she had this to say:

> I think I have inherited that from my grandmother, and, I think, her grandmother - her mother and grandmother before her, as I'm led to believe, were the salt of the earth. They knew what was good for them, and they were healthy, and they valued their health and were willing to give up everything, you know, for to be well.

Grandmother was 'fisher' (from a fishing village), the 'good old religious kind of people'.

During the same conversation, her heart condition also emerged. She had had the condition for fifteen years, and had suffered a coronary within the last three - 'the pain, I'll never forget it all the years of my life'. Again spontaneously, she commented on the dietary restrictions which had followed from her condition:

The weight doesn't help, but for years I haven't taken a spot of sugar. I'm starting to take butter now, because my mother says that margarine is of no use to anyone, so I have started to take butter.

A month later, Mrs Nigg had a heart attack in the early hours of the morning. The doctor was called out, and he decided to treat her at home. She had been severely frightened, however, and 'thought she was going'; and when I saw her a few days later she was grey in the face and very weak. Almost immediately she commented:

All this about food - it doesn't make any difference. I've been very careful about food. Jim has butter - I don't. I never take it.

As the conversation progressed, however, she grew more cheerful, and re-asserted the value of food without apparently remembering that she had just denied it. This resilient mood persisted over the ensuing months, and she commented that when she had last seen me she was very depressed; indeed six months after the attack she was so much her old self that in a conversation at that time she repeated what she had said about food and health when I first met her, and in particular the value of that traditional Scottish diet which, in the shock after her coronary, she had rejected and even, in regard to the butter, denied that she ever took.

Two things are evident in the pattern of Mrs Nigg's ideas before, during and after this coronary crisis. First, her beliefs about health food, based as they were on the premises of what I have called the Scottish rural tradition, had a structure sufficiently deep to survive intact a life threatening event which was, as she felt for a time, in flat contradiction with them. Secondly, these beliefs about health food, because of this strength in depth, were able to overrule contrary beliefs about the food appropriate to her illness, one of which, emerging only in the immediate aftermath of the attack, was the harmfulness of butter.

CONCLUSION

This was not a study aimed at giving estimates of the number holding particular beliefs; it was designed rather to elicit some of the logical structures lying behind those beliefs (Williams, 1981) and the ways in which those structures may be reinforced by a particular social circle. The weakness of the logical structures underlying beliefs about illness food, which are based on medical authority, and the strength of those underlying beliefs about health food, which are based on a conception of a way of life, form one main indication of this evidence; and if dietary instructions are to be convincing to the elderly, it seems that a knowledge of their beliefs about health food may be necessary. Secondly, the evidence has indicated that the logic of health food is tied up, through conceptions of a way of life, with

corresponding ideas about health activity; food and activity habits
are shaped into a balance, and each has to be understood in the light
of this balance with the other. Finally the third conclusion which
suggests itself is that there are at least three separate systems of
belief which relate to health food and health activity amongst elderly
Aberdonians - a mainly middle class code which is differentiated by
sex, and a rural tradition which continues to inform working class
values, and which generated, between the wars, a specific Communist
critique. It is interesting that these patterns of belief among older
people take forms which seem to have been laid down some decades ago -
the rural tradition and its Communist reinterpretation are, for
instance, memorably portrayed in Lewis Grassic Gibbon's trilogy of
1933-4, describing contemporary life in the North East.[3]   Correspondingly, these beliefs owe little to the so called health food
movement of the younger middle classes. It is tempting, on this basis,
to speculate that these various ways of thinking may represent
historical strata in British life, and that patterns of historical
progression in such ideas about health, food and activity might be
revealed by wider research.

NOTES

[1] Department of Health and Social Security. Prevention and health:
     everybody's business, HMSO, London, 1976.
[2] ibid. p.40.
[3] Lewis Grassic Gibbon (1973) A Scots Quair, Pan Books, London.

11 An Apple a Day ... Some Reflections on Working Class Mothers' Views on Food and Health

ROISIN PILL

The conviction that nothing can possibly be so good for you as home cooking is sometimes poignantly illustrated on the admission of a child to hospital when, to the annoyance of staff and even possibly to the detriment of a treatment plan, the mother will bring food from home to give to the patient. This example highlights the immense symbolic importance of food. The mother's reluctance to relinquish her control over the child to strangers in a strange place and her ambivalence towards them are expressed by reasserting her role as the prime caring, responsible nurse figure through the medium of food.

But how far and in what way do mothers regard diet as important for health? American data suggest that people clearly link nutrition and health maintenance (Stolz, 1967; Cornely and Bigman, 1961; Hassinger and McNamara, 1960; Litman, 1971; Harris and Guten, 1979). But the scanty British evidence leaves open the possibility that a significant proportion of women do not perceive food as particularly relevant for health, or the prevention of illness. (Salmon, 1979; Kraft, 1978; Blue Band, 1978). If so, what are the socio-demographic characteristics of this group, what are their wider health beliefs, and what are the practical implications of their attitudes? This chapter[1] deals with such questions, taking the view that acceptance of the relationship between food and health, however it is conceived, is a necessary, if not sufficient, condition for making dietary choices designed to maintain health. (Whether or not these choices are medically approved or objectively effective is a separate issue). Here the focus is on awareness of the link between food and health, an emphasis which is particularly relevant in the light of growing concern in official circles about the possible implications of current nutritional behaviour for the long term health status of the community.

Food choices (DHSS, 1979) are currently seen by health professionals and policy makers as an aspect of daily behaviour where individuals can take preventive action and thereby demonstrate acceptance of responsibility for maintaining their health. Personal responsibility for health is now a crucial theme of recent official policy (DHSS, 1976) and represents a major reorientation of emphasis from the comprehensive provisions offered in the nationalised Health Service after the Second World War to one where the individual may be expected to hold the key to his/her health.[2] This policy switch to the twin platforms of preventive care and individual responsibility for health provided the stimulus for a small pilot study[3] carried out by myself and Dr N.C.H.

Stott. We argued that this change was taking place without any clear understanding of what existing health attitudes and practices were and that, in order to devise more effective strategies of attitude and behaviour change, it would be necessary to develop techniques for measuring beliefs and behaviours among specific target groups.

This study was an attempt to explore how one might go about collecting this kind of material and, as such, was not primarily concerned with nutrition; although we expected that food choices would be one of the areas in which ·our respondents might exhibit awareness of the relevance of lifestyle. For the purposes of this chapter I have drawn together material on the concepts of food and diet held by our respondents, a sample of working class mothers [4] in South Wales, and related these to their theories about health and illness. The tentative proposition is advanced that definitions of 'good food', and indeed whether food choices are perceived as relevant for future health at all, are linked to the women's theories of aetiology. It is obvious that the material available in no way permits an adequate testing of this hypothesis but it does provide a basis for discussion and a useful way of organising some descriptive data. Accordingly the following sections deal first, with the division of the sample according to their beliefs about illness causation, then an examination of concepts of 'good' food, third, the evidence for correlating concepts of food and attitudes towards diet and health is reviewed.

LIFESTYLE AND DIET IN THEORIES OF ILLNESS CAUSATION

One of the most interesting things to emerge as analysis progressed was the dichotomy between those women who spontaneously referred to life-style when asked for their reasons for people falling ill and those who only mentioned causes external to the individual, causes over which she had no control. Further analysis of the transcripts examining all statements imputing a cause for illness confirmed the view that these two groups were operating with different levels of aetiological theories - the one being distinctly more ready than the other to accept that individual behaviour played a part in illness. These issues are discussed more fully elsewhere (Pill and Stott, 1982) where it is argued that those who accept lifestyle as a relevant factor in aetiology are more ready to accept the notion that they are morally accountable if they fall ill. They also recognised the long term implications of neglect and held a concept of 'resistance' to illness which reflected this view of health as a process, requiring to be worked at and main-tained. (This is in sharp contrast to the women expressing external aetiological theories who might mention 'resistance' but saw it clearly as a relatively immutable personal characteristic). In order to simplify discussion this latter group will be referred to as the 'Fatalists', while those for whom lifestyle is more salient will be described as the 'Lifestyle' group.

This rather crude and provisional classification is illustrated in Table 11.1. The first five categories may be regarded and are so regarded by the respondents, as being factors which are essentially outside individual control whereas 7 to 11 show an awareness of the relevance of individual choice. (Category 6 is somewhat ambiguous since allocation to the Lifestyle or Fatalist group of hypotheses about

Table 11.1

Types of response given to the question: 'What do you think are the main reasons for people falling ill?' (No. of respondents = 41)*

1. Environmental factors, e.g. the weather, pollution, pesticides	8
2. Heredity and family susceptibility	6
3. Individual susceptibility	4
4. Germs, bugs, viruses and infections	13
5. Stress, worry	6
6. Type of person you are, e.g. 'more nervous type', 'unhappy'	6
7. Being 'run down'	10
8. 'Way of life'	3
9. Diet	6
10. Hygiene	4
11. Neglect, not looking after yourself properly	7
12. Don't know/'you can't help it'	4

* Respondents gave more than one reason

causation depends on whether one believes that individual personality characteristics are genetically controlled and hence immutable, or not). Diet is specifically mentioned by 6 women (15 per cent), for example

Well, I think a lot to do with it - I don't mean obvious illnesses like blood diseases or something like that, but I think a lot of trouble is not the right food - not the right diet. I think if your constitution is low it's a lot to do with diet. (No. 4)

However, it is clear that diet is strongly implicated in two other categories 'run down' and 'neglect'; for these mothers 'letting oneself get run down' was almost synonymous with not eating properly as was 'not looking after yourself properly', e.g.

Not looking after yourself in a way, that is what I seem to think...yes, neglecting yourself and not eating properly at proper hours.... (No. 13)

I think the general health has got a lot to do with it because I think if your general health breaks down or we don't look after ourselves as we should, you know, the way we eat, the type of way we live, maybe not going out enough, the type of foods we eat...will bring our immunity down because the body isn't strong enough to cope.... (No. 24)

These Lifestyle mothers held different concepts of resistance and health. They saw people falling ill because they had become vulnerable as a result of their own actions and were more likely to view health as a dynamic relationship between individuals and their environment and therefore susceptible to a variety of influences, some of which were under individual control. Of these factors, dietary behaviour was undoubtedly the most important and this emphasis is reflected again in the way they talked about food. For example (see Table 11.2) they were more likely than the Fatalists, on the one hand, to mention foods they avoided, usually sweets, cake, etc., and, on the other, to make a point of including foods for health reasons, e.g.

I try to get them to eat brown bread as much as white because
white doesn't do you any good...well, brown as a wholemeal
because this white bread and some just ordinary brown hasn't
got any roughage in it. I give them brown about once a week
which they have in their cereal mainly because I know that in
a lot of our junk food that we have today - when I say that,
you know, your beefburgers, hamburgers and convenience stuff -
there's not enough roughage or fibre they say. Um, I'm not a
fad or anything, but I just try and get them to eat sensibly.
They hate eating green vegetables, at least the two boys do. (No.32)

The Lifestyle group appeared to be controlling their families' diet in
a much more planned way making conscious decisions about when, how much
and what was to be eaten so that their own and their children's 'level
of resistance' would be maintained. In sharp contrast, it was only

Table 11.2
Differences in the regulation of food between the two groups of mothers

	Fatalists	Lifestyle	Total
	N = 21	N = 20	41
No. who:			
Mention specific foods avoided	4	9	13
Mention specific foods included for health reasons	2	8	10
Avoid frying/use of grilling as cooking method	1	5	6
Stress importance of regular meals at regular hours	-	4	4
Permit child to choose what s/he likes/allow snacks between meals	4	-	4

among the Fatalist mothers that anyone admitted to asking the child what
he or she felt like eating today - in other words, allowing the child's
tastes rather than any abstract notion of what was best to dictate the
pattern of meals.   Here the rationale seemed to be that there was no
point in making something that would not be acceptable, and therefore
not eaten.

This pattern of letting the child eat what s/he wants when s/he wants
it may be viewed, from a middle class perspective, as an abdication of
responsibility or an example of the immediate gratification characteristic of socialisation in working class families. However, if the mother
does not consider food as particularly important in the prevention of
illness - which, in her view, will happen despite whatever she does -
she may well feel that letting the child choose reflects a good standard
of care on her part, e.g.

He don't like just his breakfast and then his dinner, he eats in
between like. And all mine seem to do that. This is the way
I've always given in to them because I think, well, if they want
it they can have it. I agree with that. (No. 2)

120

Half our sample did not perceive 'diet', or any other area where individual choice could be exerted, as relevant in the causation of illness, yet the majority of these same women considered food to be important in keeping their families fit and healthy. It is possible that this discrepancy reflects a belief that food is important, particularly for the proper development of children, and also as 'fuel' for adults, but can have no part to play in the strengthening of the body against disease because illness cannot be prevented. As noted earlier, Fatalists rarely mention the concept of 'resistance' or else see it as something determined at birth. This approach to food would mean that while it was considered necessary to give the 'right food' to a child to ensure correct growth, individual likes and dislikes might be given freer rein. After all, there is little point in being unduly restrictive or 'faddy' because if a child is going to fall ill, he or she will do so anyway. For adults the need to provide special foods for healthy development would no longer apply so that the likelihood of making food choices for health reasons would become even more remote. It was noted, for instance, that many of the mothers in our sample expressed an ideology of maternal sacrifice stressing the duty of 'fighting off illness', 'not giving in', 'keeping going', 'working it off'. (cf. Blaxter and Paterson, 1980).

One of the implications of the strong possibility that most mothers would tend to place the health needs of their families before their own is that those mothers with fatalistic views on aetiology would have even less incentive to give their own diet any priority in practice, although they may well pay lip service to the notion. Not only does the type of food consumed have no bearing on whether one stays healthy or falls ill, but one has a positive duty, as a caring mother, to 'keep going' for the sake of the children. This means adopting the 'right attitude' rather than making dietary changes.

This line of reasoning would also suggest that such mothers might well hold very different conceptions of what constitutes 'good' food from those more inclined to see diet as a way of building up one's resistance.

Whenever the mother mentioned 'good food' or the 'right food' an attempt was made to probe what she meant by this. This drew two types

Table 11.3
Terms used to describe 'good food'

Good food is:	Fatalists N = 18*	Lifestyle N = 20	Total N = 38
'cooked'	9	–	9
hot	1	1	2
having a variety of foods	3	4	7
'fresh' food	10	12	22
sufficient food/substantial meals	3	1	4
Not poor quality	1	2	3

*Three of the Fatalist mothers did not mention food at all during the interview

of response, one essentially a descriptive category (Table 11.3) and the other a list of foods she considered 'good'.

The commonest definition was that 'good food' was 'fresh food', usually contrasted with frozen or tinned food. Several of the mothers commented that they did buy frozen vegetables for convenience sometimes but preferred, where possible, to use fresh. There was a slight suggestion that the Fatalists were more inclined to favour fresh food because they thought it tasted better or was 'better' in some unspecified way, which may simply reflect habit and attitudes derived from their own mothers' beliefs and practices.

> All I buy usually is the frozen peas which is just to do a quick thing when I can't be bothered to do the vegetables. You know, I don't have a lot of it because I don't like a lot of it. I buy fresh meat and fish.
>
> (RP) But you are not a believer in frozen food generally?
>
> Well, I don't like the taste of a lot of it. (No. 12)
>
> Fresh vegetables are good for you.
>
> (RP) What do you think of frozen vegetables then?
>
> I don't buy them.
>
> (RP) You don't think they are as good?
>
> No, no. Tinned peas I buy but I don't buy many frozen veg. I like the fresh stuff, it's better. (No. 10)

Lifestyle mothers, on the other hand, seemed more likely to defend their choice on the superior quality of fresh food mentioning specific reasons like more vitamins in fresh food and suspicious about the implications of the processing of food for health.

> I think the natural sort of foods, they're trying to change them now a bit, aren't they, sort of like school dinners - part of the meat being soya. You know, packet type of food.
>
> (RP) What do you think about that?
>
> Not so good really - I don't think it can possibly be as good as fresh. (No. 41)
>
> I reckon when you eat these good foods - I mean, not frozen vegetables, fresh vegetables and what have you - the vitamins. I still reckon you need vitamins. They say there are vitamins in frozen food but obviously there can't be as much as in fresh food, can there? (No.26)

The most striking feature of Table 11.3 is the fact that half of the Fatalist mothers defined good food as 'cooked food'. At the beginning of the interviewing I was unaware of the significance of this then and assumed it to be a synonym for 'hot' as opposed to cold or uncooked food. However, subsequent interviews revealed that it referred to a specific pattern of meal preparation, consisting of roast meat and gravy with potatoes and other vegetables, which is accorded particular value (cf. Murcott, 1982a).

The following exchange reveals the extent of my original confusion. The respondent had been stressing the importance of good meat and vegetables.

But I do like them to eat their vegetables. I don't know why, but I do.

(RP) So you think as long as they have meat and vegetables... is there anything that you try and avoid?

Not really. I haven't got fussy kids, they're pretty good really. I mean they come home and I say 'Have this' and they say 'Yes, that's alright', you know. I mean it's cooked dinners they're not too fussy on. I don't know why. You know, they say, 'Oh, we've got cooked tonight, have we?', you know.

(RP) They don't like it?

They're not very fussy, no. They eat Tuesdays and Sundays, when I do cooked like, you know. I would do it more often but what's the point?

(RP) What do they like then?

Chips! My oldest one likes beefburgers and chips, and the other one likes cooked ham and chips, you know, or soup or beans on toast, something like that.

(RP) When you say 'cooked', then you mean...what? A roast of meat or something like that?

Yes, boiled potatoes and gravy, you know.

(RP) And they'd rather have something more like chips?

Chips, yes. But I do like them to have a cooked you know.
(No. 10)

Once I was alerted to this definition the following exchanges also make more sense. For example,

(RP) What do you think are the most important things you do to keep your family healthy?

Well, I think keeping them clothed as they should be, you know, not silly clothes. Plenty of good food, you know... I think that's about it really. Make sure they've got plenty of fruit and stuff like that.

(RP) When you say 'good food', what do you think of?

Good meals, you know, cooked meals and that.

(RP) You like to give them a cooked meal?

They have a cooked meal, say, three times a week, and then they have something in between the rest of the day and plenty of fruit and that - I've always got fruit and that here for them. (No. 6)

Well, food, you know, I mean, giving them good food. Dressing them warm in the winter, things like that. I don't know other than that, just sort of keeping them clean like.

(RP) You said food - what did you have in mind?

Well, a cereal I'd say for breakfast, if you get them to

123

eat it. Mine are marvellous on that. The oldest one I do
have a little bit of trouble with. Cooked food I'd say,
cooked dinners.

(RP) By cooked dinners you mean, what sort of things?

Well meat, you know. Meat and vegetables. I think
vegetables are important. I mean that's the hard part,
you can't force them to eat it can you? (No. 20)

Well, I liked cooked meals - roast dinners. I'm very much
for cooked meals. I mean the children would rather have
chips, you know, the moment they come in. But I think
fresh greens and things are important. (No. 17)

One possible interpretation of the difference is that the Fatalist
group of mothers have a more traditional view of food and meal
preparation, placing great stress on the virtues of meat, cooked in
certain ways, and fresh vegetables presented with it. In contrast the
Lifestyle mothers do not appear to attach the same symbolic significance
to 'a cooked', being more prepared perhaps to recognise the nutritional
value of other protein foods and to experiment with ways of serving food.

The mothers were also asked to give examples, if they had not
spontaneously done so, of what they considered to be good foods. There
were no marked differences between the two groups except that the
Lifestyle mothers gave proportionately more and also a rather wider
range of examples. Interestingly enough, fruit and vegetables dominate
the replies (see earlier quotations) with less stress on the protein
foods of fish, meat, eggs - even more surprisingly, perhaps, is the lack
of emphasis on milk. (By contrast cf. Blaxter and Paterson, 1980,
pp.207-9). Thus the one clue to different concepts of food held by
groups who differ in their perceptions of the relevance of diet in
aetiology is given by the emphasis whereby 'cooked food' equals good
food in the Fatalist group. It was suggested that this might indicate
a more traditional approach to food, one possibly rooted in working
class beliefs about the value of (real) meat, i.e. a roast as opposed to
the convenient, processed beefburgers, etc. with all the appropriate
trimmings. Manual workers doing heavy physical work and possibly
exposed to the elements need solid and nourishing meals. Hoggart
comments that the prime duty of the working class wife was to provide
warmth and a tasty meal on the table for her husband when he comes home.
(Hoggart, 1958). The 'cooked' dinner because it is hot and contains
meat, symbolising virility and strength, epitomises all the best of that
tradition. The housewife who provides such a meal for her man and
children is doing her best to prepare them to face the outside world.

Another theme which may also be rooted in older working class images
of food is the greater emphasis on quantity rather than quality when
discussing food. Here the stress lies on providing 'enough', with its
underlying view of food as fuel both for the growing child and the man
engaged in heavy physical work. This contrasts with the greater
emphasis on 'quality' and the greater concern expressed by Lifestyle
mothers about methods of growing and processed foods. The evidence for
making this distinction came partly in the responses to the question
inviting respondents to compare the health of their own with their
grandparents' generation. The advantage of this open question was that

it allowed the mothers to raise spontaneously the factors they considered relevant to health and fifteen of the sample mentioned diet/ food. Nine fell into the Lifestyle group while six were classified as Fatalists.

The Lifestyle mothers differed about whether they were in fact healthier than previous generations, some seeing the diet of years ago as infinitely better than the adulterated, processed foods available now, while others felt they ate a better quality diet than their parents.

Well, I think they have a lot more in the food line, I think that would help us now. Like my mother had five of us and we didn't - we ate fresh food, you know - but I don't know, with my children they eat a lot more meat, cheese and things like that that we didn't have.... (No. 36)

They were probably healthier than we are now, although of course, they still had the things like smallpox and diptheria, TB which we've now found cures for. But I think they lived more from the land than we do, they had a cleaner atmosphere then, which we haven't got now with all these chemicals and whatever bursting in the air...(you said they lived from the land more?) Well, you know, basic foods, whereas we don't. Everything we eat, if it still comes from the land now, you know, and it's not man-made and a lot of our food is - um, it's always being sprayed by stuff, you know, pest control stuff and whatever. (No. 32)

The Fatalists were equally undecided on the issue of comparative healthiness but the conclusions they drew were based on interpretations of the social and economic situation. People got less food because of rationing or because of the pressure of family circumstances.

I mean going back years ago, even back to my mother's time, going back to when I was a child, my mother's problem was only - she had four children and only my father working - her problem was just managing the food from one week to the next. Now you don't find many families who have got problems with food - it's more like - well, I can see my mother's point of view that it is unnecessary worries. It's more like you want to buy something, or you want this or that.... (No. 20)

However, although we have much more food available nowadays and very few people are perceived as not getting enough to eat there is some unease expressed about 'too much' food and its consequence, overweight. The above respondent also said:

Well, I would say we are healthier now myself. I mean there's not so many illnesses - well, not the serious illnesses that were going around then, I don't think. But the only thing I do think in my own way is that people tend to be more over-weight going back to years ago aren't they, you know? And I think that probably is too much food, not so many money problems as there were.... (No. 20)

This emphasis on overeating came up again in response to a question on the reasons for heart attacks. The respondents were invited to comment on the statement that 'More people nowadays seem to be getting heart attacks' and also asked if they knew what 'the experts' thought were the reasons for this. Again, the same proportion of mothers in both groups mentioned diet in their answers but the Fatalists saw the problem largely in terms of over-eating and excess weight whereas the Lifestyle mothers were much more likely also to invoke current theories about fats, cholesterol, etc. (8 Lifestyle, 2 Fatalists). In other words, they were more likely to invoke multiple factors in their theories of causation. Thus, both groups had a concept that over-eating led to weight increase which, coupled with a stress (usually defined as over-work, pace of life, 'rat race'), led to a heart attack. The body gets overloaded and breaks down.

> They said its weight and lack of exercise. I'm not a doctor so
> I don't know (What do you think about that?) It's quite likely
> really, isn't it? It varies I think...I think a lot is to do
> with weight. The actual heart itself might be faulty. It gets
> over-stressed - it gets bunged up. (No. 19)

The Lifestyle mothers recognised also that particular types of food, as well as the sheer amount, might contribute more to the likelihood of suffering a heart attack. Thus, using the metaphor of body as a machine, not only can too much fuel overload the system but certain types of fuel are more likely to cause damage.

So within a very homogenous group of working class mothers significant differences were found between those who had a more positive definition of health and were prepared to concede some role to individual behaviour (lifestyle) in the aetiology of illness, and those who viewed health either as absence of illness or in purely functional terms and do not consider lifestyle as salient. It was suggested that their perceptions of food with the emphasis on 'cooked' meals and 'quantity' rather than 'quality' might reflect more traditional attitudes, typical of working class women a generation or so earlier when social conditions were rather different.

At the same time this cannot be the whole story. I would hypothesise that these mothers also held rather different views from the Lifestyle mothers about the nature of the relationship between food and health. This topic was not however explored in the pilot study and the only clue afforded was the different attitudes displayed towards the choice of foods and control over family eating patterns. It seems plausible that mothers who do not hold a positive view of health, have no concept of 'resistance' or 'reserve of health' and see illnesses as caused by external agencies over which they have no control, are less likely to place importance on monitoring family food intake. Further data are needed to clarify respondents' models of the function of food, e.g. food as fuel, food for development, food for building up resistance, and will be available in the main phase of the study currently in progress.

The point to be stressed is that beliefs about food need to be studied and interpreted within the much broader context of systems of health beliefs and practices. Such an approach appears to offer greater potential for understanding the complexities of food beliefs and behaviour and would have practical relevance both for health professionals and health educators. Not only must any attempts to modify nutritional beliefs and behaviour first take into account the pattern already existing in the target group, but also show an awareness of how this pattern relates to the lay system(s), the ethnomedical understandings of the group. Quite different strategies would seem to be required to produce behavioural change in groups like the Fatalist and the Lifestyle mothers described above.

For both practical and theoretical reasons lay systems of health beliefs and practices in Britain today merit greater research attention than has been the case up till now. One of the purposes of this chapter has been to suggest that nutritional beliefs and practices are also best studied within this broader topic area; many of the observed variations and discrepancies between knowledge and behaviour within the population as a whole may best be explained by using health beliefs as intervening and mediating variables.

NOTES

[1] I would like to express my gratitude to Dr N.C.H. Stott for the interest and enthusiasm he unfailingly displayed when together we were battling with the problems of methodology and interpretation during the project. His comments on this paper, as well as those of Anne Murcott in her capacity as editor, have been much appreciated although I must take full responsibility for the final version. Professor Robert Harvard Davis and our other colleagues in the Department of General Practice also deserve appreciation for their support and interest throughout.

[2] But cf. Davis, 1979; Graham, 1979; Stacey, 1980 and for the US Crawford, 1977.

[3] Funded by a grant from the DHSS to whom thanks are due. The data were collected during semi-structured interviews conducted in the homes of a sample of 41 mothers living on a housing estate in South Wales and attending a health centre there. These interviews were recorded on tape and later transcribed for analysis although the original tapes were used to check interpretation.
For further details of the study see Stott and Pill, 1980; also Pill and Stott, 1981 and Pill and Stott, 1982.
It must be stressed that this was a pilot study, designed to explore possibilities and generate hypotheses, and our categorisation and analyses may well need modification when further data are collected from a large sample.

[4] Aged between 30 and 35 years, living with their husbands, with either two or three children at least one of whom is of primary school age.

12 The Sweet Things in Life: Aspects of the Management of Diabetic Diet

TINA POSNER

Diet is a key factor in the aetiology and management of diabetes - a metabolic condition in which there is too much sugar in the blood. Looking at the role of diet, and in particular, carbohydrate, highlights important aspects of the diabetic's experience of the condition and medical management of it.

This chapter will focus on the way in which sweet foods, and diabetic products promoted as substitutes, have been presented and goes on to relate this to the role of diet generally. It will draw on interview, observational and documentary material collected (while in receipt of an SSRC studentship) for a study of diabetics as a system of medical control (c.f. Posner, 1977).[1] These data illustrate the ambiguities of the moral judgements about sweet foods and differences of dietary policy involved in diabetic ideology.[2]

It is well known that diabetics have dietary restrictions. There are restrictions on how much is eaten - the level of food intake in terms of calories and/or carbohydrates, and on what is eaten. The limitation in the amount of carbohydrate has been traditionally the main restriction in the diabetic diet. Diabetics are given a daily carbo- hydrate allowance and encouraged to space out their intake of carbohydrate so that it is evenly distributed between meals. Sugar and sugar or glucose-containing foods are proscribed because they are highly concentrated forms of carbohydrate too rapidly absorbed into the system.

The common expectation about the diabetic way of life is clearly illustrated in the following case. The interviewee and her youngest son were both diabetic. She said that she did not eat sweets, her son no longer liked sweets, and that they neither of them had sweet puddings. Sunday tea with jelly, ice cream, biscuits and cakes was a ritual with the family and she bought diabetic biscuits and cakes so that she and her son did not miss out. She felt that all would be well so long as she stuck to the rules,

> If you cheat you suffer for it....Aren't all diabetics
> different? I find with me if I've got a lot of sugar I'll fall
> asleep all over the place. I get a terrible taste in my mouth
> and I'm a very irritable and nasty person to be with when I've
> got a lot of sugar. If I'm grumpy at the family they're going
> to be irritable, and then the whole house is upside down.

She explained that one of the restrictions of being a diabetic was that

activities had to be carefully planned - you could not just get up and
go out for the day - and she complained about the cost of diabetic
foods.

Diabetics' daily lives are hedged by special rules and restrictions in
which the question of diet becomes explicitly one of morality. Advised
to exclude a wide range of sweet foods[3] diabetics must deny themselves
the contents of the patisserie, bon-bons and other 'goodies'. The very
words, bon-bons, goodies, are indicators of a social valuation of these
foods. Etymologically the word sweet can be traced back to a root
meaning 'pleasing to the senses or mind, dearly loved or prized'.[4]
The 'sweet' has been equated with the 'good' for a long time. Diabetics
learn that, for them,'sweet' must equal 'bad'. They have too much sugar
in their systems. Indeed it is proposed that this is the result of over
indulgence in sugar or, at any rate, carbohydrate, in the past,[5] so
it seems logical to cut down on the current amount eaten - retribution
for past dietary wrongdoing. The medicine may not taste so good. As
sweets are given as rewards in our society, there is an undeniable
element of punishment in the withholding of sweets from diabetics, even
if it is symbolic rather than physiological.

Sweet, however, is not always 'bad' for a diabetic any more than sweet
is always 'good' for a non-diabetic. As I will show, the medical
authorities' attitude towards sweet foods for diabetics appears
ambiguous, and the valuation of sweet foods in our society may be
undergoing a change. Recent indictments of sugar - whether in health
education campaigns (DHSS, 1978), whether as temptation for slimmers
against which Jean Nidetch in The Story of Weight Watchers rails, or
among advocates of whole foods, nutritionists (Yudkin, 1977) or critics
of the policies of the food industry (e.g. the Politics of Health Group
pamphlet 'Food for Profit') - contribute to valuations of sugar as bad.
In the absence of a fuller study of social meanings of 'sweet' I can
only speculate that an ambivalence in the diabetic world reflects
contrasting conceptions in the wider culture.[6]

Examination of the symbolic significance of 'sweet' in the diabetic
diet also reveals another aspect of morality involved in diabetic
ideology. As already noted the medical theories about disease implicate
diet. As a result its management involves an important element of
'medicalisation' of diabetics' daily living. In common with other
chronic conditions, sufferers are faced with a continuing dilemma - am I
'normal', am I 'ill'?

These questions are confronted in Balance, a bi-monthly magazine
published by the British Diabetic Association (BDA). A content analysis
of two years' issues of this publication[7] showed that its pages were
full of encouragement to diabetics to lead a full and normal life in
spite of possible restrictions, and many denials that diabetes
represented any kind of handicap. In most issues there was a feature
on a celebrity, or someone who had achieved some distinction, who was a
diabetic. There was often an article on a strenuous sport in which
diabetics had successfully taken part. The overall message from these
articles seemed to be: 'Anything a 'normal' person can do, a diabetic
can do as well, if not better'. One could get the impression that far
from being a handicap, diabetes could be a spur to achievement. A
health visitor, who gave health education talks to diabetics, wrote in
an article in Balance:

And by the way, we prove that most diabetics are better than non-diabetics.[8]

A diabetic correspondent ended his letter to the magazine:

Diabetics are quite able to compete with non-diabetics and come out on top.[9]

Every issue of Balance carried advertisements, often in colour, sometimes a whole page. The advertisements were mostly for foods and drinks produced especially for diabetics and dieters, without sweetening, or containing a sucrose substitute. Their wording reflected not only the struggle for normality in a diabetic's life, but also the idea of going one better than non-diabetics precisely because the products were in some way special and superior - thus making a virtue of necessity!

The following advertisements for Frank Cooper products illustrated the theme that diabetics need not be restricted in their diet, nor miss out on the good things, life's treats:

Dieting need not mean giving up the sweet things in life. Here's something to keep you sweet. After all, by only adding water to our fruit, we're adding variety to your diet. Just because you're a diabetic, doesn't mean you can't be a gourmet.

In the same style, others stressed joining in as usual, staying in touch with the normal world of real honey, beer and biscuits:

The Ale that allows you to be in with the crowd (Low C)

For the first time Zeese brings you the full taste and aroma of real honey - but without sucrose....

Diabetics like to enjoy the good things in life - like a long, cool glass of lager....(Konig Diabetic Lager)

Diat Pilz is the beer for people who want to stay in good shape. They no longer need to forego their normal glass of beer....

Now you can enjoy all those soft drink flavours (Boots).

Sample the sweet life (Boots pastilles, chocolate and biscuits).

Count yourself in for a taste of the sweet life - with Vivil, the sugarless sweets.

Then there were those slogans which referred to the superiority of the products - often in the same nostalgic terms, both 'whole' and mass-produced foods are promoted (c.f. Atkinson, 1979):

They contain no added sugar whatsoever. Just the natural sugar that's present in the fruit itself. As a result their calorific value is exceedingly low.... (Frank Cooper).

Fructose is the sweetest of all naturally occurring sugars, about 1½ times sweeter than ordinary sugars - more than twice as sweet as sorbitol. It leaves no after-taste or unpleasant side effects.

Ideal in all slimming diets. Fruit sugar is better too for all members of the family. Not only is it excellent in all sweet dishes, accentuating the natural flavours of fruit jams, etc. but it causes less tooth decay than ordinary sucrose, and it's ideal for athletes and others who need to build up reserves of energy. (Dietade).

Your special lemon curd still made the good old-fashioned way. Nothing but good things go into our diabetic lemon curd (Ratcliffe's).

Savour the tang of the world's most prestigious marmalade.... Discriminating palates around the world choose Frank Cooper products. Not from necessity but from a simple preference for better things.

If the 'sweet' often equals 'good' according to wider cultural values, it might be expected that this would be reflected in advertisements, and that, in its attempt to encourage diabetics to feel they can lead a 'normal' life, the BDA magazine would carry adverts which suggest that diabetics need not miss out on 'goodies'. A difficulty arises because, of course, in the diabetic 'sub-culture', 'sweet' is to mean 'bad' - something to be excluded from a diabetic's life. The result is editorial ambivalence. On the one hand, considerable space is given over to advertisements for diabetic products, thus seeming to condone their message. On the other, there is recognition that they are an expensive and unnecessary part of a diabetic's diet. The editorial line on diabetic foods has tended to vary.

An editorial in the June 1976 issue in a letter complaining about the high price of special diabetic products such as sweets and preserves commented that diabetic foods are not necessary for diabetics. In December that year, in the Question and Answer section of the magazine was the following observation under the heading "Bad Ads?":

It seems to me, having read Balance for many years, that you are rather hypocritical in your attitude towards the special diabetic foods. On the one hand you advertise them on almost every page - on the other hand, you say that they are not an essential part of a diabetic's diet.

The anonymous dietician providing the answers in that issue replied:

Diabetic foods are indeed not an essential part of the diet, yet we do not feel that they can be described as luxuries. Such things as jam and chocolate are, after all, commonly used in everyday diets. Many diabetics are overweight particularly the middle-aged and elderly and so for them foods such as jam, sweets and biscuits are not allowed. For those who are not overweight they help to make the diet more normal.

Four years later, in December 1980, diabetic products were being presented as luxuries. A new section was started in the magazine in which a dietician (with name and photograph this time[10]) answered questions about diet. Part of the section under the heading 'Christmas gifts' was a list of suppliers of diabetic cakes and chocolates. A note heading the list said:

As always we do emphasize that diabetic confectionery is not essential but nevertheless recognise that on special occasions such items may be a welcome gift.

131

And on the letter page there was an editorial note[11] headed 'important' in bold letters:

> Readers are asked to note that food products advertised in Balance are not essential for a diabetic diet. Overweight diabetics are reminded that (with the exception...fruits canned in water...) these products are completely unsuitable for them. Those who do buy these products must remember to note the carbohydrate content and count it into their diet.

What is never questioned is that 'sweet' is 'good'. In the same way Stretham et al. (1981) conclude from their study of the presentation of sugar in health education literature:

> It is a universal assumption that an acceptable adult diet (apart from slimming diets) will routinely contain pudding, sweetened spreads, biscuits, cakes, confectionery and sweetened drinks....The assumption that sugar is a highly desirable food is taken completely for granted. Not only is it never questioned, but it is thoroughly reinforced.

This reinforcement comes most explicitly, the authors suggest, from routine assumptions that it is especially acceptable as a treat or gift and highly effective as a bribe or reward:

> Generally the leaflets accept the view that if you want to be somewhat indulgent, and give something that will be really appreciated, confectionery or sweet foods are an ideal choice.

The emphasis in health education literature, they report, is on avoiding 'excess' sugar consumption, that is, eating no more than the norm for the average British adult.

The way diabetic products are presented, illustrates an important aspect both of diabetic's experience of the condition - the struggle for normality, the attempt to overcome restrictions involved, and the denial of handicap. It also illustrates aspects of the medical management of the diet. The ambivalence of the official line is indicative of an uncertainty about the basic ideological stance to be taken. This can make a crucial difference to diabetics' attitudes to their condition and way of coping with it - what it means in day to day terms. The whole issue of 'forbidden foods' is related to the emphasis of dietetic and medical policy, but this has varied between one authority and another. Whether the diet should be suited to the diabetic, or the diabetic to the diet, has been a key question.[12]

Readers' letters to Balance illustrate some of the resulting 'debates':

> Many thanks for my copy of Balance. I do love reading every article. It is so helpful especially to think that I can at last have a Yorkshire pudding and pancakes. I must admit that I have missed having them for about 4 years. I also wonder if it is possible to have a small pie - all my life I have been fond of them and now my mouth waters when I see them. (April 1976).

To which the dietitian responded:

> Of course you can have a small pie so long as you watch the carbohydrates and if you are overweight, the calories.

132

Another letter sympathised:

> I feel sorry for the diabetics in Belfast who receive the Food
> Plan Card (reported in the previous issue). I couldn't
> believe the list of foods under "Foods not allowed". My
> husband has been a diabetic on insulin for 3 years and usually
> has a 20g. pudding allowance which he takes often as fruit,
> sometimes as quite a large helping of icecream, jelly, apple
> tart sweetened with fructose etc. Sausages and tinned soups
> can easily be worked into his diet using 'Carbohydrate
> Countdown'. He eats chocolate when he is out walking. We
> usually go out for a drink on Saturdays, when he eats less
> carbohydrate at his evening meal and has a couple of pints of
> beer instead. And surely there is no reason why a diabetic
> not on a weight-reducing diet should not drink dry wine and
> spirits. I thought the days of 'NOT ALLOWED' were behind us.
> (August 1976).

The dietician who had written the original article was allowed a
rejoinder:

> Obviously exchange portions have their place in the diabetic
> regimen, but they should always be used with discretion...On
> a clinical basis diabetics should preferably not take alcohol....

Similar inconsistency is illustrated in the experience of a man in his
twenties who was a representative for a firm of market consultants, one
of the study interviewees. He explained how the hospital where he was
admitted and stabilised after he was first diagnosed as a diabetic,
helped to prepare him both technically and psychologically for coping
with his condition after discharge. He was told:

> You mustn't go away thinking the diabetes is going to rule your
> life. You must go away thinking "I will carry on almost
> completely normally and I will sort of rule the diabetes". I
> mean you didn't sort of be given a diet and you had to stick to
> it.

He explained that the dietician asked what he normally ate and the diet
was fixed on that basis, and then the insulin dose fixed on the basis of
his own dietary pattern. He had been worried about how he would manage
to cope with his diet, because his job involved entertaining clients,
and lunch would sometimes be a five-course meal, sometimes a canteen
lunch, and at others, consist of a pint and sandwich in a pub. He was
reassured by being told that he could always adapt to whatever circumstances he was in. He said:

> I generally have more or less whatever I want to eat....As long
> as you stick roughly to your diet, you rule your diabetes and
> not the other way round.

He said that he had not eaten sugar or lemon meringue since he had been
diagnosed as diabetic, but that he ate lots of things that he thought
the dietician at the hospital he now attended (for out-patient checkups
every six months) would not approve of. He often ate a doughnut or a
'Milky Way' for his mid morning or mid afternoon snack, finding that it
did not affect him badly and that it was convenient. He pointed out
how different the attitude at the hospital he had first attended was
from that of the dietician he was currently seeing at the hospital: 'A
doughnut – you're not supposed to eat things like that!' (His diabetes

was very stable and he was not overweight, and he did consider the
possibility that he might have been lucky and that it was possible some
other diabetics could not eat what he did, with impunity).

The medicalisation of diabetic life extends even into the kitchen.
Doctors have a say in how much, what and when to eat - or drink - and
now food is to be prepared. The Diabetic's Handbook (published by the
BDA) reminds diabetics to ask the doctor first before following a
particular diet or including alcohol, any special slimming or diabetic
product in their diet. It spells out clearly how the diabetic's diet is
to be determined:

> The doctor in charge of your case will assess how many grams
> (or portions) of carbohydrate food you are allowed during the
> day, and you will also be told how these are to be distributed
> between the various meals. You may also be told the total
> number of calories you are allowed each day. The rest of
> your diet will be composed of free foods, that is to say the
> foods that contain little or no carbohydrate - so they need
> not be counted.[13]

There is widespread agreement among medical authorities on diabetes
that diet is an all important aspect of management of the condition.
However, there has been disagreement about the best dietary policy[14]
and considerable differences in practice in the emphasis on diet in the
control of the disorder. Observations in out patient diabetic clinics
in two different hospitals bore this out.

In hospital A patients saw the dietician for a session of instruction
when diabetes was first diagnosed. A diet was worked out with the
patient within the level of restricted carbohydrate intake set by the
doctor, and completely prohibited foods identified. Patients were given
some explanation, advice and encouragement, but no follow up appoint-
ments were made because insufficient staff were available. They were
told to come back to see the dietician if they had some dietary problem.
The doctor could refer them back if s/he thought it necessary: but only
one of the four doctors observed was seen to do so.

At this outpatient clinic the blood sugar level was measured routinely
at every visit. It was the main criterion for judging the degree of
control of the diabetic condition even though it was recognised that
such a spot check could be arbitrary. Alteration in treatment,
bargaining between doctor and patient, congratulations and rewards,
complaints and punishments, all depended on the blood sugar level.
"How's my diabetes doctor?" meant "Is my blood sugar level up or down?".
Controlling the diabetes mostly meant attempting to manipulate the
blood sugar level by altering the amount of insulin or number of tablets
taken.

In hospital B, patients saw the dietician on every visit. The blood
sugar level was not routinely measured, and when it was a test was done
after the consultation. The blood sugar level did not have the same
importance in the transactions as in the first hospital, and more
emphasis was placed on diet and the results of urine testing. For the
consultant, in particular, diet was the aspect of treatment around
which everything revolved. Weight reduction was praised and rewarded
and the bargaining here was about weight:

- Your weight's good.   You've done very well.
  You've got thinner - delighted.

- Because if you lost weight, you see, you might be able to
  do without it (insulin).

- If you want to keep your diabetes under control you've
  just got to lose weight.

- If you keep putting on weight your diabetes will get worse.

The importance of diet was constantly stressed:

- The thing is - don't give up on the diet....Keep it up
  because it's the key thing.

- We want you to get thinner - that's the best way to get rid
  of the sugar. I'd like you to have a blood test and...an
  X-ray...but the most important thing is to see the dietician.
  Provided you look after your weight, you'll be OK.

- The control of the diabetes will almost always depend on
  your weight.

The important attached to diet in Hospital B was unusual - and partly
explained by the staff's involvement in research on the use of gel-
forming fibres and complex carbohydrate in the control of diabetes.
Generally, however, the status of diet (and dieticians) in the eyes of
doctors (and patients)has not in practice been in accord with the
importance attached in theory to diet in the management of diabetes. As
already reported (Posner, 1977, p.146) one doctor attributed this to the
feeling shared alike by doctors and patients that putting someone on a
diet is not 'real medicine' like prescribing tablets or giving insulin.
Aware that a higher proportion of patients could control their diabetes
by dietary means without medicine, doctors may put the onus on the
patients saying that they will not stick to a diet anyway.   Prescribing
is in the hands of the doctor, and the level of a hypoglycaemic agent
can be more easily manipulated than the patient's diet. The diabetic
is - after all - supposedly in control of his or her own kitchen.   A
greater emphasis on dietary management of diabetes would give patients
more autonomy, and allow a more 'normal' sense of self.

There has always been agreement among medical authorities that the
unrestricted consumption of sugar or sugar containing foods is bad for
diabetics.   Though, as we have seen, there have been differences of
policy about whether occasional consumption is to be entirely forbidden
or simply 'allowed for'.   Recently, however, there has been an
important change of dietary policy in regard to the ideal level of
carbohydrate in the diabetic diet.[15] Previously diabetics were told
to cut down on the carbohydrate in their diet - the implication being
that carbohydrate in general, but sugar in particular, was bad for them.
Now they will be told, in effect, 'carbohydrate is good for you', and
encouraged to increase their level of carbohydrate intake.[16] However,
an important distinction is made between simple carbohydrate (e.g.
sweets, chocolates) which is still proscribed, and complex carbohydrate
(e.g. bread, potatoes), which nutritionists recommend - not just for
diabetics but for everyone.

This chapter has, in sum, looked at ambiguities of diabetic ideology
which are reflected and symbolised in the ambiguities centred on sweet

foods in the diet. Sweet foods have long been held to be one of life's pleasures. In the Golden Age honey dripped from the trees, honey was a word given to one's sweetheart (*sic*) in the fourteenth century, newly-wed couples were fed honey, a luxury food, for a 'honeyed moon' and promised lands flowed with milk and honey. Now that sugar is no longer a precious food, and consumption of sugar in Wester diets has dramatically increased, it seems to be the case that we have had too much of a good thing. There is now much evidence that a food which is seen symbolically as valuable and good, is nutritionally bad except in small quantities. Sugar is implicated in aetiological theories not only of diabetes but also heart disease. Indeed it has been suggested that white sugar has nothing to offer nutritionally, but, on the contrary, leeches the system of essential vitamins and minerals for its digestion (Dufty, 1975). In diabetes a high blood sugar level predisposes to gangrene and other infections. In other words for diabetics to be sweet can be, quite literally, to be bad. Should a wider cultural devaluation of sugar take hold, however, some of the ambiguity may be resolved. Diabetics' dilemmas could thus be eased, allowing them to take some comfort that the sweet life may well no longer be considered one of the quite so good things in life.

NOTES

[1]   This paper is based on work done while I was receiving an SSRC postgraduate award at the Social Research Unit, Bedford College, London University. The original version was read at a conference in February 1981 organised by the British Medical Anthropology Society. I am indebted to Anne Murcott for her help with re-shaping this paper.

[2]   The term 'ideology' is here being used in the narrow sense of a set of shared beliefs promoting a particular way of thinking about the condition, and acting in relation to it.

[3]   The typical list of 'forbidden foods' would include: sugar, glucose, jam, marmalade, honey, sweets, chocolate, ice cream, cakes, pastries, sweet biscuits, puddings made with flour, thickened soups, sauces and gravies, soft drinks, fruit tinned in syrup, sweet wines and sherries and liqueurs.

[4]   Oxford English Dictionary.

[5]   Western diet is importantly implicated in theories of the aetiology of diabetes but there is no agreement as to which aspect of diet is the most important - a total excess of calories leading to obesity, the amount of sugar in the diet, or the amount of refined carbohydrate.

[6]   The UK has one of the highest levels of per capita consumption of sugar in Europe.

[7]   1976 and 1977.

[8]   Balance No.33, p.5.

[9]   Balance No.41, p.2.

[10]   It may be that this reflected an increase in the status of diet and the dietician in relation to the management of diabetes, possibly connected with recent dietary research and the importance of the findings.

[11]   In 1981 the Nutrition Sub-Committee of the Medical Advisory Committee of the British Diabetic Association acknowledged saccharine as the only currently available non-calorific sweetener, and recommended restricted use only of sorbitol and

136

fructose, adding: '...the use of special foods for diabetics
which contain sorbitol and fructose is not recommended. Most of
these products are expensive, unpalatable and of questionable
value'. (Dietary Recommendations for Diabetics for the 1980s, p.9)

[12] The question was not posed in this way in the issues of Balance
examined. 'Forbidden foods' symbolised a more traditional and
less flexible approach to diabetic diet. The use of the
carbohydrate exchange list allows a diabetic flexibility within
a limit in terms of the number of calories per day (and sometimes
per meal) coming from carbohydrate food. So long as s/he does not
exceed that limit s/he can have what s/he likes, with a few
exceptions. The BDA's Nutrition Sub-Committee's Dietary
Recommendations for Diabetics for the 1980s (pp.11/12) came down
on the side of suiting the diet to the diabetic: 'Dietary advice
for diabetics should be tailored to individual needs, in
circumstances and preferences...In those requiring insulin the
insulin regimen used should, wherever possible, be chosen to fit
in with a patient's existing eating habits rather than attempting
to adjust the diet to a fixed insulin prescription'.

[13] The Diabetic's Handbook: Introduction to Nutrition (DH.110), p.4,
British Diabetic Association, 1972.

[14] The medical disagreements about diabetic diet have centred around
the question of whether restriction of carbohydrates or calories
is the more important and whether it is important to restrict
saturated fats.

[15] The BDA's Nutrition Sub-Committee's first two recommendations in
1981 (op.cit. p.10) were:
1. The traditional view that restriction of carbohydrate is an
essential part of dietary management of diabetics can no longer
be regarded as correct. Provided that the energy content of the
prescribed diet does not exceed individual requirements, the
proportion of energy consumed as carbohydrate is immaterial to
diabetic control.
2. Most of the carbohydrate consumed should be in the form of
polysaccharides (e.g. bread, potatoes, cereals) and the use of
foods which are rich in fibre is strongly encouraged. Isolated
sources of mono- and di-saccharides (e.g. sweets, chocolates,
sweetened drinks) should be excluded from the diet (other than in
cases of hypoglyaemic emergency or illness).
A high carbohydrate, high fibre, low fat diet was recommended for
all diabetics because of the accumulating evidence that such a
diet could reduce the risk of the development of complications.
The evidence has come from epidemiological findings, and dietary
research, e.g. Simpson et al. (1981) who concluded: 'The most
important practical conclusion is that carbohydrate restriction
still recommended for most diabetics in the UK is unnecessary and
may well be preventing patients...from achieving better diabetic
control.' (The Lancet vol.1, no.8210, 3 January 1981, pp.1-5).

[16] From approximately 40% of the calories consumed per day to
approximately 70%.

137

SECTION III

COOKING, GENDER AND HOUSEHOLD

13 Lobster, Chicken, Cake and Tears: Deciphering Wedding Meals

SARA DELAMONT

Special foods, such as 'wedding cakes' or 'roast turkey and
cranberry sauce' have special easily recognised associations
with particular occasions. (Leach, 1976, p.60)

Between breakfast and the last nightcap, the food of the day
comes in an ordered pattern.   Between Monday and Sunday,
the food of the week is patterned again.   Then there is the
sequence of holidays and fast days through the year, to say
nothing of life cycles of feasts, birthdays and weddings.
(Douglas, 1975, p.251)

INTRODUCTION

While all the papers in this collection can claim to be innovative in
that they deal with food, most focus on a relationship or topic which
has received sociological attention.   Domestic violence and the
elderly are legitimate subjects of sociological enquiry on which there
is a literature.   Thus Rhian Ellis (q.v.) can use the work extant on
battered women to examine food in violent marriages.   This paper is
rather different, in that sociological consideration of weddings and
wedding receptions is minimal.   The neglect of wedding rituals by
sociologists is odd when over ninety per cent of the population marries
at least once, and looks odder in comparison to the larger literatures
on 'minority' issues such as strikes, children in hospital, old age and
domestic violence.   This paper, therefore, is doubly a voyage in
uncharted seas.   It examines menus suggested for weddings by the mass
media, and the messages they carry about marriage, kinship systems and
the role of women in modern Britain.[1]

 The general perspective is structuralist, following Leach (1976) and
Douglas (1975), whose statements head the paper.   Both of them refer to
'wedding food' as a special social category yet neither actually
analyses how marriage meals differ from other menus.   This chapter
begins the analysis for Britain.   It falls into sections:
1   Mass media recommendations and wedding practice.
2   Wedding menus.
3   Menus as message systems.

MASS MEDIA RECOMMENDATIONS AND WEDDING PRACTICE

There are four sources of public advice on appropriate food for weddings. These are general women's magazines (Good Housekeeping), glossy wedding periodicals (Brides), cookery books (Entertaining with Elizabeth Craig) and books on marriage (Wedding Etiquette Properly Explained).[2]   Using books and magazines is obviously no substitute for researching into what people actually do and believe. However, Diana Leonard (1980, p.34) found that:

> most of the information and advice on the actual organisation
> of weddings contained in these magazines and books...is quite
> close to what I observed to happen in practice.

In the absence of recent sociological studies of marriage ceremonies (Leonard's data were collected in 1967-9) the mass media sources are all we have.   What follows is, therefore, an analysis of the messages carried by the media, and I am not claiming that people slavishly follow them.

The source material used is aimed at different markets.   The etiquette books and glossy magazines are specialist, aimed at the bride to be. In contrast cookery books and magazines like Woman's Realm are intended for any woman, whatever her marital status.   Media presentation of wedding clothing and behaviour can be gathered best from the specialist publications, such as Brides and Wedding Day, but the specialist wedding magazines do not cover wedding food.   They have cookery pages, but these deal with preparing food after marriage not what to eat at the wedding. The reception menu is the concern of the bride's mother or caterer, not the bride herself.   Similarly the advertisements in these magazines are not for food, but for dresses, makeup, and equipment for the new home.

This is, in itself, a significant 'finding'.   The bride is expected to leave both the detailed planning of the reception, and paying for it, to others.   Her father traditionally pays for it, and the food - although she may choose it - is not cooked by her.   At her wedding, the bride does not show off her skills as a cook/hostess.   She is a guest at a meal provided for her by her family, at substantial expense.

Wedding Day publishes a questionnaire every summer for couples getting married to return.   The survey receives a sizeable response (although there is no way of knowing how representative respondents are): in 1977 351 couples returned questionnaires while in 1980 they had 'over 1,600' replies.   The results shown in Table 13.1 provide the best available details of wedding practices and costs.

Table 13.1
Average Reception Costs from Wedding Day Surveys

	1977	£	1980
Food	215		400
Drink	108		158(1)
Cake	22		42
Premises	28		46
	383		646

(1)   £242 in London

In 1980 one bride reported that her reception had cost £6,626.   In

Brides (UK) (Summer 1981) an article on 'Planning your Wedding
Reception' warned:

> A lavish affair with campagne flowing freely, lots of flowers
> and first-class food could easily cost £3,000 for 100 guests
> ....For tighter budgets, a reception held in a local hall for
> 100 guests with food, flowers and cake organised by family
> and friends, sparkling wine to drink, would come to about
> £400.

The task facing the bride, or engaged couple, is to decide where the
reception will take place, and who will cook the food. According to
the magazines and books, there are two choices of cook: the bride's
mother, or a paid outsider, the caterer. There are three possible
locations: the bride's family home (house or garden), a public hall,
or a commercial club, hotel or restaurant. A paid, non-family, caterer
may provide the meal in any of these three types of location: the
bride's mother cannot cook in the commercial setting. Figure 13.1
shows the possible cook/setting combinations.

```
                        LOCATION:

                        Private

             Bride's Mother    |  Caterer
             Bride's Home      |  Bride's Home

MOTIVE:                        |
                               |
Food Provision                 |
for                            |
                               |
Love _____|_____ Money
                               |
                               |
                               |
             Bride's Mother    |  Caterer
             Hired Hall        |  Hotel/Restaurant

                        Public
```

Figure 13.1 Location and motive

The decisions about who provides the food, and where it is served,
affect the menu, the number of guests and the cost, and are affected by
them. The 'experts' are divided about whether or not it is a 'good
thing' for the bride's mother to do the cooking. Heaton's (1975)
Wedding Etiquette Properly Explained argues for a hotel or restaurant
because the modern house is too small, and

> Probably too, the bride's mother is unwilling to be burdened
> with the chores of cooking and acting as waitress and dish-
> washer on the side....(p.116)

Heaton stresses the conflict between the roles of 'cook' and 'hostess',
and emphasises cooking as a drudgery, a chore and a burden. Similarly
Gilliatt (1973, pp.48-9) talks of a hotel taking 'all the catering

worries off your shoulders' because feeding 60 to 100 guests is 'a far
bigger problem than most people imagine, especially if hot food is to
be served'.

The general women's magazines, addressing the bride's mother, have
argued the case for a 'home' fixture and all stress how easy, and how
much fun, running a daughter's wedding can be.   Thus <u>Woman's Journal</u>
(August 1981) announces cheerfully that:

> A beautiful buffet may seem like a huge undertaking. Actually
> it's only a matter of enlarging the same plans you would make
> to entertain a small group of friends at home. A buffet
> style menu is easy if you select dishes that can be completely
> or partly made ahead.

Their only warning is

> Avoid catering by yourself for more than 50.

Similar articles were found in <u>Woman's Realm</u>, <u>Woman and Home</u>, <u>Good
Housekeeping</u> and <u>Woman</u> aimed at the bride's mother, not the engaged
couple. The contrast is considerable between Heaton's woman – a drudge
– and the Bride's Mother who is <u>organised</u> to provide better food than a
commercial caterer and still enjoys the reception.   One is doing a
chore, the other is Shirely Conran's <u>Superwoman</u> (1975).   All the media
sources examined argue that the bride's duty is to look beautiful,
while other people do the work of food preparation.

We have no data on what proportion of engaged couples choose the
bride's home or a hired hall or an hotel, and who cooks for them, but
Leonard's (1980).   Most weddings in Swansea were in the morning, and
the reception was, therefore, a lunch.   Ninety-seven per cent of her
religious ceremonies were followed by a reception on commercial premises
(with around sixty guests).   The register office weddings were unlikely
to have a 'public' reception but a private meal at home.   Receptions
after church were centred on a sit-down meal, with waitress service in
a club, hotel or restaurant, that is, cooked by a commercial caterer.
The data we have suggest that the option in the bottom right of Figure
13.1, a public reception where food is provided for money, is the most
popular.

In the next section, the actual menus recommended for wedding meals
are considered, and the 'private with love' versus 'public for money'
dichotomy becomes heightened.

WEDDING MENUS: PRIVATE AND PUBLIC

The bride and those planning the wedding still have at least two other
decisions to make: the time at which the meal is to be served and
whether it is to be a sit down knife and fork meal or a standing buffet.
All the magazines and books argue for a morning wedding followed by a
lunch, and this was the pattern Leonard found in Swansea.   Accordingly
this paper ignores 'tea' menus and concentrates on lunches.

All suggested menus for wedding lunches traced are similar.   Table
13.2 shows the basic structure of the lunch menus suggested by a
variety of magazines and cookery books, from the 1915 edition of Mrs

Table 13.2
Suggested Menus

Source	Suggested Guest Nos.	Hot or Cold	1st/Fish Course	2nd/Meat Course	Pudding
Woman's Journal August 1981	25	C	Salmon	Chicken	Fruit Flan
Wedding Day Summer 1981	8	C	Salmon	Chicken	Trifle/ Meringues
Woman and Home June 1981	30	C	Salmon	Gammon	Gateaux Fruit Salad
Living April 1972	40	C	Smoked Salmon	Chicken	Gateaux
Woman's Realm 10.5.80.	50	C	Melon	Pork/ Chicken	Savarine Meringues
Good Housekeeping Cookery Book	?	C	Salmon	Chicken	Gateaux
	?	C	Melon	Mixed Cold Meat	Lemon Souffle
	?	H	Hot Lobster Vol au Vents	Turkey	Lemon Chiffon
Woman 3.4.82.	60	C	Smoked Salmon	Turkey	Chocolate Sponge
Mrs. Beeton 1915 edition	?	C	Oyster Sole Turbot Salmon Lobster	Chicken Turkey Lamb Veal Pigeon Beef Foie Gras	Fruit Creams Fruit Salads Meringues Ices
	?	H	Lobster Sole	Quails Sweetbreads Chicken Foie Gras Turkey Partridge Game Pie Pheasant	Fruit Creams Fruit Salads Pastries Ice Creams Fresh Fruit

Beeton up to the present day magazines. While Mrs Beeton's menus are more lavish, the basic structure of the wedding lunch has remained remarkably stable for a century. There may be a soup/fruit juice/ melon course before the fish, and the number and variety of vegetables varies, but the basic menu is clearly:

1) Salmon/Lobster
2) Poultry
3) Light Pudding (fresh fruit, aerated dish)
4) Wedding Cake

Accompanying such a menu should be a succession of appropriate liquids: sherry, wine, tea/coffee, champagne. The full sequence of the reception is, therefore:

1   Sherry
2   Salmon/Lobster and Wine
3   Poultry and Wine
4   Light Pudding
5   Cake and Champagne
6   Coffee and/or Tea

All but the Mrs Beeton 'winter' menu are cold meals, and a luxury food - salmon or lobster - features in many of them. They are also different from the meals in commercial places served to Leonard's sample. Leonard (1980, p.182) gives a typical menu as follows:

1   Sherry
2   Soup
3   Roast Turkey with bacon rolls
     Roast and Mashed Potatoes
     Peas
     Bread Sauce
4   Pears and ice cream
5   Coffee
6   Sherry and Wedding Cake

This menu is more like those offered by hotels to inquirers and those in Heaton's (1975) etiquette book, than those in the general magazines and cookery books. Heaton was a hotel manager, and one of his five specimen menus for a reception in a hotel or restaurant is shown in Table 13.3, along with some menus from Ladbroke Hotels (with 1981) prices. This table shows menus like Leonard's sample are typical of

Table 13.3
Commercial Menus

Source	Starter	Main Course	Pudding	Coffee?
Heaton 1	Tomato Soup	Roast Chicken Bread Sauce Potatoes, Sprouts Carrots	Peach Melba	Yes
Ladbroke Beef Menu 4 (£7.00)	Melon	Roast Beef Sprouts, Parsnips Roast Potatoes	Profiteroles	Yes
Chicken Menu 9 (£6.00)	Soup	Chicken Supreme Peas, Carrots Potatoes	Sherry Trifle	Yes
Turkey Menu 12 (£6.50)	Tomato Soup	Roast Turkey Sprouts, Carrots Roast Potatoes	Gateau	Yes

'catered', public receptions. They are also proper, cooked dinners (assuming there is gravy) as analysed by Murcott (1982a and q.v.). They could not be provided by the bride's mother (unless she missed the ceremony) because they are hot and demand constant and last minute

attention. The proper dinner is what the bride's mother would/should/
does provide on other 'special' occasions - e.g. Christmas - but cannot
on the wedding day. So she either provides a different kind of special
meal in the home or her cooking is delegated to a professional who
provides a proper dinner away from the bride's home.

The mass media are proposing two different kinds of wedding lunch
which can be represented thus:

Location	Cook	Temperature	Posture	Meal Type
Home	Bride's mother	Cold	Stand	Unusual Food
Hotel	Caterer	Hot	Sit	'Proper Dinner'

This gives us two different ideal types, one where strange food in
familiar surroundings marks the 'special' occasion, the other where a
'strange' location is familiarised by 'proper' food, albeit of a
celebratory kind. If we repeat Figure 13.1 with the food types added,

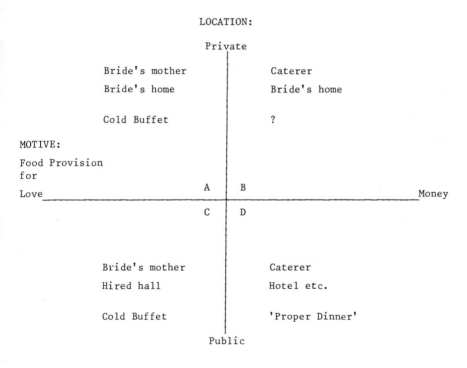

Figure 13.2 Location, motive and food types

we get Figure 13.2 above.   There is one menu which has not been
analysed, that provided by the caterer in the bride's home.   The books

147

and magazines studied all advised the bride to be guided by her caterer, who is the 'expert'. Material gathered suggests the caterer coming to the bride's home will bring a cold buffet,[3] which leaves the two message systems intact. If the reception is a 'home' fixture the food is cold and exotic, if it is in an hotel or restaurant then a 'proper dinner' is served. Both these forms emphasise the dislocation of the bride's mother from her usual role of cook: the first by the unusual foods and posture, the second by the changed location. Her role at the 'home' fixture is made strange by the bizarre menu, and at the 'away' fixture by the fact that she is a guest.

In the next section I turn to the two alternative meal plans as two different message systems and examine their meanings.

MENUS AS MESSAGE SYSTEMS

Monica Wilson (1972) has analysed the wedding ritual of the Nguni people of South Africa, paying particular attention to the apparently incongruous appearance of:

> two ornately iced cakes suggestive of a French patisserie...
> in a remote homestead, dominated by a cattle byre.

Nguni marriage parties had adapted some 'white' customs from missionaires and settlers, and among these was wedding cake. However Nguni have two cakes, one provided by each family, and the mothers of bride and groom distribute pieces of each cake to absent kin. Two cakes became new symbols of traditional ideas about lineages and fertility.

Wilson is unusual in focusing upon a food item - wedding cake - which we 'recognise', although she shows it 'means' something rather different among the Nguni. The position of this paper is similar to Wilson's, and in agreement with Leonard's (1980, p.2) comment:

> If white weddings are alive and well in the second half of the
> twentieth century, it is not because they are outdated
> charades, but rather because they make important statements
> about, among other things, the nature of marriages and family
> relations.

The two types of reception - in terms of location and food - have to be seen in this way. What is being transmitted is a statement about proper food and the proper role of women. At the wedding reception the bride's family are both despatching the bride into a new family unit and demonstrating what kind of people they are. Receptions show the groom, his kin and the guests what life style the bride has and therefore what she should be entitled to in future. That far the two kinds of reception are similar. Both cost money, and show that the bride's father can afford to provide a good meal. But the bride is about to become responsible for feeding the groom so it is also important to show what kind of food her upbringing has led her to treat as proper. The two kinds of reception symbolise this transfer - from a girl who is cooked for, to a woman who does the cooking - in different ways.

The hotel-based 'proper' dinner conveys two clear messages. First the bride's family know what a proper meal looks like, therefore the bride does, and therefore she can and will provide proper dinners for her new

husband (Murcott, 1982a and 1983b). The second 'message' is that –
because this meal is in a public place outside the home – the bride is
no longer entitled to have meals cooked for her by her mother in her
natal home. The phase of 'keeping close and spoiling' so well described
by Leonard (1980) is over, and this is captured by the last financial
indulgence which is not accompanied by domestic labour from the parents.

Leonard's sample saw a commercial reception as necessary for a proper
wedding. Registry weddings did not have an hotel reception, and meals
cooked by 'mum' were second best. Magazines which advocate a stylish
home reception challenge hotel domination, by offering a different
message. The bride's mother is Superwoman, a cool, calm, collected
hostess with organising ability and technological resources (such as
freezer, mixer and microwave) (c.f. Murcott, 1983a). She saves money
for her husband by catering herself, and displays that she is a better
cook than the professionals. This reception shows the world (and the
groom) that the bride has been raised by, and hence will be, the perfect
hostess, the highly organised wife. Only a family in good housing will
contemplate a reception at home from choice so the financial standing of
the bride's father is displayed by the setting of the reception, against
which the home produced food is a kind of 'symbolic' economy, negated by
the expensive food items in it.

To summarise: the message system of the two kinds of wedding
reception is that 'traditional working class' and 'middle class
superwoman' have produced two rather different kinds of bride. The role
of women is not the same in all classes, but varies along the lines
proposed by Dorothy Smith (1977). Smith argues that 'Industrialisation
cannot...be treated as a unitary factor in interaction with other
factors'. As far as women are concerned she has suggested that the
working class family relates to industrial capitalism in a different
way from the managerial/bureaucratic middle class (who do not own
capital). The working class woman is 'central to the home as an
enterprise' because:

> Her achievement as a housewife was apparent in her ability to
> set a good table and in having plump, healthy and clean
> children...Her work still has a vital significance in that
> the order of the home as moral and material order is the
> product of her labour and primarily her responsibility.

The wedding reception provided on commercial premises is, therefore,
highly symbolic. It makes the wedding as an especially 'sacred',
'unusual', 'non-normal' occasion, when the working class woman does not
cook. Because it is special, it reinforces the usual, profane, mundane
meal provision which is the normal woman's usual task. Having a meal
'out' is a rite of reversal commonly used to make important status
passages (e.g. Leach, 1976). It is like donning a carnival mask, or
the officers waiting on the men in the mess once a year, or wearing
clothes inside out.

Smith proposes that the relationship of the middle class family 'to
the corporation becomes an enactment of the moral order legislated by
the corporation'. The job of the corporation wife is 'to manage this
imaged order'. The media have become increasingly dominant as a source
of 'definition of form', and 'an autonomous source of stylistic
determination'. These media present a 'display order' that:

is oriented toward an externally defined system of household
decor, taste, standards of cleanliness etc....It is not
sufficient that the clothes and bedding be clean, they must
be seen to be clean....The internal decor of the house
becomes an end in itself which may have little to do with
the comfort or convenience of the inhabitants.

Because the 'corporation wife' is affluent, her work is not essential.
Services are bought, not performed by the woman herself. Smith says
this is why 'creative' hobbies are so characteristic of the middle
class wife. She produces only for display, not for the market or for
essential use. In short:

the corporate enterprise establishes women as its 'executives',
analogous to their husband's position as managers. Nothing is
left to women but the execution of an order, whose definition
is not hers.

For Dorothy Smith, then the:

middle class woman has been alienated from all that was once
hers. In the time when existence was difficult, it was an
enormous accomplishment for a woman to create and maintain a
family....The home was a place she created, usually with her
own hands....

Today, however, when the home is a media created image:

her skills become irrelevant with the elaboration of
technology....She is honoured for her taste or her ability
to "find bargains"....The home, its concrete arrangements,
is the woman's product in which she is objectified....

The media image of the bride's mother who has created the 'perfect
wedding buffet' for her daughter is exactly this 'objectified' woman.
The wedding meal, full of luxury foods presented in a beautiful home or
garden, is indeed 'oriented' to 'the values and standards of an
externalized order'. She normally buys services, but for this meal she
performs them herself. Organising the meal, but appearing at the
ceremony, is a public statement of her managerial skills. She demonstrates that not only can she organise and cook, but also that she can
be seen to organise and to have cooked.

Thus the two contrasting types of wedding menu suggested in the mass
media are actually appropriate for two different sorts of woman, who
are related to the capitalist system in two rather different ways.

NOTES

[1] I am grateful to Paul Atkinson and Anne Murcott for incisive
criticisms of the early versions of this chapter. Edmund Leach,
Esther Goody and Marilyn Strathern taught me the anthropology it
draws on, though the latter may dislike this analysis. Kathleen
Edwards and Val Dobie typed my disorganised manuscripts into a
publishable form and I am very grateful to them.
[2] This article is based on the following sources:
i. General women's magazines: Woman's Journal August 1981, 'The
Wedding Breakfast'; Woman and Home June 1981, 'Wedding Reception
in the Garden'; Living April 1972, 'Wedding Buffet'; Woman's

150

Realm May 3rd 1980, 'The Perfect Wedding Cake' and May 10th 1980 'The Perfect Wedding Buffet'; Good Housekeeping August 1981 'Your Wedding GH Style'; Woman April 3rd 1982 'Artful Ways to a Grand Wedding'.

ii. Specialist wedding magazines: Brides and Setting Up Home (UK edition) Summer 1981, and Autumn Preview 1981; Brides (American edition) June/July 1981; Wedding Day and First Home Spring 1981, Summer 1981, Early Autumn 1981. These were augmented by an earlier analysis of the 1977 issues of the magazines used in Delamont (1980).

iii. General cookery books: Mrs Beeton's Household Management, 1915 and 1923 editions; Entertaining with Elizabeth Craig (1933) Collins London; The Best of Good Housekeeping.

iv. Wedding etiquette books: Planning your Wedding, E. & D. Woods (n.d.); Wedding Etiquette Properly Explained, V.Heaton (1975) 4th ed. Paperfronts, Elliot Right Way Books, Kingswood, Surrey; 'Brides' Guide to Planning your Wedding, M.Gilliat (ed.) (1973) Collins London.

[3] The passages on receptions abound with the phrase 'the caterer will advise you....' One caterer who advertises in Wedding Day called 'Travelling Fayre' offer menus (and a marquee with accessories) which are an example of Category B in Figure 13.2. The food is essentially similar to that recommended for the bride's mother by the magazines: that is cold buffets of the 'prawn cocktail, cold turkey' and 'chilled soup, poached salmon' kind, with the most expensive menu being: Chilled Watercress Soup, Poached Scotch Salmon, Roast Turkey, Salads (four kinds), Raspberry Flan, Cheese, Champagne, Coffee, at £10.50 in 1981 including half a bottle of wine. Thus quartile B has 'cold buffet' in it as well.

14 You are What You Eat: Food and Family Reconstitution

JACQUELINE BURGOYNE AND DAVID CLARKE

The mundane tasks of cooking, eating and clearing up - such central activities within any domestic regime - are curiously absent from existing sociological descriptions of family life. Certainly a series of studies of marriage and the domestic division of labour (Bott, 1971; Edgell, 1980; Leonard, 1980; Young and Willmott, 1973) along with some works on parenting and childcare (J. and E. Newson, 1970) do offer tangential insights into the social arrangements for cooking and consuming food, yet on the whole the very taken-for-grantedness of the subject has tended to obscure it from the sociological record. This is unfortunate, for food, meals and mealtimes can tell us much about other aspects of the domestic world. Recent research on 'irregular' families of various kinds has highlighted this and the comments of Ferri (1976), Marsden (1975, pp.43-4), George and Wilding (1972, pp.131-2) and Wallerstein and Kelly (1980, p.42) all reveal how the consumption of particular foods in particular ways may mirror other aspects of family organisation. Mealtimes are a well known and powerful symbol of domesticity: variations in food beliefs and practices may therefore point to more fundamental sources of variation in family life itself.

We have recently become interested in the manner in which food, eating and mealtimes may provide a new dimension for exploring the experiences of those who divorce and remarry and who pass, along with their children, from one domestic regime into another. Remarriage and step-families contain wellknown stereotypes of food and mealtime problems. Brenda Maddox, in her book The Half Parent remarks,

> In many stepfamilies meals are excruciating, the time when the expectation of happy family life comes up against the reality ....Just as the image of the stepmother is witch, so the image of her food is poison. (Maddox, 1975, pp.136-7)

To suggest, as Maddox does, that the mealtable may be a battlefield upon which stepfamily tensions are fought out, is to recognise that meals, food and eating can play an important part in the total process of family reconstitution after divorce. Accounts of this process may tell us something not only about divorce and remarriage but also about the more general relationships between food and family life.

In our interviews with forty divorced and remarried couples in Sheffield[1] we encountered numerous references to food and eating, invoked to illustrate a wide range of family and personal circumstances, from breakdown and separation to the experience of restarting with a new partner. Many of these references were quite spontaneous and

unsolicited, though we did ask some specific questions on the domestic
division of labour in both first and second marriage. Where references
to food occur, therefore, they allow us to tap an interesting dimension
of the divorce and remarriage process.

The most obvious way in which remarried members of our sample talked
about food was in seeking to illustrate specific contrasts between first
and second marriage. Change would usually be described in one of two
ways: either from a predominantly separate domestic regime to an
essentially shared one, or vice versa. Mrs Dunwell[2] illustrates the
first type.

> In this marriage my husband is a completely different person,
> in that he loves cooking for a start, so any time he comes home
> after he's been at work, if I've not got the tea ready...and I
> say that I didn't feel like it...he takes over and does it,
> which is smashing, it's really good. It's completely different
> from the other marriage.

Some men were similarly inclined to describe greater involvement in
culinary tasks. Mr Hurst:

> With the first wife I didn't do anything really, there was just
> no encouragement to do anything, you know. I came home, had me
> tea, read the paper, watched television, had a lazy sort of
> life. But with the present wife, if I come home and she's not
> home I cook tea, so it's usually ready for her when she gets in
> ...do what I can for her...and that's the difference.

Indeed, in some cases, this increased involvement on the part of
husbands appeared to be elevated to a full blown rhetoric of equality.
Mrs Baker:

> Well, if he comes in from work and I'm at home, then the meal's
> cooked ready for him...but I'm working two full days a week and
> I work a half day as well. But the days when I'm at home,
> then I get the tea ready, just as I could expect him to get it
> ready if I was out and he was at home. In other words we take
> equal shares in everything, more or less.

In a similar number of cases however change was apparently in the
opposite direction, away from shared tasks and joint involvement to more
clearly defined and circumscribed duties. In keeping with a desire to
maintain an overall favourable comparison between first and second
marriage, this too was depicted as a desirable state of affairs, usually
by husbands, but sometimes by wives as well. Mr Powell:

> I did far more then than what I do now...I'd wash t'pots and
> peel potatoes and things like that, which I don't do now.

> Why is that?

> Er - I don't really know...er, there were certain things wrong
> with my first marriage which I didn't think were going to
> happen and which I knew weren't going to happen again, and
> that was one of them. You know, male chauvinist and all
> t'rest of it...you know, it's summat I'd been brought up not
> to do and I did it t'first time I got married and I'll not do
> it this time.

Mrs Hutchinson:

This husband does less. - what I would call housework than the
first one did. He doesn't...well...sweep up, wash the dishes
or cook a meal. He doesn't go out on his own, unless, sometimes he does on Sunday dinner when he's in the kitchen and in
the way...Sunday dinnertime I like to do it all myself...So
yes, there is quite a radical difference as far as that's
concerned, 'cos me first husband would do washing, he'd wash
up, he'd cook...and I resented it...it was because he hadn't
got a job and he wanted something to do and I resented the
fact that he'd taken it off me.

All these examples suggest that food, cooking and mealtimes might make
up a part of the vocabulary wherein men and women explain their current
domestic circumstances, such as in the contrast between first and
second partners. A careful reading of our data reveals however that
food references occur in numerous other contexts and not merely in
response to direct queries about the domestic division of labour.
Indeed, the preparation and consumption of food are subjects which we
find accompanying numerous accounts of the entire process of divorce
and remarriage.

FOOD AND MARITAL PROBLEMS

Given the centrality of food and eating within the domestic world, it is
not surprising that a number of men and women described conflicts and
problems in first marriage which centred around mealtimes and in which
the meal itself might be the pretext for airing more deeply rooted
dissatisfactions. In many cases it is clear that these problems have
their origin in circumstances more complex than the specific mealtime
incident described. For example, Mrs Hutchinson, whom we have already
met and whose husband had refused to work from shortly after their
marriage, leading the life of a semi-recluse, described how she did not
cook any meals for him for several years: 'if he wouldn't do any work
for us, I wouldn't do any work for him'. Whilst Mr Gilmour recalled
how, after working long hours he would frequently arrive home late, eat
a meal and then fall asleep in his chair.

I was tired, it had been a very busy day, er...because I used
to start work early in the morning, I never used to get a
break or anything. I used to completely work through the
day. I ate as I worked and drank as I worked...er, I might
come home sometime, eight o'clock, nine o'clock at night...I
wasn't in the mood for talking, I'd have tea and sit down in
a chair, she'd start talking to me - next thing you know,
I'd dropped off to sleep...I can certainly appreciate that
side of it, at the same time I don't think the wife
appreciated my side of it.

In some cases, the family meal - for example the traditional Sunday
dinner - deliberately contrived as an occasion when the whole family
could be together, seemed to misfire completely and become the crucible
for disharmony and conflict. Mrs Smithson recalled her husband's
jealousy of their eldest son, Robert.

He picked on Robert a lot, it were as though he were jealous
of him, you know, er...he even, on a Sunday, he used to
count Robert's potatoes, believe it or not, and Robert loves

154

meat, he's always from being right small loved meat...and,
er...for example, he used to...I used to give him his Sunday
dinner, 'cos really that's the only time we had dinner
altogether with him working shifts, you know, and he used to
count his potatoes and more often than not, Robert used to
end up on t'stairs crying and not have his Sunday dinner
because he'd picked on him so much, so it used to upset
everybody, nobody used to eat.

Similarly, Mrs Bingham, who in her first marriage had married a widower
with two children, described her husband's jealousy towards their own
baby.

I can remember him being a bit jealous when Catherine was
born, which surprised me really 'cos he'd already got two
children and I can remember when I fetched Catherine home
there used to be rows if his tea weren't ready on the table
when he came in, you know, because I'd always had his tea
ready when he walked in and...when you're feeding a new
baby, you're sat for hours waiting and messing about with
'em and if his tea weren't ready he used to play hell....

Several other women were able to recollect similar incidents when
conflicts arose over meals not being prepared at the appropriate time
and when highly segregated role relationships served to censure a woman
who 'failed' in wifely or motherly duties.   In a few cases such
incidents spilled over into violent outbursts which found a ready
pretext in the discontents of the stomach (Ellis q.v.).   Mrs Hobson,
again recalling a father's problem of adjustment to a new baby,
described the following incident:

He suddenly changed, as soon as Jason came on t'scene. One
Christmas, Jason had got measles and he came home in a
right temper...I says well, what about his dinner, 'cos
there weren't no dinner ready, well I thought he'd had his
dinner already...and 'cos his dinner weren't ready he went
up in t'air, y'know, and throws this plastic car - supposed
to hit me - and it went through t'window and then he broke
another window chucking summat else at me.

EATING ALONE: DIET AND HEALTH

If specific mealtime incidents could sometimes act as painful reminders
of unhappiness in a first marriage, then a general description of eating
habits was frequently cited as one of the more obvious consequences of
marriage breakdown and separation.   It is important to see the ways in
which the disruption of a particular set of social phenomena can lead
to a better understanding of their normal, routine and taken for granted
aspects.   In this case, descriptions of diet, health and eating habits
during the period of separation help to reveal normal expectations of
such matters within marriage itself and also point, as we shall see, to
the manner in which problematic aspects might be overcome.

When we asked our respondents to describe their feelings, mental
states and health prior to, during and immediately after the period of
separation, one of the most common indicators of their general condition
at those times was that of a change in weight - either gain or loss.

Weight change was cited by just under a half of our divorced respondents, though the form which it took was usually related to highly specific and situated aspects of their experience of separation and family reconstitution.   In general weight loss, which was the most common, related to periods of unhappiness during or immediately after marital breakdown, whereas weight gain might be associated with either the 'relief' of ending an unhappy relationship, or more usually with the satisfaction which came from beginning a new one.

Loss of weight was frequently experienced as part of a more general state of debilitation following separation, during which physical symptoms combined with confused mental states to produce a feeling of uncertainty and disorientation.   Mr Mosely:

> I lost...I don't know...about two stone...er, I couldn't sleep very well, I didn't really feel like eating at times. I don't know, somehow at the back of me mind, I knew it was for the best, you know, that it finished, but - er, why, I just don't know.

Mrs Chapman:

> Well, I lost a tremendous amount of weight. I was on nerve tablets y'know and in fact they finally had to take t'tablets off me 'cos I were getting to such a state that I'd have took t'lot, you know, and finished it all.   And I were thin and drawn and I couldn't sleep and I wasn't eating at all.

Mrs Worthing put it very vividly:

> I just didn't...I couldn't eat...just didn't want to eat... and I dunno, I were just full up all the time and didn't want to eat anything.

Among those who lived alone for a time after the separation, such states were often compounded, especially for men who had been used to relying upon their wives for regular meals (c.f. Hart, 1976, p.145).   Mr Fox sums up the feelings of anomie and disruption:

> Well I wasn't eating regularly, not as much as what I was before, 'cos I was having to get me own meals...and I'd probably, like, say when I was on mornings, I'd probably have a sandwich at work, come home and have a drink of tea when I got home...some days it might just be a sandwich that I'd have all day.   And then probably another day, I'd say to meself, 'Well, I'm hungry, I'll have summat to eat'. And where I lived then, there were only a shop about a hundred yards from me, and I used to talk mesen into having a meal. I used to say that I'd have this and I'd have that and I used to go to the shops and get it all and come back and cook it, and then I found that I didn't really want it....

Other men found support from sympathetic parents who appeared to see their sons as incapable of adequately feeding themselves whilst living alone. Mr Browning described his experience:

> I used to buy food...but when I did that...it were just a case of mainly t'chip pan or t'frying pan...for a few months ...and then me parents said, 'Well, do you want to come and have your meals with us before you go out to work?' - like when I was on nights. I got out of doing it then...making a

decent meal.

Accounts of this sort seem to make an appeal to more widespread assumptions about male involvement in culinary tasks; the inept <u>man</u> in the kitchen is certainly a more convincing stereotype in our society than the incompetent woman. Consequently, separated men would tend to see the absence of regular meals as one of the more difficult aspects of living alone. In some cases those who could afford it would have an evening meal in a restaurant, or ate each day with a neighbour. Others benefitted from a degree of public sympathy for their plight which would be unlikely to extend to the estranged woman - such as Mr Hutchinson who described being given five Christmas dinners the year that his wife left him. An important exception to this male-female difference occurs however in the case of custodial parents' references to food, cooking and mealtimes during a period as head of a single parent household. Custodial fathers - who were over-represented in our sample[3] - show up in marked contrast to the other divorced men we interviewed insofar as they place a strong emphasis upon their success in organising regular and wholesome meals for their children - despite pressures of time, work commitments and a lack of previous experience in the kitchen. Mr Heathcote described some of the difficulties:

> Well, the work suffered in as much as I got custody of the kids, so that I had to see them at school for nine o'clock in the morning...they had lunch at school and then I had to come back to bring them home at about half past three...bring them home and feed them and what have you...and if I'd got to go out on business again in the evening, arrange a babysitter so that I could go out.

Nevertheless, he made a special point of continuing with other aspects of the family routine.

> I cooked Sunday dinner every week after my wife had gone. The lot - from Yorkshire pudding to roast potatoes - and proved to myself that I could do it.

In some instances, custodial fathers appeared to find the experience of single parenthood - 'being a mother and a father to them' - highly educative. Mr Chapman:

> It were hard for me at first, it were very hard. I mean just a stupid thing like doing a Sunday dinner, I used to have to be running about all over t'place. There'd be one thing ready before summat else, y'know, and by the time - for argument's sake - t'meat were in and that weren't done, t'potatoes and greens would be ready...they'd be cold by t'time the meat were ready y'see...so therefore I just had to adjust and with trial and error get everything right, y'know, so that everything's ready at the same time. But as I say, you gradually get used to that. I mean I suppose it's like a young couple getting married, I mean the woman's probably just in the same state as what I were in, I mean she's got the meals to get ready, she's probably never done a meal in her life before, but it gets easier as time goes on.

In certain cases this sort of involvement in domestic tasks served as a mechanism for coping with the emotional difficulties of life in a single parent family. Problems of <u>time</u> associated with lone parenthood

(Hipgrave, 1981) may be of two kinds - either too little time or too much. Mr Baker, for example, claimed he coped well with his domestic duties, but found the problem of loneliness more difficult to deal with.

> It was difficult to start off with...not the cooking, I could manage that, but the loneliness. I mean the kids were in bed for half past eight...that was it once they'd gone to bed, it was just a case of watching the television or just sitting waiting for the 'phone to ring. It was the loneliness more than anything else.

For the custodial father, to provide the children in his care with regular and properly cooked meals, is not merely to ensure their dietary and physical wellbeing, but points to a broader concern with the maintenance of a sense of stability in the home environment. For many Sheffield families, as we can begin to see here, the traditional Sunday dinner of meat, roast potatoes, Yorkshire pudding and vegetables forms an important element within the routine of a settled and stable family life. To produce the meal in its full version - something of a logistical feat in itself according to one informant - is therefore to enact a powerful ritual of reinforcement, communicating to self and children alike, that despite marital separation, 'normal life' continues much as before.

RECONSTITUTING THE FAMILY

For most of the men and women we interviewed however 'normal life' seemed only to be possible with the regular presence of a partner, and in many cases the search for a new mate - if indeed such a relationship had not itself precipitated the breakdown of the first marriage - was usually self conscious and expeditious. Courtship, cohabitation and remarriage were therefore the processes in which 'starting anew' found expression. Where the strains of living alone or the burdens of single parenthood bulk large in personal accounts of separation and divorce, it is quite common for seemingly mundane and everyday matters to be invested with considerable significance and given a pivotal place in the narrative, around which important events may turn.

Second courtships occurring among older couples with children reveal the process in an interesting way and in contrast to conventional romantic stereotypes, tend to incorporate domestic and humdrum routines. Indeed, it may be the successful accomplishment of such routines which forms an important part in the decision-making process of a new relationship. Mr Hurst, a custodial father to two children, who remarried a mother of three:

> I wanted to see how they'd get on...so er, as I say, I took them up there, Saturday and Sunday, then the following weekend they came down here...and I cooked a meal for the...you know, she cooked a meal up there, Saturday and Sunday, then I cooked down here Saturday and Sunday...and...er, everybody got on very well, so er, we knew then there weren't any problems.

Bachelors, too, appear to have had considerable involvement with their divorced partners' children during the period of courtship; and clearly in some cases these previously unmarried men, perhaps enjoying a reasonable level of material comfort, appeared attractive to children whose mothers were struggling to care for them in a single parent household. The Farmers are a case in point. Mrs Farmer describes the period when she was living alone with her four children:

> I had an awful lot of trouble with supplementary benefits...I used to receive a Giro cheque every week and this was payable on a Saturday and I found week after week I wasn't getting my Giro cheque on the Saturday and that meant that at the weekend I wasn't getting any money...I'd have to borrow all weekend. In fact some weekends there wasn't anyone to borrow off, so we'd got to manage...and the kids went without meals during the weekend, you know, so that was a really trying time....

After she met Trevor, a bachelor with his own car and a well-paid job, the situation at weekends began to alter. Mr Farmer:

> ...weekends it were nowt for me to take t'kids out – petrol at that time was 38p per gallon and...er...I used to take 'em out every Sunday really. They had their dinners – they'd have their sandwiches in plastic bags and trifle and that...I always took the kids with me, the kids took to me straightaway.

Indeed, neglect of the children during the courtship period could be a source of guilt to some men and women who felt that it was perhaps unreasonable to subjugate children's interests to their own. Mr Moseley:

> I felt a bit at times that we didn't pay enough attention to them...or we weren't with 'em as often as we ought to have been with 'em. They've suffered that way a bit... particularly before I moved here...in that Marian would come home, probably cook them a quick meal, then she'd go straight out and they'd be in bed by the time she came back.

On the whole however, the reconstitution of family life through new relationships, cohabitation and eventual remarriage was accompanied by increasing feelings of having 'done the right thing' and thus tended to produce a greater sense of personal wellbeing. If weight loss had been one of the adverse consequences of separation, weight gain was a possible concomitant of a new relationship, Mrs Moseley:

> In the last two years I've put a stone and a half on, since Graham and I have been living together...I've put a stone and a half on in that time.

> Yes, what do you put that down to?

> I think...er, just ease and comfort and no big worries... I've no big worries at all now, because we've nothing really to worry about...we've managed to get over the little stumbling blocks.

Mr Worthing's account echoes this and also places weight gain more precisely in the context of the new relationship, drawing on a number of relevant factors.

> In the two years since it finished I've put on about two stone.

> You've started putting weight on since you separated?

> Yes

How do you account for that?

Er...well there's several factors...the main one possibly is the fact that I stopped smoking at the same time and I would say that I eat more, but there again you can tie that down to the fact that I've stopped smoking perhaps...I definitely eat more.

Was there any particular reason why you gave up smoking?

Well, Diane (new partner) didn't like it and for years I've always been one of those that's er...sort of stopped every month and lasted about a day, I've really wanted to health-wise...Diane had never smoked and she didn't like it, so it gave me the added incentive - I stopped quite easily.

And your weight went up then did it?

Yes I enjoyed food more and I ate a lot more.

In some respects this sense of personal wellbeing was the touchstone whereby many of our respondents were able to construct a coherent and warranted account of their experience of divorce and remarriage. Having described the unhappiness and personal miseries of a first marriage, there was undoubtedly a strong compunction to elaborate feelings of satisfaction and fulfilment the second time around. The examples which were invoked to achieve this ranged from the particular and individualistic to those which included broader references to other types of marriage. Mr Thompson:

We don't argue, she's everything I wanted my first wife to be, you know, understanding of me as a person and how erratic I am, and very domestic in that the house is always tidy and clean... there's always food in the fridge and always something to drink ...bottle of cider, bottle of beer, bottle of whisky, always something in there to drink...me meals are always there on time ...and she cooks me meals because she enjoys cooking...she'll wash t'pots straight way and not allow me to help, things like that....

Mr Wickham, on the other hand, takes a broader view.

It depends how you look at life, varied ways of looking at life isn't there? Depends what you want...I mean I can take you to houses in this street, not what I want, they're like bleeding show houses with big car and caravan outside...they're both working, they see nowt of each other...well who wants that sort of life? We're comfortable, we've got plenty of grub on t'table, that 'fridge is full...got a little caravan to retire to when we've nowt to do in t'summer...depends what you want out of life.

Of course, not all accounts were so positive and unqualified. Re-marriage frequently involves an increased and highly self conscious investment in the pursuit of an 'ordinary family life', yet the process of 'starting again' is often moulded and shaped by constraints arising out of the emotional and material heritage of first marriage. This tension between wishing to appear 'just like any other family' and the obvious differences which may result from the number and age of children, custody, access and maintenance arrangements lies at the heart of any understanding of remarriage where children are involved.

Rebuilding a family life out of diverse and fragmented origins is a programme largely made up of mundane and everyday events – such as mealtimes. Nonetheless these events are frequently invested with considerable significance, providing a ready measure whereby members may evaluate 'success' or 'failure'. An obvious example is one where the children may simply not like a stepparent's (usually a stepmother's) cooking. Mrs Heathcote, a previously unmarried stepmother to two children:

> It worried me at first...and it still does, you know, when I sort of say 'what do you want for your tea?' and they say 'oh I don't know'. You sometimes get a bit desperate...whatever you give them they don't want. Sometimes I blow my top a bit. Anything that's different that they haven't seen before – 'ugh whatever's this?'

Frequently the difficulties are more complex. Dr Parker's ex-wife had a history of mental illness. Just before the Parkers were expecting their first child in the remarriage (his second wife had not been married before) they suddenly had to take care and control of Dr Parker's daughter and stepdaughter by his previous marriage. He draws upon an interesting food metaphor in order to explain some of the problems.

> When you live as a couple...a childless couple, er...there is an awful lot of time to relate, to understand one another, to talk about things...you have time to relax over meals and various things. Children 'eat' time and consequently they 'eat' a lot of relationships as well. I mean suddenly you have three children and here you are living in a kind of buzzing cacophony of demands and relationships...I think in those first couple of months the strain was enormous really.

In the case of Mrs Graham, the problem was reversed. After her first marriage ended she lived for some considerable time with her three daughters as a single parent. She describes one of the problems which began to occur after she remarried and her new husband had to find an appropriate place within what had become a well established domestic regime. Once again we see how mealtime incidents may crystallise underlying tensions and conflicts within the family.

> This was one fear I did have before I was married. I suppose I'd just got a nice little routine going with the girls. They came in...they used to have their tea...straight from school sometimes and I used to have a bit of tea with them and that that was it finished...there was no sort of...I don't know, I can't find the right word what I mean actually. I mean I don't begrudge cooking him a dinner, you know, he's very very fussy I must admit...with food. I find it very hard...whereas I can make do with anything or I'll have a cheap cut of meat because we're a bit skint and a little meal out of it...Martin can't eat cheap cuts of meat, because they're either too fatty...he doesn't like chicken, er...you know, there's sort of perhaps four things he likes. So all week I've got to think on these four things that he likes. It's a worry because...I'm doing something different for the children, something for him which is different again and to me it's just a worry because before that I used to do one thing and that's it, we all had the same.

161

I know I'm not alone...there must be millions of other people
in the same...but it's the temperament of the person, I suppose
that determines how they adapt to the situation and, er...my
temperament doesn't seem to be adapting to it.

CONCLUSIONS

Success in 'adapting to it' appears to find some expression in our
informants' descriptions of mealtimes and eating habits. To be 'eating
properly' is therefore symptomatic of a more general sense of personal
wellbeing, in the same way that being 'off one's food' might suggest
self neglect, disruption and a state of uncertainty. Most of the men
and women we talked to described their feelings about remarriage in
terms of a quest for a more balanced, comfortable and rewarding life,
in contrast to the unhappiness of an earlier marriage. Their references
to food (with the exception of those made in response to direct
questions about the division of labour in first and second marriage)
occurred spontaneously and unsolicited within what were often detailed
and lengthy accounts of the experience of divorce and remarriage.
Within our limited and ad hoc data, it appears that it is the arrangements surrounding the preparation and consumption of meals, rather than
the food itself, which merits attention. Few references to the content
of meals occur in our transcripts, whereas issues concerning how and by
whom meals are prepared and consumed crop up regularly. We have
therefore tried to show how the context of eating may be altered by
divorce and remarriage and have drawn upon illustrations which form a
part of more general accounts of a process which inevitably contains
contrasting sets of emotions. It is important not to lose sight of the
context of these illustrations, however tempting it may be simply to
marshal 'quotable quotes'. Naturally, space prevents us from
elaborating other aspects of our study of divorce and remarriage, though
some of these have been documented elsewhere (Burgoyne and Clark 1980,
1981a, 1981b, 1982a, 1982b). It is necessary, however, to underline
that the food references which we report fit into a broader framework of
interpersonal and structural relationships.

Marriage breakdown and its concomitants are frequently perceived as
private troubles, isolated within the confines of a particular family.
Yet divorce on a mass scale inevitably produces a public response in
the legal, economic and bureaucratic arenas. This tension between remarriage as both a 'private trouble' and a 'public issue' (Wright Mills,
1970) would have to be more fully explored in any subsequent analysis
of divorce and family reconstitution in relation to diet, food and
eating habits; for as some of the literature, as well as our own
findings suggest, post-divorce arrangements - particularly those
relating to children - may have direct consequences for the diet and
health of family members. In this paper, constrained by the limitations
of our data, we have chosen to focus upon the more personal and private
aspects of remarriage and have tried to show how the various experiences
encountered by those who divorce and marry again may find echoes in
descriptions of their food and eating habits.

NOTES

[1] This research was sponsored initially by the Sheffield City Polytechnic and was completed with the aid of a grant from the Social Science Research Council. Details of sampling and the content of the interviews can be found in Burgoyne and Clark (1981a).

[2] All names are pseudonymous and were chosen by the sample couples.

[3] Of the 24 divorced fathers in our study, 13 had custody of their children, whereas national norms suggest that custody goes to perhaps 10-15% of all fathers (Eekelaar and Clive, 1977).

15 The Way to a Man's Heart: Food in the Violent Home

RHIAN ELLIS

> There are only about 20 murders a year in London and not all
> are serious – some are just husbands killing their wives.
> (Commander Hatherill of Scotland Yard, 21.2.54)

Despite a large body of writing on domestic violence[1] both in Britain
and the USA in the last few years (Marsden and Owens, 1975; Pahl, 1978
and 1981; Dobash and Dobash, 1980; Martin, 1980; Elsey, 1980;
Steinmetz and Straus, 1974; Gelles, 1974; Borowski, Murch and Walker,
1981) its causes and genesis are still shrouded in obscurity. This
paper is one attempt to develop a perspective on domestic violence,
both the extreme kind dismissed by Commander Hatherill and those attacks
which do not lead to the woman's death.[2] The argument here is that
the purchase, preparation and consumption of food form a significant,
but neglected, factor in many violent marriages. As Murcott (q.v.) has
shown, the woman's role in meal provision is a symbolic, as well as a
material, task. In this paper the woman's role as homemaker, house-
keeper and especially as cook, is examined in cases where perceived
failures of performance have led to aggression in the family. The
focus is, then, on incidents such as the following:

> He dragged me out of bed. 'Get down the f__ing stairs and get
> me summat to eat, you f__ing whore', he says. So I went down-
> stairs and put something on the cooker. Then he came downstairs
> and started on me again. He got me bent over the clothes horse
> so I couldn't move....And he just kept on hitting me and hitting
> me and I was screaming and screaming.   (Pahl, 1978, p.29)

This attack on a woman (who fled to the refuge in Canterbury) can be
considered by researchers from many angles. Here the focus is on food,
as one aspect of the marital relationship. The paper is in three
sections. First it shows that the buying, cooking and serving of meals
is one important element in many violent relationships, next the nature
of marital disputes about food is examined and then the issue of food
is widened to consider how, in such families, cooking relates to trouble
over money, time and power. The data used in this paper are drawn from
the published research material on battered women, including the
author's own (Ellis, 1982). While the data are not new, the analysis
is, although it relates to the more global argument of Dobash and
Dobash (1980).

These authors have claimed that:

the girl is taught to combine domestic skills with deference to
the authority of those males to be served. (p.79)

To illustrate this they quote women pressed into large amounts of housework as young children. One described how, at the age of seven, she
served her father his Sunday lunch:

> my mother came out and she said, 'Go get his plate and give him
> his pudding'. I'll never forget it because it was apple tart
> and custard. And I went in and I said 'Oh, I need the toilet',
> and I gave him it. I just gave it to him like that and I ran
> up the stairs to the toilet....

Her father called her back and:

> he took that plate of boiling hot custard and apple tart and
> smashed it right in my head...because I didn't hand it to him
> right. (1980, p.80)

This incident is typical in that domestic work is not just any one or
other household task but a service often and centrally concerned with
food. From an early age girls are taught to cook for and how to serve
food to men. As Murcott (1983b) points out, men conventionally play
little part in food preparation which is seen as being 'woman's work'.

Interviews carried out with battered women (Pahl, 1981; Dobash and
Dobash, 1980; Elsey, 1980) show that violence often results directly
from a perceived failure of the woman to perform 'women's tasks' such
as cookery, at the command of the man. In her study, Oakley (1974)
shows that, although women's work in the home has not received much
attention from sociologists, it is surrounded by widely held attitudes
and norms which govern, not only who does it, but how and when it is
done. For instance, where food is concerned, Murcott's (1983b) work
shows that women are expected to prepare 'good' food, on time, for men.
In violent relationships when women are perceived to fail to live up to
their wifely expectations they are beaten. While this may be seen as
an extreme sanction, it does nevertheless show that men see it as
appropriate that they should control the tasks women do and the time
these tasks are done. An examination of the literature on domestic
violence shows that first, trouble often centres on meals and second,
lack of money to buy food is a frequent complaint of the victims. Many
accounts by battered women mention trouble occurring because of their
'non-performance' of housekeeping tasks. A careful scrutiny of such
accounts shows that buying, cooking and serving food is the most
tension-ridden of these tasks.

MEALS AND THEIR TIMING

There is a clear expectation in many working class subcultures that
good wives have a hot meal on the table when the man comes home. The
Newsons (1965) capture this:

> for the man who works all day cramped at the coal face, in the
> hot vibrating cab of a heavy vehicle, standing at a clanging
> machine on the factory floor, or out of doors in all weathers
> ...the wife's first function is to feed him. Whether or not
> the rest of the family is due for a meal, the manual worker
> expects his dinner to be ready on the table within a few

minutes of his return home....If there are grown up sons living
at home, the same treatment will be accorded to them, and, if
necessary, the housewife will provide hot meals at regular
intervals as the men come in. (p.220)

One of the main issues triggering off violent episodes is violations of
this norm. Thus nearly every researcher has data on battered women who
say their husbands attacked them for failure to have a hot meal ready.
Melville (1978) reports a battered woman who:

> did not have supper ready in time - and the man attacked her
> with a hammer.

Elsey (1980, p.20) interviewed a woman who got beaten if meals were not
ready when he came home and another who reported:

> You've got to run about after him, he'd say 'I want my dinner
> and if it isn't ready I'll throw it all over you'. When I
> gave him his dinner he'd throw it all over me so I used to
> leave it. (p.24)

And in Pahl's (1981) follow-up study of 42 women who had been through
the Canterbury refuge is an interview with Doris, who said of her
husband:

> He doesn't like waiting for his meals, so if his supper's not
> being walked on to the table as he walks in the door - there's
> trouble. I have to have the meal so I just have to dish it
> up. (p.8)

Similarly, Russell and Rebecca Dobash (1980, p.101) interviewed a woman
who said:

> He had come home from work and he'd been drinking. He was
> late and I'd started cooking his meal, but I had put it
> aside, you know, when he didn't come in. Then when he came
> in I started heating it because the meal wasn't ready. I
> was standing at the sink...and he just came up and gave me
> a punch in the stomach....It was only because his tea wasn't
> ready on the table for him.

This incident is notable in that the husband had violated the wife's
expectations by returning late, after drinking. The literature reveals
that the more violent incidents occurred when the man was late, but
still expected a hot meal. Thus one of Elsey's sample (1980) said her
husband would disappear on drinking bouts for several days, but:

> If he'd spent 4 days out and come and say 'I want my bloody
> dinner', he'd expect it to be there cooked. (p.62)

Similarly a woman told Erin Pizzey (1974)

> On 10 occasions he hasn't bothered to come home all night. He
> rolls in sometimes the next afternoon after the pubs have shut
> at lunch, expecting his meal to be put on the table. (p.35)

And one of the cases reported to Borowski, Murch and Walker (1981) was
a woman whose

> boyfriend is out most nights, coming in several hours late
> for meals. (p.108)

Dobash and Dobash (1980) recorded an incident where a neighbour had

166

come to remonstrate with a violent man who

> says to her, 'I never done nothing. It's her - she never had
> my tea ready'. She says 'You dinnae expect your tea at two
> o'clock in the morning cos that's what time the car drew up
> outside the door'. He says, 'She'll have my tea ready when I
> go into this house, not when she feels like it. Going to her
> bed and all this. She doesnae work. I work. She should be
> up for me'. (p.172)

This appears to be a commonly held male belief. All the researchers
report incidents of men coming home late at night and rousing sleeping
women to cook food. Thus, Elsey (1980) reports

> there were also arguments about getting her up in the middle
> of the night to cook a meal for him. (p.20)

And, another of her sample said

> I was in bed asleep and he just woke me up and said 'your
> place is downstairs at that cooker when I come in'. That
> would be about 3 or 4 am. I told him I wait until midnight
> and if he's not in, I go to bed...he'd drag me out of bed
> by the hair, drag me downstairs and make me cook him a meal. (p.63)

Pahl (1981, p.9) interviewed a woman, who was expected to get up at
3.00 am to make her husband a cup of coffee.

The Dobash's research (1980, p.100 and also p.95) includes similar
reports to which a further issue is added - i.e. the quality of the
food provided.

> 'There's never anything in this bloody house to eat. Is
> that all you've got?'....I said we might have a bit of
> boiled ham or something...or if there's cheese. 'There's
> never anything but bloody cheese....'

Others are reported by Pahl (1981)

> I had a poker thrown at me - just because his tea was too
> weak. It's part of being a wife. (p.54)

Pizzey (1974)

> A month ago he threw scalding water over me, leaving a scar
> on my right arm, all because I gave him a pie with potatoes
> and vegetables for his dinner, instead of fresh meat. (p.34)

and Elsey (1980 - also pp.12-14)

> The meal had not been to her husband's liking, and he had
> thrown it out of the door. (p.62)

A WOMAN'S TIME

Such trouble over mealtimes is only one part of violent relationships.
Some of the men expected to control their spouse's timetable - as the
man in the Dobash study (quoted above) did when he said 'She doesnae
work. I work. She should get up for me'. Thus Binney et al. (1981)
quote a victim saying

> You did what he said or else. You went to bed when he said,

you got up when he said, you ate when he said....(pp.3-4)

Another told Elsey (1980)

> He started talking to me just like a dog, as though I was a
> servant....He'd say 'I want a cup of tea and I want it now,
> and I mean now'. (p.24)

Such attempts to organise wives' time extends beyond cooking and
serving meals to shopping:

> He used to time me when I went shopping and accuse me of going
> with other men. (Elsey, 1980, p.14)

The Women's Aid group in Kettering reported that victims:

> can't even go to the shops unless they are back in 5 minutes
> ....One woman had a packet of bones from the butcher...for
> the dog, and her husband said, 'How does the butcher know you
> have a dog? You must be having an affair with him'. He then
> beat her. (Melville, 1978)

Similarly

> If I went to the shops, I'd got to be back in half an hour,
> otherwise he'd go up the wall. (Elsey, 1980, p.26)

Dobash and Dobash (1980) report a parallel example

> We were two miles from the village. He allowed me half-an-
> hour to go up to the village and half-an-hour to walk back
> and ten minutes to get what I needed in the shops...If I
> wasnae back inside that hour and ten minutes, I got met at
> the door saying where the f__ing hell have you been....I
> used to marvel at women that could go down shopping...and
> having a cup of coffee....(p.129)

Elsey (1980) interviewed one woman whose husband planned her whole day

> I can't do anything in the kitchen...without him telling me
> how to do it...he wants everything to be planned out to the
> last minute....He used to tell me when I could have a bath
> and tell me when I could wash my hair, tell me when I could
> wash and iron clothes. (pp.61-5)

It is important to note that several authors frequently call domestic
'failures', which trigger violent incidents, 'trivial'. Thus Binney et
al. (1981) write

> Violence was likely to be used against women for trivial
> actions which in some way offended the man - for example, not
> having a meal on the table the instant he arrived home from
> work, asking for housekeeping money, or talking to the
> postman. (p.3)

They quote one victim who seemed to share this view

> You'd get knocked about for missing the milkman or not ironing
> a shirt - that sort of trivial thing.

Melville (1978a) also talks of 'trivial' incidents, for example:

> a husband wanted his trousers, and the wife said, 'I know I
> should have ironed them, but I had to get the dinner'.

168

My argument is that in the men's eyes these are not trivial derelictions
of duty and consequently social scientists cannot 'write them off' as
unimportant. The task is to understand why such apparently minor faults
are seen as major crimes deserving punishment. One argument is that
many men expect personal domestic service exclusive to them done only by
their wives, and feel the marital contract is broken if this is not
forthcoming. The men may be unreasonable, but so few data are available
on marital norms it is hard to be sure. Perhaps most marriages are
based on such 'bargains'. Certainly, breaches of male views of proper
wifely conduct cannot be called trivial if they result in broken limbs.
An example of domestic service contracts being 'broken' include the
following (and see also Pahl, 1981, p.75)

> Jane's husband refused to allow her to be ill - when she had
> flu he decided she was mentally disturbed and took her to a
> doctor. He diagnosed flu but the man made her get up and
> cook for him. (Elsey, 1980, p.34)

Although these may seem to be extreme cases of male attitudes about
domestic tasks, such attitudes are underpinned by contentions inherent
in our society about who should rightfully do housework. Thus, it is
only recently that boys have begun to be taught domestic subjects in
school (and cf. Coxon [q.v.])

Interviews with battered women reflect the total unwillingness of
many men to do even minor housework tasks; to do so is regarded as an
affront to their masculinity and their authority in the household.
Such attitudes reflect wider issues of male authority in our society
and underline the point made by Oakley (1974) that housework is seen as
one of the 'inbuilt' functions of women and not of men.

POVERTY, MONEY AND FOOD

A related source of conflict hinges on family finance and the provision
of food within the household. Most authors have emphasised the
financial aspect of this 'problem', but here food is seen as equally
important, both materially and symbolically. Binney et al. (1981)
write

> Twenty per cent of women said one of their reasons for leaving
> home was that their partner kept them in extreme poverty,
> regardless of how much he was earning. (p.5)

Over one third of 636 women interviewed living in refuges said they
were better off on Social Security than they had been with their
husbands. The authors comment

> Women who had been given meagre amounts for housekeeping were
> sometimes forced to spend most of it on steak and such like
> for their husbands, while they and their children lived on
> milk and biscuits. (p.6)

One third of the victims said their health had improved, and Binney et
al. (1981) say

> This was often due to the women eating and sleeping better.
> Women often felt their appetites had increased and they could
> also often afford to buy more and better food: 'When I came
> here I was really skinny, and now I've found I've put on a

169

hell of a lot of weight. My husband always wanted steak and
chips every day, so me and the kids had to make do with what
was left. Now I have my own pocket money in my pocket and
that's a big achievement!' (p.58)

Such troubles are also reported by other researchers

He did not work, I didn't have enough money, and our children
would go hungry...he wanted me to be a general housewife for
him, to stay at home, and cook and wash....(Melville, 1978)

and in Elsey's (1980) sample, a woman recounted how

On occasions when she asked him where the money was for food,
he would turn round and hit her. (p.25)

Perhaps the most poignant is the woman Pahl (1981) interviewed who
explained that her husband had been 'smoking half our food money',
whereas in the refuge

One thing I've found, since we've been here, my little girl
starts to sleep all night. I think some of it is that we
were that short of money that I couldn't give her as much
to eat as what I can here. I've found that now I'm on my
own with Mandy - I'm financially better off. (p.14)

The issue of families' money management has, as Pahl (1981) notes,
important policy and practical implications. Many women and children
entering refuges live in extreme poverty and suffer from an inadequate
diet because of the husbands' refusal properly to provide for them.
The Dobash research found that there was a fundamental difference
between husbands and wives about making decisions: women favoured
joint decision making, the men favoured 'separate spheres of decision
making'. If, however, any disagreement arose it was the wishes of the
man which prevailed. So when women continued to ask for money, although
the man had already refused,

...she may find that he views this as an unacceptable
challenge to his authority and stops the negotiation by
force. (Dobash and Dobash, 1980, p.129)

CONCLUDING REMARKS

It is clear from the data on battered women that domestic organisation
and in particular the purchase and preparation of food plays an
important part in triggering violent incidents. It is also clear that
in these relationships there exist inequalities arising out of the
control of financial resources. There emerge from these researches
obvious indications that those women interviewed were under the
financial and domestic control of their husbands. Thus, they were
allocated what money those men thought would be enough; their time and
movements were monitored and they were expected to prepare meals when
and how the men demanded.

In violent relationships controls are exerted by physical force. It
would, however, be wrong to see this as being unusual, first because
violent homes are probably more common than we would care to believe
and secondly because the convention that men have authority over women
is sufficiently strong for violence not to be needed. In their
examination of women and power Stacey and Price (1981) point out that

170

power within the family is in the hands of men. Dobash and Dobash (1980) conclude that physical violence is the outward manifestation of the control and oppression of women. This control is nowhere more apparent than in the home particularly when domestic organisation is at issue. As they put it,

> The use of physical violence against women in their position
> as wives is not the only means by which they are controlled
> and oppressed but it is one of the most brutal and explicit
> expressions of patriarchal domination. (p.ix)

NOTES

[1] In this chapter I have used 'domestic', 'marital' and 'family' violence synonymously. This is for convenience. I do not imply that all victims are married, or that all women are battered by husbands or co-habitees - some are harmed by sons, brothers and fathers. Nor do I wish to minimise the issue of child abuse. However, in this chapter I am focusing on women attacked by husbands or male cohabitees.

[2] I am grateful to the DHSS/Welsh Office who funded me during 1977/78 to do full time research on domestic violence. The views expressed in this chapter are not necessarily those of the DHSS/Welsh Office or any other local or central government department. I also wish to thank the other UK researchers who provided unpublished material during the last five years. Constant enthusiasm for the work has been provided by my MSc supervisor Sara Delamont. Myrtle Robins typed the paper with her usual skill and attention to detail.

16 Men in the Kitchen: Notes from a Cookery Class

TONY COXON

> What sort of man are you? Why <u>are</u> you living alone? Why <u>aren't</u>
> you married? That last question is usually put by women, and
> intended to undermine your rugged masculinity and cause grave
> doubts. (p.9)

Willie Rushton poses these questions in the forward to his book
<u>Superpig</u> (1976). He then tells the reader that the book is intended
for:

> Widowers, divorces, old lags, separatists, unmarried fathers,
> pooves, hermits and trappists. (p.9)

<u>Superpig</u> is a guide to domestic survival, covering cleaning, travelling
and of course cooking. 'How the kitchen was won' and 'The Entertaining
of Ladies' suggest a lone but intrepid male's approach to the task.
Cookery for men is also the focus of this chapter but reveals less
gallantry and rather more ambiguity and uncertainty. The data used
consist of firsthand observation of an evening class called 'Cookery
for Men' attended by the author in the 1970s together with some material
from the mass media.[1] The argument is that the <u>abnormality</u> of such an
evening class and the anomalous status of its students, neatly reveal
quite how, despite the course's title, cooking is thought of as woman's
work.

This chapter is divided into two main sections. There is a brief
description of the evening class (participants, layout, timetable,
curriculum etc.), followed by an examination of the social status,
interaction patterns, and motivation of the students who attended.
Before embarking upon these, a few *caveats* must be given.

This contribution is deliberately brief for two reasons. First, the
argument can be stated succinctly precisely because it is so closely
in line with the conclusions of the companion chapters in this section.
Second, the data drawn on were collected in an incidental and un-
systematic manner, so it would be improper to place too great a
reliance on them. The evidence was collected, like that reported in
Davis and Horobin (1977) in the medical context, as a subsidiary
activity while attending an evening class called 'Cookery for Men'
which I had joined to widen my culinary repertoire. At the time,
sociological questions were not of paramount concern, but an abiding
interest in social networks led me to note how the students formed
working groups and cliques within the class. Like Davis and Horobin's

contributors I was a participant observer in the 'purest sense', bringing my 'training in social science to the analysis of (my) experiences'. Also like theirs, the present account differs 'from other participant observation studies in that the situations were not deliberately chosen for their research potential'. (1977, p.11). Clearly some serious research on different kinds of cookery class for males (such as home economics in schools, commercial catering courses and other evening classes) compared to classes for females is needed before firm conclusions can be drawn.

The underlying argument of this paper is that men will usually only learn domestic cooking, and have to practise their skill, when there is no woman in their household. The public admission of needing to learn how to cook is potentially stigmatising for, as the Rushton quote implies, 'real' males have females to cook for them. Men in this evening class had damaged social identities of one kind or another (cf. Davis and Strong's 1977 discussion of bachelors as a social problem) and formed friendship groups on the basis of shared stigma.

Male cooks are, conventially, public cooks. That is they are employed in the catering industry, the armed services, or as famous chefs. The ordinary man does not regularly cook at home, nor do men whose paid employment involves cooking and many men are happy to boast that they cannot cook. As the other contributions in this section show, domestic cooking is conventionally construed as women's work. A few items from cookbooks and contemporary issues of women's magazines will serve as illustration:

> Are you hungry?....Do cookery books scare the pants off you?
> Are you aged between 15 and 90 - preferably male?....this book
> is for you....No matter whether you wish to impress your
> latest girlfriend with a slap-up dinner or merely have to
> survive while your wife is in bed with flu, this book will
> show you exactly what to do.

So runs the blurb on the dustjacket of Donald Kilbourne's Pots and Pants: a Cookbook for Men. It is, once again, womanless men who need to cook. But the author, as the note records, is married. He also 'enjoys cooking occasionally and looks upon it as a production job that must be got through as efficiently as possible'. Not only does he not cook as a matter of routine, the way he cooks has the hallmark not of the domestic but of the industrial processes. Margaret Powell achieves a similar effect in the introduction to Sweetmaking for Children (1972) when reporting that her son 'eventually became a very good cook indeed and (don't laugh!) a very good tailor and dressmaker. He makes a lot of his own and his wife's clothes, although in his job he's an atomic scientist'. (p.6). Although skilled domestically doing such tasks is incidental to his proper employment. Indeed, his work is characteristically manly, for as Weinreich-Haste (1979) has shown, science is regarded as hard, complex and masculine, in diametric opposition to cooking. The theme that men cook as work and only on occasion at home is also found in a feature Woman (12 June 1982) ran on well-known chefs and their wives. Readers are offered brief interviews with 'Christine Shepherd, wife of Richard Shepherd' (of Langan's Brasserie); 'Lady Bradford who is married to Lord Bradford (Porters in Covent Garden)'; and Katherine Mossiman, wife of Anton (master chef at the Dorchester)'. All three women insist that cooking is work, and that the man has the right to leave his work behind him when he comes home. Additionally however all three face critical scrutiny of their cooking, saying typically:

I've always got to concentrate that bit harder for him.

Christine Shepherd says Richard 'never cooks for me'; the other two will cook 'If we have a dinner party' or 'If we've got guests coming for dinner'. The Woman reader is left in no doubt that the children's meals, the ordinary food, and the washing up, are women's work. It is not, however, that men cannot do routine domestic cooking. 'Me and My Freezer' (Annabel July 1982) reported three 'busy ladies and one brave houseperson dad' with families to feed. Alongside a 'working housewife' who regularly gives dinner parties for ten, 'proud grandmother' caring for the grandchildren and 'mother of two' is a father bringing up two children alone. As a single parent this man has to cook. But the article makes clear that help is at hand, for his daughters Savannah (14) and Belinda (12) 'do home economics at school' and now 'practise some of their favourite recipes'. We are also told that Roger's 'meal times are planned' and that 'he doesn't neglect gourmet, chef-style meals'. Whether this justifies calling him a 'brave houseperson' or not, the message is clear. Men can do it, but only when they have to.

Annabel and Woman are highly traditional magazines, but the readers of the latest glossy monthly for women Options are equally likely to be the cooks in their households. In June 1982 the magazine offered an article on the 'myth' of shared housework in contemporary marriage which included the following:

In our supposed household co-op the jobs are apportioned equally (but) sharing seems to mean that I peel the carrots while he woos the seven-year-old's idolatry creating origami paper frogs ....I, the wife, cook, because I'm the one who best knows how ....Tell you what, he says expansively, if you're tired...why don't I treat us all to a take-away? Doner Kebabs or McDonalds, he queries, while the children cheer. What I hoped was that just occasionally he too would roast, garnish and serve up a sliver of wholesome loving care instead of fetching it home in cardboard cartons....

It was in part to avoid that feeling in my own family that I enrolled in the evening class. I saw a notice at the local comprehensive school advertising the course saying that 'it would cover a wide range of cooking, from beginners upwards'. While I could cook some dishes, I lacked a whole set of basic skills - particularly making gravy and pastry.

THE CLASS

The evening class took place along with a variety of others at a comprehensive school. The tutor, a friendly, cheerful woman in her late 30s, began most of the 2 hour classes with a lecture and demonstration of the evening's dish. She was well prepared, bringing a completed version of the dish along so that the students could see the ideal result. After a coffee break, the students cooked the 'dish of the day' working in small groups. Recipes were distributed, typed on sheets, each week; guidance on the ingredients needed was given a week ahead and students could collaborate over bringing them. Among the dishes taught were tuna mousse, banana and walnut loaf, chicken Maryland, Quiche Lorraine, mince hot pot and Pavlova.

Throughout the two terms certain tensions arose over the syllabus. These had two different, though possibly related sources. Some members of the class were such beginners that certain dishes were seen as difficult or unnecessarily elaborate. Other members of the group held strong views about 'funny foreign food', and wanted to learn how to prepare a straightforward 'cooked dinner' of the kind discussed by Murcott (1982a). This cultural difference (which may be age-based, or class-based) is neatly captured in Good Housekeeping for August 1982. In an article about Blackpool, Hunter Davies interviewed the Landlady of the Year. She won the title by coming top of a course for Guest Housekeepers, the exam involving planning for a buffet for 150. Davies says:

> She included lots of fancy things like Tuna Fish Mould,
> Crunchy Garlic Chicken, Quiche Lorraine, which she would
> normally never serve....
> 'I stick to meat and two veg. They've got to be knowing
> what it is....'
> She always rotates the same seven meals...so if you stay
> two weeks you get everything twice –

'everything' being: steak and kidney pie, roast beef, lamb chops, roast pork, salad, chicken and fish (on Friday). These menus are the kind of food that many of the class wanted to be able to cook, rather than quiche with Gruyere in it. There was, then, a tension between the kind of dish wanted by the older, the inexperienced, and the broadly working class students as opposed to the younger, the more experienced, and the more bourgeois class members. These tensions crystallised when the class cooked a Christmas dinner, becoming obvious less through the menu for that heavily traditional meal than through the choice of wine, and the manner of serving the food. The class differed – for example – over the question of serving mince pies on a doily.

There is, clearly, scope for much more work on the implications of different syllabuses in such classes, both for men and women. In this chapter, however, it is more important to move on to the social relations among the students.

STUDENT GROUPINGS

The precise dishes cooked and the students who enrolled for the course interacted in a way which concentrates the focus of this paper. Two kinds of student came along for the course, who wanted rather different kinds of menu. One group of men were absolute beginners, and they wanted to learn basic 'survival' cooking: mince hot pot rather than Pavlova. Another group already had some skill, and wanted to learn either specific skills (e.g. 'I could not make pastry') or more elaborate Cordon Bleu dishes. Virtually all students, however, lived in all-male households. Two kinds of males live in such households – heterosexual and gay – and a second division within the class grew up between 'straights' and homosexuals. A men's cookery class could have divided itself between those who had no woman to cook for them, and

those who wanted to become part of a 'symmetrical' family by sharing
food provision, but this one did not.

If I was alone in wanting cookery skills primarily to be able to
share the task of feeding a family, the other men in the class did not
share a single motivation beyond wishing to feed themselves. Some
students - mostly the beginners - had found themselves womanless. This
group wanted 'survival' skills, because they were widowed, divorced, or
had lost the female relative (mother, sister, aunt) who had been
cooking for them. The most extreme example here was a man in his 50s
whose wife had died in the same year as the death of his mother, when
his children also moved away from Cardiff. This group included some
men who had become fed up with opening tins and frying eggs. These men
had presumably run out of substitute 'wives' and 'mothers' among female
kin and affines, because as Rosser and Harris (1965, pp.153-22) showed,
the extended family survives in South Wales because women feed males,
even distantly related ones. Rosser and Harris found adult males who
visited their mother for lunch every working day, and when deaths
occurred, other relations, such as affines, substituted for the deceased.
So men enrolling in a cookery class due to a death or divorce were
especially socially isolated. The majority of students, about twelve,
fell into the category 'heterosexual but without a woman in the house'
and were suffering varying degrees of social isolation.

The class also contained a smaller group of which I was a member -
which over the two terms developed into a clique - of gay men who
chiefly lived alone from choice, and here the motivation was to learn
more creative, advanced cooking. For the gay man, learning to cook for
oneself is necessary; in a 'womanless' household, somebody has to cook.
One man, for example, was even delivered to the class by his older
partner like a new bride being sent to learn cooking by a demanding
husband.

However friendly they were, the majority of the class tended to
distance themselves from our group. This was evident in three ways. As
in most classrooms, students soon staked a claim to 'their' desk,
'their' table. From early in the first term the smaller clique regularly
shared a table in the corner. Second, this went with observably less
conversational contact, beyond greetings at each end of the evening,
between that clique and the rest of the students. And while most of the
class would at some time talk sport - especially football - as they got
on with their cooking, the clique in the corner never did. These
groupings were repeated to some extent in the seating arrangements
students chose for the Christmas dinner. Third, the cleavages in the
class were also observable in patterns of co-operation. Most noticeable
was the way students who chose to work alongside one another also
collaborated in providing ingredients for the following week - each of,
say, three people would bring three times the amount of selected items,
and cut down on the amount of shopping etc. each had to do.

CONCLUDING REMARKS

It would be foolhardy to draw firm conclusions from the observational
and documentary material presented here. The present purpose is to
provide an example which endorses the argument of the other chapters in
this volume. It also serves as a reminder of the lines of enquiry that

need to be pursued. While others have considered a relationship between food and sex - whether novelists such as Gunter Grass in <u>The Flounder</u> or commentators like Bates (1958) or the anthropologist <u>Back</u> (1976) - and Murdock has updated his cross-cultural survey of the division of labour by sex (Murdock and Provost, 1973), what has yet systematically to be studied is the manner in which gender on the one hand and cooking on the other is conceptualised and socially organised. If it turns out that men do not routinely cook, leaving it to women and if cooking is thought of as unmanly, then a symmetrical family and democratic household do indeed remain a long way off.

NOTES

[1] Thanks are due to Sara Delamont and Anne Murcott for the loan of items from, respectively, their collections of magazine cuttings and cookbooks, and for their suggestions and comments on an earlier draft of this chapter.

17 Cooking and the Cooked: a Note on the Domestic Preparation of Meals

ANNE MURCOTT

Both Lévi-Strauss (1966) and Douglas (1972) have, in their own ways, advocated analysing cooking as language. Sooner or later this also involves analysing the language of cooking. But one of the many objections to the work of Lévi-Strauss is that his understanding of specific cooking terms is, if not ethnocentric, at least selective and idiosyncratic (cf. Lehrer, 1972). There is scant space in his theoretical and methodological approach for empirical investigation of the usages from which his analysis proceeds. To value the ethnographic exploration of folk concepts is a perhaps more 'Anglo-Saxon' pursuit, the beginnings of which is attempted here.

The very term 'cooking' provides an appropriate enough instance. Merely as a preliminary, the following definitions can be seen to capture quite different emphases. The first is from the Oxford English Dictionary

> Cook v. Intr. To act as cook, to prepare food by the action of heat
> Trans. To prepare or make ready (food); to make fit for eating by due application of heat, as by boiling, baking, roasting, broiling etc.

the second the opening paragraphs of a cookbook for children.

> Cooking is the way people turn raw food into things that look and taste different and sometimes better.
> Heat is most often used to alter raw food. Other foods are just changed by the way they are mixed together. Cold can be used sometimes too.
> There is no one way to cook. All over the world people have worked out different things to do with food that tastes good.
> (Cooking: making things to eat, Puffin, 1976)

More analytically Lehrer (1969) has pointed out that the word 'cook' has three levels of generality. The first is most general and refers to the preparation of meals as one of a number of household tasks; the second contrasts cooking with baking, and the third, the most marked sense of the term, involves the application of heat which produces an irreversible change in the food cooked.

Exploration of the meanings of the verb 'to cook' is the focus of this chapter.[1]. The concern, however, is with everyday, folk usages

and derives from a small single-handed empirical investigation of some
younger women's ideas and concepts of food and eating.[2].

This essay provides an aside, a comment, on analyses of part of that
study presented elsewhere. (Murcott 1982a and 1983b). The first paper
shows that informants continually stressed the importance of what they
mostly termed a 'cooked dinner'. Such a meal is reportedly proper for
a husband's (and children's) homecoming, ideally provided three or so
times during the week, absent on Saturdays, rather special on Sundays.
The following exchange from an interview illustrates the gist:

> (On Sundays) we'll have cooked
>
> (AM) Like what?
>
> Pork, potatoes, cabbage, peas, beans
>
> (AM) Anything after?
>
> No
>
> (AM) How about Saturdays? - do you have cooked on Saturdays?
>
> We usually have fried

It also illustrates a shorthand to describe a meal apparently in terms
of the technique used to prepare it.

The cooked dinner, I argue, symbolises the home, a husband's relation
to it, his wife's place in it and their relationship to one another.
This theme is taken up in the second paper which examines the
conventions that women do the cooking as a service for their husbands,
in deference to his tastes, to fit in with his timetable - i.e. her
part of the marital contract. The discussion in each paper is located
within the familiar assumption also shared by informants that domestic
cooking and oversight of the kitchen is women's work.

In the present chapter I take up two points of evidence noted in
passing in those discussions. The first is a particular meaning of the
verb to cook, the second is report that husbands can and do prepare
food, albeit as will be seen, in a firmly circumscribed fashion. In so
doing I shall argue that one folk usage of the term cooking is both
specific to the cooked dinner and simultaneously reflects the gender
based domestic division of labour. It may be that this usage is class
related - the meaning may be well understood by members of all social
classes, but the expression used in this rather specific way confined
to local[3] and/or working class sub-cultures.

My argument is extremely speculative - the analytic tactic adopted
warrants no more. It is based on a selection of material from a series
(not a representative sample) of interviews only with women, only in a
specific age group. The justification for marshalling the data in this
way, however, is to concentrate attention on empirical nuances of
usages and attempt imaginatively to expand understanding that may
provide leads for future enquiry. I claim nothing more.

It was then in the spirit of exploratory study that I asked informants
if they thought cooking was important, neither knowing what sort of
responses the question might yield nor whether those responses would be
at all illuminating. In the event it elicited answers that illustrate

a range of interpretations of the term cooking.

I had expected that one version would endorse cooking as self evidently necessary - for instance

Well mainly that's how our meals are done through cooking... isn't it, if you didn't cook it would never be done. (P 07; her occupation is categorised in Registrar General's Class V, her husband's IIIb) [4],

and without a trace of irony

Well yes, you've got to eat (M 21 II/II).

But I was surprised by

Yes, well I suppose you'd starve otherwise (M 22 V/IIIb)

and

Well yes you've got to cook or you'd starve

(although this immediately raised the further question of what was meant by 'starve'). Introducing two of the oppositional pairs that also feature in the responses she continued after a long pause

Unless you had salads and cold stuff all the time (M 20 IIIb/V)

Raw and cold regularly cropped up in contrast to cooked (hot) - salads were occasionally favoured as low in calories by some women, disliked by as many others and reported insufficiently filling for men. As for hot food, few talked so eloquently of its symbolic significance as a mother of a two year old.

I always try and give him something warm anyway...he's out in the garden all day...if there's something warm inside him... (mind you) knowing (him)...it's probably cold when he eats it, but I know it's gone in that oven and it was warm when I put it on his plate (P09 IIIa/IIIb)

Cooking was also reckoned important - and preferable - as opposed to tinned and convenience foods.

A further range of answers dealt with the techniques and craft of cooking. Hygiene was important; food, especially meat that is half cooked is not safe, so timing needs care. Meals too have to be attractively presented and made to look appetising. Good cooking needs patience and is a matter of practice - you have to

learn by your mistakes, you know nobody's just a good cook automatically (P13 IIIa/II)

It needs application

you got to be interested...you got to want to do it (M01 IIIa/II)

you have to be 'bothered' to do it and 'can't cut corners'. Cooking is important in providing variety and enjoyment, but 'plain' cooking does as well as 'fancy'.

Given especial stress was the expression of the importance of cooking in terms reflecting gender, the home and marriage - a feature I discuss more fully elsewhere (1983b). Essentially, cooking is important in that a wife is to provide the meal for a man's return home from work.

It is proper that as often as not a cooked dinner is ready for him and
it is proper that preparing it is the wife's work. In this light being
a good cook does matter

> To a man, yes...a woman doesn't bother that much, she's used to
> her own cooking. But to a man if their mother is a good cook
> and they go and get married to somebody who is a poor cook, well
> they do see the difference.

adding unexpectedly

> Well everybody has said that I'm a good cook, so I can't deny
> that because we're all still living. (PO7 V/IIIb)

Cooking is securely anchored as the responsibility of women as wives
and as mothers. Informants all affirmed that conventionally this is
so. They also reported that they did the cooking. For all informants
the kitchen was their domain, shopping and stocking their responsibility, routine planning and daily oversight of meals their work. When
before the first baby's arrival the wife was employed the task of
cooking the evening meal still fell to her. Her husband might help,
but if instead he read the paper or watched TV until it was ready,
women would get on with <u>their</u> work now that he had finished his.

To be sure, husbands in the now well worn phrase, were 'very good
really', willing to take over if she were doing the washing, seeing to
the children, down with flu or expecting a baby. This, in some
instances, if he is declared redundant while she still has employment,
extends to his having a meal ready for her return - an arrangement to
reverse again when he once more finds work. But informants were
emphatic that such eventualities were exceptions to the fundamental
rule that, in the ideal, men primarily are responsible as the bread-
winners, women primarily responsible for the home, the kitchen and the
cooking.

All this might give the impression that men in the usual run of
things never prepared any food, or were only understudy cooks. This
was not, however, the picture informants presented. Certainly men's
competence was, on the whole, considered limited. Left to their own
devices they would fail to eat vegetables and risk their health, shop
quite unsuitably and extravagantly, leave the kitchen in a mess or be
unable to prepare anything without a woman's supervision. (One
informant did however consider that men made <u>better</u> cooks - women are
'moody', to do with the menstrual cycle, and thus less methodical than
men).

Yet the women also reported that men did prepare food and would do
some kitchen work. Some make the breakfast at weekends; one, when
they were first married used to take his wife breakfast in bed

> which was very nice, but again the novelty wore off, we tend
> to take it in turns now (PO6 IIIa/II)

Another informant, living with her parents explained that if neither
she nor her mother or sister was about, her father would always get his
own supper - sandwiches or a tin of soup, around 9.30 pm. Partly
because she likes neither the taste nor even the smell of any 'spicy
stuff' another woman's husband cooks curry for himself

I wouldn't have anything to do with it at all...he'll sometimes
cook supper, y'know, sort of bacony things, y'know (MOS II/II)

By and large informants reported that they cooked according to their
husbands' not their own preferences (cf. Murcott 1983b). This practice
did not, in the few instances where it occurred, extend to meals both
regarded as unconventional and disliked by the wife. As in the case
just noted, it was the husband, if he wanted to eat in this style, who
prepared the curry. An even more marked instance is the following: I
had asked whether they ever went out for 'an Indian', had a 'Chinese
take away' or ever cooked anything like that at home

No, if my husband wants it, he does it himself...he's got them
Supercooks (cookery magazines)...he'll go down the supermarket
and come back with things and go and make a curry or something
like that....If like he has a friend to come here...he'll make
curry and buy the stuff...out of his own pocket because it's
not for me and him, it's for his friend and it's nothing to do
with the family. A friend to me is if they've been friends for
years, a friend is part of the family to me, but to him it's
not so he'll go out and he'll take it out of his own pocket.
(P15 IVb/IVb)

Patently this is not reckoned a routine family event.

Effectively it appears that men's participation in the kitchen is
marginal to the regular and central provision of the main family meal.
Men make chips or cheese on toast, but not, day in day out, the
homecoming meal.

Now I've got his tea ready whereas before he had to wait
for it (when she too was out at work)...I do all of it
(cooking)

(AM) Does he do any as well?

No. It, when, I mean he'll, he has done breakfasts but
he's never cooked the gravy dinner...he said he can but
he's never proved it...he'll cook chips (M10 IVb/IIIb)

I did not ask whether he had been invited to but declined or whether he
had not been offered the opportunity. But the extract illustrates
clearly the gender based division of labour. Men do prepare food, do
get in to the kitchen, but what they do there is distinct from the
cooking with which women are charged.

At least, so it would seem. A closer look at further data reflecting
the meaning of the verb to cook introduces another dimension. Still
discussing the domestic division of kitchen labour an informant answered
that she nearly always cooks

he helps y'know, he'll clean the vegetables and things like that
but he doesn't actually do the cooking. I'm the cook. (M07 II/II)

Explaining that when she went in to hospital to have the baby another
remarked

My mum will come up and give a hand...(he follows directions)
but to leave him he's absolutely hopeless....

adding in passing

182

he makes lovely custard, but he can't cook anything (P14 IIIb/IIIb)

In these instances it seems as if subtly different meanings of 'cooking' are being employed. And these are echoed in separate sections of the interview where women described typical eating patterns and identified what they meant by a cooked dinner.

Time and again informants would explain that weekday lunch on their own may be a 'snack' and then 'I cook in the evening' or 'teatime I cook' and proceed to describe the version of the cooked dinner planned for that day, the one the family liked best or whatever. One woman used the verb 'to eat' in parallel fashion with describing the same arrangements saying

> Usually we eat in the evening...lunch time could be a sandwich ...something snacky rather than two meals. (MO5 IIIa/IIIa)

A second woman commented on the habits of a couple she knew

> She doesn't bother to cook at all, really, y'know, properly, coz he's quite happy to have cold meat with a few boiled potatoes and he's not bothered y'know whether he is dished up chips everyday with fish fingers or something...to me it's not cooking ...it's producing the bare necessities for a meal. (MO9 IIIa/IIIa)

A somewhat similar distinction is made by a third informant, already quoted above

> Absolutely convenience food tonight. I quite often buy things like that...little individual pies y'know and I keep them in the freezer for the nights when for one reason or another I don't feel like cooking in inverted commas...when I go to Marks and Spencer I think oh I'll put those two in for an emergency. That isn't cooking to me you see. (MO7 II/II)

These last two instances illustrate something of the meaning of cooking, noted earlier, that refers to craft and technique. But the next fixes another interpretation of the term

> (Lunchtime) y'know snack...egg and toast and a yoghurt... or I have tomato soup...the evening meal we have together. A cooked meal...roast, grill, whatever.

(AM)   Would a sort of thing like the kind of meal you'd have in the middle of the day – does that count as a cooked meal?

> No...well it is cooked – but it, I wouldn't class it as a meal...I don't know whether I'd cook lunch time...just have cheese on toast or something...but I wouldn't feel that I'd eaten a meal. (MO4 IIIa/II)

Here the verb to cook (and the noun a meal) is plainly linked to the cooked dinner. Lunch or a snack is not a real meal, nor is its preparation properly cooked.

Such an example provides the key to this chapter's argument and the basis for summarising what has been said. First, from among the variety of meanings attributed to 'cooking' and 'cooked', informants laid strenuous emphasis on the cooked dinner, explaining the importance of cooking most especially in relation to women's responsibility for preparing that dinner ready for their husband's return. Other household

food events[5] breakfast, snacks etc. turn out to be far less
specifically women's work - the same food events to which informants
refer as distinct from a cooked dinner (cf. Murcott, 1982a).

As hinted at the beginning of this discussion, such usage may be
class cultural. The term cooked dinner was used less often by
informants with non manual occupations - but it was not absent.
Furthermore it refers to a meal reportedly taken regularly by informants
of all social classes and the meal also appears to have the same
symbolic significance among them all.

Possibly it is a matter of repertoire - among non manual informants a
cooked dinner can take its place alongside a much larger range of
possible styles of meal which are also accounted proper, homecoming
meals. The handful of interviews (6) conducted with wives of senior
professional men in medicine and the law bear this out but also quite
strikingly indicate a continuity with the main series of interviews.
So the same division of kitchen labour prevailed - one man taking over
(sic) as necessary, insisting on still doing a Sunday roast for the
children, another taking no part whatsoever making not even a cup of
coffee. The husband's work comes first - although as students, or when
newly married, men proved domestically capable, but the subsequent
demands of a busy practice led wives not to expect any help. Here too
couples assumed that the wife would make a suitable meal for her
husband's return from work. Such a meal however, could equally be steak
and salad, lasagne'al forno' or a cooked dinner.

The data however provide no more than a suggestion - they are not
sufficiently extensive and include no examples of recently geographically mobile households. But I would hazard, that not only is a
class dimension relevant, but that it is cross cut by another,
reflecting local more parochial cultural orientations on one hand and
cosmopolitan viewpoints on the other.

As promised this chapter has been highly speculative. Its purpose is
to indicate future lines of enquiry. Much more systematic and thoroughgoing work needs to be undertaken exploring not only the meaning people
attach to cooking and kitchen work but also the relation of those
meanings to the social organisation of households and the social
relationships involved in a gender linked division of labour. Just
possibly, it will turn out that it is not so much that women do the
cooking, as what is called cooking is the work that women do.

NOTES

[1] I would like to thank all those necessarily anonymous people who
made the research possible, Martin Read for his computing help and
advice, and Lisa Lowe for the loan of her cookbook.
[2] Unstructured, tape recorded (with one exception) interviews were
held with a series of 37 expectant mothers attending a health centre
in a South Wales valley for ante natal care (22 pregnant for the
first time) 20 of whom were interviewed again after the baby's
birth. A wide range of occupations was represented amongst
informants and their husbands/boyfriends, stretching the length of
the Registrar General's (RG) classification. A further 4 interviews
were carried out with wives, who had at least one child under eleven

184

at primary school, of men in senior positions in the legal and medical professions. I am grateful to the SSRC for their financial support of this research.

[3] I do not mean that usage is specific to the locality in which I conducted the research - but rather that it is likely to be current among those attached by orientation to, and birth and/or length of residence in, the area in which they live.

[4] Following each quotation is the informant's reference number, then note of the social class the RG's classification of occupations categorises first the woman's and second her husband's/boyfriend's current or main occupation.

[5] Douglas and Nicod (1974) coined the term 'food event' which avoids begging the question and allows any distinction informants might make between something other and a 'real meal'.

[6] See note 2.

Bibliography

Allen, D.E. (1968) British Tastes, Hutchinson, London.

Angyal, A. (1941) 'Disgust and related aversions', Journal of Abnormal and Social Psychology, vol.36.

Arnott, M.L. (ed) (1975) Gastronomy: The Anthropology of Food and Food Habits, Mouton Publishers, The Hague.

Atkinson, P. (1978) 'From honey to vinegar: Lévi-Strauss in Vermont', in Morley, P. and Wallis, R. (eds) Culture and Curing: Anthropological Perspectives on Traditional Medical Beliefs and Practices, Peter Owen, London.

Atkinson, P. (1980) 'The symbolic significance of health foods', in Turner, M. (ed) Nutrition and Lifestyles, Applied Science Publishers, London.

BNF (1975) Report of a Survey of Housewives' Knowledge and Attitudes: food and nutrition, British Nutrition Foundation, London.

Back, W.K. (1977) 'Food, sex and theory', in Fitzgerald, T.K.(ed) Nutrition and Anthropology in Action, van Gorcum, Assen/Amsterdam.

Balaam, D.N. and Carey, M.J. (1981) Food Politics: the Regional Conflict, Croom Helm, London.

Barkas, J. (1975) The Vegetable Passion, RKP, London.

Barker, T.C. et al.(eds) (1966) Our Changing Fare: two hundred years of British food habits, McGibbon and Kee, London.

Barker, T.C. et al.(1970) The Dietary Surveys of Dr Edward Smith 1862-3: A New Assessment, Staples Press, London.

Barthes, Roland (1967) Elements of Semiology, Tr.Annette Lavers and Colin Smith, Cape, London.

Barthes, Roland (1973) 'Wine and milk' in Mythologies, Tr. Annette Lavers, Paladin, St. Albans.

Bates, M. (1958) Gluttons and Libertines, Random House, New York.

Batstone, E. et al. (1977) Shop Stewards in Action, Blackwell, Oxford.

Batstone, E. et al. (1978) The Social Organisation of Strikes, Blackwell, Oxford.

Batstone, E. (1982) 'Motivation, legitimacy and nutrition: a history of food in industry', Mimeo, Oxford University.

Bendix, R. (1963) Work and Authority in Industry, Harper, New York.

Berger, P.L. and Luckman, T. (1966) The Social Construction of Reality, Penguin Books, Harmondsworth.

Binney, V. et al. (1981) Leaving Violent Men, Women's Aid Federation England, London.

Blaxter, M. and Paterson, E. (1980) Attitudes to health and use of health services (with special reference to children) in two generations of women in Social Class IV and V, Final report DHSS/SSRC Joint Working Party on Transmitted Deprivation.

Blaxter, M. and Paterson, E. (1982) <u>Mothers and Daughters: A three-generation study of Health Attitudes and Behaviour</u>, Heinemann Education, London.

Blue Band (1978) <u>Lifestyle Study</u> and <u>Lifestyle Study of Working Women</u>, Blue Band Bureau, 25, North Row, London.

Borowski, M. et al. (1981) <u>Community Response to Marital Violence</u>, University of Bristol.

Bott, E. (1971) <u>Family and Social Network</u>, Tavistock, London, 2nd ed.

Boyd Orr, J. (1936) <u>Food, Health and Income: report on a survey of adequacy of diet in relation to income</u>, Macmillan, London.

Braverman, H. (1974) <u>Labor and Monopoly Capital</u>, Monthly Review Press, New York.

Burgoyne, J. and Clark, D. (1980) 'Why get married again?', <u>New Society</u>, vol.52, no.913.

Burgoyne, J. and Clark, D. (1981a) 'Starting again? Problems and expectations in remarriage', <u>Marriage Guidance</u>, vol.19, no.7.

Burgoyne, J. and Clark, D. (1981b) 'Parenting in stepfamilies', in Chester, R. et al. (eds) <u>Changing Patterns of Child-bearing and Child-rearing</u>, Academic Press, London.

Burgoyne, J. and Clark, D. (1982a) 'From father to stepfather', in O'Brien, M. and McKee, L. (eds), <u>The Father Figure</u>, Tavistock, London.

Burgoyne, J. and Clark, D. (1982b) 'Reconstituted families in the family', in The Family Research Committee (eds), <u>Families in Britain</u>, RKP, London.

Burnett, J. (1979) <u>Plenty and Want: a social history of diet in England from 1815 to the present day</u>, Scolar Press, London, revised ed.

Butler, C. (1923) <u>Benedictine Monachism</u>, London.

CIS (1975) <u>Unilever's World</u>, Russell Press, Nottingham.

Carter, A. (1976) 'The new vegetarians', <u>New Society</u>, 4th March 1976.

Chang, K.C. (ed) (1977) <u>Food in Chinese Culture: anthropological and historical perspectives</u>, Yale University Press, New Haven.

Clark, D.C. (1982) <u>Between Pulpit and Pew</u>, Cambridge University Press, Cambridge.

Cornely, P.B. and Bigman, S.K. (1961) 'Cultural Considerations in Changing Health Attitudes', <u>Medical Annals of the District of Columbia</u>, vol.30, no.4.

Cosminsky, S. (1977) 'Alimento and Fresco: Nutritional concepts and their implications for health care', <u>Human Organization</u>, vol.36, summer.

Crawford, R. (1977) 'You are dangerous to your health: the ideology and politics of victim blaming', <u>International Journal of Health Services</u>, vol.7.

Crawford, W. and Broadley, H. (1938) <u>The Peoples Food</u>, Heinemann, London.

DHSS (1976) <u>Prevention and Health: Everybody's Business</u>, HMSO, London.

DHSS (1978) <u>Eating for Health</u>, HMSO, London.

Darling, G. (1941) <u>The Politics of Food</u>, Routledge, London.

Davis, A. (1979) 'An unequivocal change of policy; prevention, health and medical sociology', <u>Social Science and Medicine</u>, vol.13a.

Davis, A. and Horobin, G. (eds) (1977) <u>Medical Encounters</u>, Croom Helm, London.

Davis, A.G. and Strong, P.M. (1977) 'Working without a net: the bachelor as a social problem', <u>The Sociological Review</u>, vol.25, no.1.

De Castro, J. (1969) <u>The Black Book of Hunger</u>, Beacon Press, Boston.

De Garine, I. and Hladik, C.M. (eds) (forthcoming) <u>Anthropology of Food</u>, Cambridge University Press, Cambridge.

Delamont, S. (1980) <u>The Sociology of Women</u>, Allen & Unwin, London.

Delphy, C. (1979) 'Sharing the same table: consumption and the family', in Harris, C. (ed) The Sociology of the Family: New Directions for Britain, Sociological Review Monograph no.28, University of Keele.

Dennis, N. et al. (1956) Coal is Our Life, Eyre & Spottiswoode, London.

Djang, T.K. (1942) Factory Inspection in Great Britain, Allen & Unwin, London.

Dobash, R. and Dobash, R. (1980) Violence Against Wives, Open Books, Shepton Mallet, England.

Douglas, M. (1975) 'Deciphering a meal' in Implicit Meanings, RKP, London.

Douglas, M. (1966) Purity and Danger, RKP, London.

Douglas, M. (1976-1977) 'Structures of gastronomy' in The Future and the Past, Annual Report 1976-77, Russell Sage Foundation, New York.

Douglas, M. (1977) 'Beans means "thinks"', The Listener, 8 September.

Douglas, M. and Nicod, M. (1974) 'Taking the biscuit: the structure of British meals', New Society, 19 December, vol.30, no.637.

Drummond, J.C. and Wilbraham, A. (1958) The Englishman's Food, Jonathan Cape, London.

Dufty, W. (1975) Sugar Blues, Abacus Press, Tunbridge Wells, Kent.

Dumont, L. (1970) Homo Hierarchicus, Weidenfeld & Nicholson, London.

EEC (1975) A Study of the Evolution of Concentration in the Food Industry for the United Kingdom, parts I and II, EEC, Brussels.

Edgell, S. (1980) Middle Class Couples: a Study of Segregation, Domination and Inequality in Marriage, Allen & Unwin, London.

Eekelaar, J. and Clive, E. (1977) Custody After Divorce, Centre for Socio-Legal Studies, Oxford.

Elias, N. (1978) The Civilizing Process, Basil Blackwell, Oxford.

Elliott, A. (1965) 'Company Welfare Benefits' in Reid, G.L. and Robertson, D.J. (eds) Fringe Benefits, Labour Costs and Social Security, Allen & Unwin, London.

Ellis, R.M. (1982) Battered Women: A Case Study of Social Control, Unpublished MSc Econ thesis, University of Wales.

Elsey, A. (1980) Battered Women - An Appraisal of Social Policy, Unpublished MSc thesis, Cranfield Institute of Technology.

Farb, P. and Armelagos, G. (1980) Consuming Passions: the Anthropology of Eating, Houghton Mifflin, Boston.

Fenton, A. and Owen, T.M. (1981) Food in Perspective, John Donald, Edinburgh.

Ferri, E.L. (1976) Growing up in a One-Parent Family, National Foundation for Educational Research, Slough.

Fitzgerald, T.F. (ed) (1976) Nutrition and Anthropology and Action, van Gorcum, Assen/Amsterdam.

Ford, C.S. (1964) A Comparative Study of Human Reproduction, Yale University Publications in Anthropology, no.32, Human Relations Area Files Press,

Forster, R. and Ranum, O. (1979) Food and Drink in History: Selections from the Annales Economies, Sociétés, Civilisations, John Hopkins University Press, Baltimore.

Fox, A. (1974) Beyond Contract, Faber, London.

Friedman, G. (1955) Industrial Society, Free Press, New York.

Fung, Y. (1953) A History of Chinese Philosophy, Princeton University Press, Princeton, tr. Derk Bodde.

Gelles, R. (1974) The Violent Home, Sage, New York.

George, S. and Paige, N. (1982) Food for Beginners, Writers and Readers, London.

George, V. and Wilding, P. (1972) Motherless Families, RKP, London.

Gideon, H. (1962) 'A baby is born in the Pinjab', American Anthro-
  pologist, vol.64.
Goody, J. (1982) Cooking, Cuisine and Class, Cambridge University Press,
Graham, H. (1977) 'Images of pregnancy in antenatal literature', in
  Dingwall, R. et al. (eds) Health Care and Health Knowledge, Croom
  Helm, London,
Graham, H. (1979) 'Prevention and health: every mother's business: a
  comment on child health policies in the 1970s in the 1970s', in
  Harris, C. (ed) Sociology of the Family: New Directions for Britain
  Sociological Review Monograph no.28, University of Keele.
Graham, H. (1980) 'Family differences in early years on the eating
  habits of children', in Turner, M. (ed) Nutrition and Lifestyles,
  Applied Science Publishers, London.
Harris, D.M. and Curten, S. (1979) 'Health-protective behaviour: an
  exploratory study', Journal of Health and Social Behavior, vol.20.
Harrison, F. (1982) Strange Land, Sidgwick & Jackson, London.
Hart, N. (1976) When Marriage Ends, Tavistock, London.
Hartley, D. (1954) Food in England, Macdonald, London.
Hassinger, E.W. and McNamara, R.L. (1960) The Families, their Physicians
  their Health Behavior in a Northwest Missouri County, College of
  Agriculture Research Bulletin 754, University of Missouri, Columbia.
Health of Munitions Worker Committee (1916) Investigation of Workers'
  Food and Suggestions as to Dietary, HMSO, London.
Herzlich, C. (1973) Health and Illness, Academic Press, London, tr.
  H.D.Graham.
Hipgrave, T. (1981) 'Child rearing by lone fathers' in Chester, R. et
  al. (eds) Changing Patterns of Child-bearing and Child-rearing,
  Academic Press, London.
Hoggart, R. (1958) The Uses of Literacy, Penguin, Harmondsworth.
Homans, H.Y. (1980) Pregnant in Britain: a sociological approach to
  Asian and British Women's Experiences, Unpublished PhD thesis,
  University of Warwick.
Homans, H.Y. (1982) 'Pregnancy and birth as rites of passage for two
  groups of women in Britain', in MacCormack, C. (ed) Ethnography of
  Fertility and Birth, Academic Press, London.
Hugh Jones, C. (1978) 'Food for thought: patterns of production and
  consumption in Pirá-Parená Society', in La Fontaine, J.S.(ed) Sex and
  Age as Principles of Social Differentiation, ASA Monograph 17,
  Academic Press, London.
Hytten, F. and Leitch, I. (1964) The Physiology of Human Pregnancy,
  Blackwell Scientific Publications, Oxford.
Information Services Division (1979) Scottish Health Statistics, HMSO,
  Edinburgh.
James, A. (1981) 'Confections, concoctions and conceptions', in Waites,
  B. et al. (eds) Popular Culture: Past and Present, Croom Helm, London.
Jerome, N.W. et al. (eds) (1980) Nutritional Anthropology: Contemporary
  Approaches to Diet and Culture, Redgrave, New York.
Johnson, J.P. (1977) A Hundred Years Eating: Food, Drink and the Daily
  Diet in Britain since the late Nineteenth Century, Gill and Macmillan,
  Dublin.
Kerr, M. and Charles, N. (1982) 'Food as an indicator of social
  relations', paper presented to the Annual Conference of the BSA,
  University of Manchester, April.
Knowles, D. (1940) The Monastic Order in Britain, Cambridge University
  Press, Cambridge.
Knowles, D. (1948) The Religious Order in England, Cambridge University
  Press, Cambridge.

Kotz, N. (1971) Let Them Eat Promises, Doubleday, New York.

Kraft (1978) Survey of Attitudes to Foods and Health, Kraft Foods Ltd., St. George's House, Bayshill Road, Cheltenham, Glos.

Kraft (1979) 'The Kraft survey of attitudes to food and health', Nutrition Bulletin 26, BNF, vol.5, no.2, May.

Kuper, J. (1977) The Anthropologists' Cookbook, RKP, London.

Leach, Edmund R. (1976) Culture and Communication, Cambridge University Press, Cambridge.

Lehrer, A. (1969) 'Semantic cuisine', Journal of Linguistics, vol.5.

Lehrer, A. (1972) 'Cooking vocabularies and the culinary triangle of Levi-Strauss', Anthropological Linguistics, vol.14.

Leonard, D. (1980) Sex and Generation, Tavistock, London.

Lévi-Strauss, C. (1966) 'The culinary triangle', New Society, 22 December, 166.

Lévi-Strauss, C. (1970) The Raw and the Cooked, Jonathan Cape, London.

Lévi-Strauss, C. (1973) From Honey to Ashes, Jonathan Cape, London.

Lévi-Strauss, C. (1978) The Origin of Table Manners, Jonathan Cape, London.

Litman, T.J. (1971) 'Health care and the family: a three generational analysis', Medical Care, vol.9, no.1.

Llewelyn Davies, M. (ed) (1978) Maternity: Letters from Working Women, Virago, London. (First published 1915).

Macintyre, S. (1981) 'Expectations and experiences of first pregnancy: report on a prospective interview study of married primigravidae in Aberdeen', Occasional Paper no.5, Institute of Medical Sociology, Aberdeen.

McKillop, M.and A. (1917) Efficiency Methods, Routledge, London.

McLaughlin, T. (1978) A Diet of Tripe, David & Charles, Vancouver.

Maddox, B. (1975) The Half Parent, Andre Deutsch, London.

Marsden, D. (1973) Mothers Alone, Penguin, Harmondsworth.

Marsden, D. and Owens, D. (1975) 'The Jekyll and Hyde marriages', New Society, 8 May.

Melville, J. (1978) 'Women in refuges', in Martin, J.P. (ed) Violence and the Family, Wiley, Chichester.

Mennell, S. (forthcoming) The Sociology of Taste - Eating in England and France, Basil Blackwell, Oxford.

Merkle, J. (1980) Management and Ideology, University of California Press, Berkeley.

Merrill, R. (ed) (1976) Radical Agriculture, Harper, New York.

Mills, C. Wright (1970) The Sociological Imagination, Penguin, Harmondsworth.

Mitchell, J.C. (ed) (1969) Social Networks in Urban Situations, Manchester University Press, Manchester.

Molony, C.H. (1975) 'Systematic valence-coding of hot-cold foods', Ecology of Food and Nutrition, vol.4.

Morpeth, R. (1979) 'The Village Midwife in the Prijab', Unpublished paper, Cambridge.

Murcott, A. (1981) 'Cravings and aversions: conceptions of body and diet in pregnancy amongst some women in South Wales'. Paper presented to the joint conference of the British Branch of the International Commission on the Anthropology of Food and the British Medical Anthropological Society, February, London.

Murcott, A. (1982a) 'On the social significance of the "cooked dinner" in South Wales', Social Science Information, vol.21, no.4/5.

Murcott, A. (1982b forthcoming) 'Menus, meals and platefuls: observations on advice about diet in pregnancy', The International Journal of Sociology and Social Policy.

Murcott, A. (1983a) 'Cookbook's images of technique and technology in the British kitchen', Women's Studies International Forum, vol.6, no.2.

Murcott, A. (1983b forthcoming) '"It's a pleasure to cook for him....": food, mealtimes and gender in some South Wales households', in Garmarnikov, E. et al. (eds) The Public and the Private, Collected Papers, 1982 Conference British Sociological Association.

Murdock, G.P. and Provost, C. (1973) 'Factors in the division of labor by sex: a cross cultural analysis', Ethnology, vol.XII, no.2.

Nelson, D. (1980) Managers and Workers, University of Winconsin Press, Madison.

Newby, H. (1977a) The Deferential Worker, Allen Lane, London.

Newby, H. (1977b) 'In the field: reflections on the study of Suffolk farm workers' in Bell, C. and Newby, H. (eds) Doing Sociological Research, Allen & Unwin, London.

Newby, H. and Utting, P. (forthcoming) Agribusiness in Britain, Hutchinson, London.

Newson, J. and E. (1965) Patterns of Infant Care in an Urban Community, Penguin, Harmondsworth.

Newson, J. and E. (1970) Four Years Old in an Urban Community, Penguin, Harmondsworth.

Nichter, M. (1977) Health Ideologies and Medical Cultures in the South Kanara Areca Nut Belt, Unpublished PhD Thesis, University of Edinburgh.

Nicod, M. (1979) 'Gastronomically speaking: food studied as a medium of communication', in Turner, M. (ed) Nutrition and Lifestyles, Applied Science Publishers, London.

Oakley, A. (1974) The Sociology of Housework, Martin Robertson, London.

Oddy, D.J. and Miller, D.S. (eds) (1976) The Making of the Modern British Diet, Croom Helm, London.

Pahl, J. (1978) A Refuge for Battered Women, DHSS, London.

Pahl, J. (1981) A Bridge Over Troubled Waters, University of Kent at Canterbury.

Paterson, E. (1981) 'Food-work: maids in a hospital kitchen', in Atkinson, P. and Heath, C. Medical Work, Gower, Farnborough.

Pilgrium Trust (1938) Men Without Work, The University Press, Cambridge.

Pill, R.M. and Stott, N.C.H. (1981) 'Relationship between health locus of control and belief in the relevance of lifestyle to health', Patient Counselling and Health Education, vol.3, no.3.

Pill, R.M. and Stott, N.C.H. (1982) 'Concepts of illness causation and responsibility: some preliminary data from a sample of working class mothers', Social Science and Medicine, vol.16.

Pizzey, E. (1974) Scream Quietly or the Neighbours Will Hear, Penguin, Harmondsworth.

Politics of Health Group (1979) Food and Profit, Politics of Health Group, London.

Posner, T. (1977) 'Magical elements in orthodox medicine', in Dingwall, R. et al. (eds) Health Care and Health Knowledge, Croom Helm, London.

Proud, E. (1916) Welfare Work, Bell, London.

Report of the Committee on Indigenous Systems of Medicine (1948) Ministry of Health, Government of India.

Richards, A.I. (1939) Land Labour and Diet in Northern Rhodesia, Oxford University Press, London.

Richards, A.I. (1948) Hunger and Work in a Savage Tribe, Free Press, Glencoe, Illinois.

Robson, J.R.K. (1980) Food, Ecology and Culture: Readings in the Anthropology of Dietary Practices, Gordon & Breach, London.

Rosser, C. and Harris, C. (1965) The Family and Social Change, RKP, London.

Salmon, J. (1979) 'If they tell us what we're eating, do we care?', British Public Opinion, Autumn.

Sheiham, A. et al. (1981) Sweet Nothings, Health Education Council, London, 3 vols.

Simoons, F.J. (1961) Eat Not This Flesh: Food Avoidances in the Old World, Madison, Wisconsin.

Sinha, R. (1976) Food and Poverty, Croom Helm, London.

Smith, D. (1977) 'Women, the family and corporate capitalism' reprinted in Stephenson, Manyhee Women in Canada, General Publishing Co.Ltd., Ontario, revised ed.

Stacey, M. (1978) 'Sociological concepts of health and disease and critiques of such concepts'. Paper presented at SSRC Symposium, Sheffield.

Stacey, M. (1980) 'Realities for change in child health care: existing patterns and future possibilities', British Medical Journal, 280.

Stacey, M. and Price, M. (1981) Women, Power and Politics, Tavistock, London.

Steinmetz, S. and Strauss, M. (1974) Violence in the Family, Dodd Mead & Co., London.

Stevens, C. (1979) Food Aid and the Developing World, Croom Helm, London.

Stolz, L.M. (1967) Influences on Parent Behaviour, Stanford University Press, Stanford, California.

Stott, N.C.H. and Pill, R.M. (1980) Health Beliefs in an Urban Community Report to DHSS, Mimeo, Department of Central Practice, Welsh National School of Medicine.

Tabor, D.C. (1981) 'Ripe and unripe: concepts of health and sickness in Ayurvedic medicine', Social Science and Medicine, vol.15B.

Tan, S.P. (1982) Food Ideology and Food Habits of Chinese Immigrants in London and the Growth of their Young Children, Mimeo, Department of Human Nutrition, London School of Hygiene and Tropical Medicine.

Tan, S.P. and Wheeler, E. (1982) 'Concepts relating to health and food held by Chinese Women, Mimeo.

Tannahill, R. (1975) Food in History, Paladin, St. Albans.

Tremolieres, J. (1970) 'A behavioural approach to organoleptic properties of food', Proceedings of the Nutrition Society, vol.29, no.2.

Tudge, C. (1979) The Famine Business, Pelican, Harmondsworth.

Turner, B.S. (1982) 'The government of the body: medical regimens and the rationalization of diet', BJS, vol.33, no.2.

Twigg, J. (1981) The Vegetarian Movement in England, 1847-1981: A Study in the Structure of its Ideology, Unpublished PhD thesis, London School of Economics.

Urwick, L. and Brech, E. (1949) The Making of Scientific Management, Management Publications Trust, London.

Wallerstein, J.G. and Kelly, J.B. (1980) Surviving the Breakup, Grant McIntyre, London.

Wardle, C. (1977) Changing food habits in the UK, Earth Resources Research Ltd., London.

Warren, G.C. (1958) The Foods We Eat, Cassell, London.

Wedderburn, D. and Craig, C. (1974) 'Relative deprivation in work' in Wedderburn, D. (ed) Poverty, Inequality and Class, Cambridge University Press, Cambridge.

Weinreich-Haste, H. (1979) 'What sex is science?' in Hartnett, O. et al. (eds) Sex-Role Stereotyping, Tavistock, London.

Wellin, E. (1953) 'Child Feeding and Food Ideology in a Peruvian Village' Mimeo, WHO, Geneva.

Weymes, H. (1981) 'Concepts of Food in Times of Crisis' Paper given at the British Medical Anthropology Conference, May, London.

Williams, R.G.A. (1981) 'Logical analysis as a qualitative method', Sociology of Health and Illness, vol.3.

Wilson, A.C. (1976) Food and Drink in Britain, Penguin, Harmondsworth.

Wilson, Monica (1972) 'The wedding cakes: a study of ritual change', in La Fontaine, J.S. (ed) The Interpretation of Ritual, Tavistock, London.

Wright, H. (1981) Swallow It Whole, New Statesman Report 4, New Statesman, London.

Wynn, A. and Wynn, M. (1979) Prevention of Handicap and the Health of Women, RKP, London.

Wynne-Tyson, J. (1975) Food for a Future, Abacus, London.

Young, M. and Wilmott, P. (1973) The Symmetrical Family, Penguin, Harmondsworth.

Yudkin, J. and McKenzie, J.C. (eds) (1964) Changing Food Habits, McGibbon and Kee, London.

Yudkin, J. (1977) Pure, White and Deadly: the problem of sugar, Davis-Poynter, London.

Index

Agribusiness 16, 31, 36-38, 43
Alcohol 3, 50, 59, 68, 70, 92, 160
Angyal, A. 22
Anthropological studies of
   food 1, 4
Appearance of food 47, 79
Appetite, changes in during
   pregnancy 57, 59-67, 71
Aversions, revulsion to food 22,
   26, 29, 59, 61-3
Ayurveda 74

'Balanced' diet 2, 79-80, 92, 112
Barthes, R. 10-12
Berger, P.L. 5
Blood, beliefs about, as food
   22-24, 26

Carter, A. 14-15
Children 3, 84-5, 89, 96, 101,
   107, 159; beliefs about food
   suitable for 10, 24, 86-8, 93,
   99; food preferences of, 91,
   103-4, 120
'Codes' of food and drink 10
Controlling eating, in pregnancy
   60, 81; in diabetes 128
'Convenience' foods 9, 14, 38,
   97, 100
'Cold' foods 74-6, 79, 86-7, 89,
   93
'Cooked dinner' 3, 98, 102, 122-4,
   146, 179, 181, 183
'Cooked meals' see 'Cooked dinner'
Cooking: significance of, 11, 25;
   as 'good' 96-8; as 'important'
   180; of meat 25, 180; techniques
   25-6; Chinese, 87-8; and women's
   role 103, 179
'Cooling' foods see 'Cold' foods
Cravings in pregnancy for food,
   57, 61-3, 67, 73
'Culinary triangle' 12

Diabetic ideology 128-9, 135-6
Diet: car workers' 48; after
   childbirth 90; company directors'
   47; farmworkers' 2, 31, 33, 112;
   diabetic 136; of older
   generation 97, 107, 111; in
   pregnancy 69, 78, 80, 86;
   weight reducing 69
Dietary advice 94; in pregnancy
   58, 63, 77-9, 81
Domestic division of labour 3, 32,
   59, 102, 153-4, 174, 181
'Domestication' of work place
   eating 48-9, 51
Douglas, M. 1, 4, 16, 18, 141, 178

Eating, abnormalities in, see under
   appetite
Equilibrium, of the body 85, 88,
   90, 94, 106
Exercise, for health 17, 109-110,
   126

Femininity and food 3, 24, 27-28
Food, as 'fuel' 32, 124, 126
Food beliefs 1, 3, 79, 84, 106, 117,
   126-7, 152; valuations as 'good':
   'cooked', 96-7, 121-3, 180,
   'country' 16, 111-2, 'fresh'
   121-2, 125, 'homemade' 111, 117,
   'moderation' 111, 'natural' 14,
   29, 96, 122, 'plain' 96, 111,
   'pure' 15, 'raw' 29, 'sweet'
   129-32; valuations as 'bad':
   'convenience' 14, 100, 180,
   'cooked' 29, 'frozen' 122,
   'packaged' 114, 'processed' 14,
   31, 96-8, 125, 'sweet' 98, 100,
   119, 129, 'tinned' 95-6, 98, 111,
   122, 180
'Food ideology' 1, 18
Food, meanings of in pregnancy 73,
   75-6
Food prices 35-36

Food processing industry 38-43
Food production, structure in
  Britain 36-43; absence of rural
  self-sufficiency 31, 34

Goody, J. 1, 4
'Grammar' of eating 27
Guilt, of not providing 'proper'
  diet 9, 92, 94

Health: in the 'Chinese system'
  85-6, 88, 94; in Ayurvedic
  philosophy 74-5, 77-9
Health beliefs 3, 85-6, 110, 127
'Health food' 3, 108-9, 113-5
'Health' foods 2, 12-17, 104, 108-9,
  116
Health maintenance 17, 74, 89,
  109-10, 117
Historical studies of food 1, 4
Honey, symbolism of 11, 135
'Hot' foods 74-6, 78-9, 86-7, 93,
Husbands in the kitchen 3, 181-2,
  184
Hytten, F. 63

Illness causation, popular beliefs
  about 3, 118-20
'Illness Food' 3, 108-9, 114

Leach, E.R. 11, 141, 149
Lehrer, A. 178
Leitch, I. 63
Levi-Strauss, C. 4, 11-12, 18, 26,
  178
'Life-style' and diet 106, 118-120
Luckman, T. 5

Marital obligations, food and, 3,
  32-3, 48-9, 59, 90, 102, 108,
  124, 154, 165-7, 169, 179-80
Masculinity and food 3, 24, 27, 33,
  124; and cooking 157, 169, 172
Maternal obligations, food and
  92-3, 103, 117, 155, 181
Mealtimes, and absence of family
  33, 66-7, 102, 155-6; changes
  in 66, 102; control of 2, 45, 50;
  and domesticity 152; length of
  47-8; and marital conflict 154,
  167; meaning of 33
Meat, symbolic significance of
  21-26; 'goodness' of 97, 99, 124
'Meat and two veg' 33
Men, beliefs about food suitable
  for 10, 24, 86, 99; meals for
  103, 169
Message of wedding menus 148-50

Milk, 'goodness' of 3, 10-11, 80
  97, 99-100
Moral meaning of food 1-3, 15, 17,
  29, 92, 95, 105-6, 110, 128
Mythology, of food 10-11, 15-16

Nicod, M. 102

Overeating 3, 106, 125-6

Paternal obligation, food and
  157-8
'Philosophies' of eating 1-2
'Proper meal' 96-7, 99, 102-3, 113,
  148. See also 'cooked dinner'
Raw food 29, 180
'Repairing' foods 87-8

Sex and food 24, 117
Sexual division of labour, and
  food 3, 117, 179
Shopping 35-6, 103, 168, 181
Smith, D. 149-50
Social Class 79-81, 104-5, 107,
  113, 116, 118, 149-50, 165, 184;
  and perceptions of diet in
  pregnancy 74. See also diet of
  company directors', and
  carworkers'
Sociological study of food and
  eating 1, 4-5
Soup, 'goodness' of 3, 96-7, 99,
  107, 114
'Starve' 111, 180
Sunday dinner 102, 154, 157-8, 184

Teenagers see children
'Time thrift' 46
Tremolieres, J. 5

Vegetarian, vegetarianism 2, 18-19,
  78; 'modern' version 20, 28
Victorian invalid diet 25
Vitamins, belief in value of,
  13-14, 81, 93, 96, 100, 122

Weight, change in 33, 66, 155-8,
  169-70
Weight control 68-9, 113, 134-5
Wellin, E. 1, 18
Weymes, H. 79
'Wholefoods' 12, 28 see also
  'health' foods
Wife, proper role of 3, 148-50
  see also femininity, women
Women, beliefs about food suitable
  for 24, 99; as cooks 149, 157,
  164, 173; meals for 103